# THEORIZING CLASSICAL SOCIOLOGY

# THEORIZING CLASSICAL SOCIOLOGY

Larry J. Ray

**Open University Press**
Buckingham · Philadelphia

Open University Press
Celtic Court
22 Ballmoor
Buckingham
MK18 1XW

email: enquiries@openup.co.uk
world wide web: http://www.openup.co.uk

and
325 Chestnut Street
Philadelphia, PA 19106, USA

First Published 1999

A catalogue record of this book is available from the British Library

ISBN 0 335 19865 1 (pbk)     0 335 19866 X (hbk)

**Library of Congress Cataloging-in-Publication Data**
Ray, Larry J.
    Theorizing classical sociology / Larry J. Ray.
      p.  cm.
    Includes bibliographical references and index.
    ISBN 0–335–19866–X (hbk)     ISBN 0–335–19865–1 (pbk)
    1. Sociology—Philosophy.  I. Title.
  HM585.R39  1999
  301′.01—dc21                                     99–20484
                                                        CIP

Typeset by Graphicraft Limited, Hong Kong
Printed in Great Britain by Redwood Books, Trowbridge

Dedicated to Joseph Benjamin Ray

# Contents

# Preface and acknowledgements

How are we to make sense of the competing array of theoretical approaches to sociology? I address this question here with reference to the emergence of a classical tradition, within which emerged a concept of society that allowed a play of contrasting theoretical positions. So the existence of a competing array of theories is a consequence of fundamental ways in which the social has been imagined over the past two centuries. The central theme here is sociology as a debate with the Enlightenment. Each chapter discusses the ways in which particular social theories engaged with the idea of the social that emerged out of the Enlightenment and the controversies it provoked. However, each chapter also provides a discrete account and discussion of one of the major theories in the classical tradition. This book can then be read in its entirety, as a thematic discussion of classical social theory, or it can be used as a resource for accounts of particular theoretical perspectives. I have attempted to emphasize the themes that recurred in classical theorizing while acknowledging that over the past century these have become crystallized around the works of individual writers. So there is, I hope, a balance of organizing themes and due attention to the works of canonical theorists to whom sociology continually returns for inspiration.

This book is the result of twenty or so years' teaching social theory at Lancaster University and more recently at the University of Kent. Thanks are due to colleagues and students whose shared commitment to theory has created stimulating working and thinking environments. Acknowledgements are due in particular to those who have contributed directly to this project by offering encouragement or helpful criticisms of earlier drafts. These include Howard Becker, Jon O'Brien, Mike Gane, Celia Lury, David Morgan, William Outhwaite and Alan Warde. Thanks to Randall Collins and the ASA for permission to reproduce Figure 8.1. Thanks and deep appreciation to Emma for assistance, support and encouragement throughout this project.

# CHAPTER I

# Dimensions of the social:
# an introduction

This book is about classical social theory and its legacy. My main purpose is to provide an understanding of the central themes in classical theory while showing how these set the scene for subsequent debates. But what is the classical tradition? In part it is derived from the works that have shown the longest staying power, notably Marx, Weber, Durkheim and, latterly, Simmel. But like other 'traditions' it is in part a contemporary construction and the way we view sociology's past is closely linked to our present concerns. The classical corpus is not fixed but subject to both forgetting and remembering. To Parsons' (1949: 3) rhetorical question 'Who now reads Spencer?' one could add, who now reads Giddings, Sumner, Ward, Hobhouse, Sorokin, Veblin, von Mise and many others, each of whom could at some time have claimed entry into the classical pantheon? But understanding the classical legacy is less dependent on who is read at any one time, so much as an engagement with some central intellectual and social issues, which are the main focus here. So this is not a Marx-Durkheim-Weber centred account of classical sociology. There are many such excellent critical expositions available already, to which I shall refer in due course. The trinity of founding fathers does feature here (how could it not?) but the focus is more on classical sociology as part of a long quest for social understanding.

My intention is to offer an account of classical sociology and its intellectual background in the **Enlightenment** that also points forwards to what follows. Namely, the attempt by subsequent sociology to develop and apply sociological theory to twentieth century concerns. The classical tradition, I suggest, is an unfinished enterprise of imagining the social in various ways that drew on earlier themes. We remain to a large extent within these categories, which overlap, play against each other, and combine in the works of individual theorists.

But where should a study like this begin? This is not an easy question to answer, because social theory, broadly understood, has no clear starting point. In all complex societies there were scholars who developed systematic thought about morals, social organization, people and nature, the cosmos and religion. Many of these systems of thought were concerned with understanding the origin of society and offered explanations of the existing social structure. Theorizing society has deep historical origins, which include the Egyptian prophets, Greek philosophers and, subsequently, medieval scholars in Europe and the Maghreb. Yet this volume focuses mainly on the eighteenth and nineteenth centuries, from the European Enlightenment. One reason for this, as in other histories of sociology, is convenience – a review of the past two millennia of social thought would simply be unmanageable. Another reason is that during the Enlightenment a distinct configuration of social and theoretical issues took shape. Anyway, it is not my intention simply to provide a chronology of social thought, but to offer a more synoptic approach that identifies recurrent themes and issues in classical sociological theory. These will now be briefly outlined.

## RECURRENT THEMES AND ISSUES

Sociology emerged with the conditions of modernity, that is, the modes of social life and organization which emerged in Europe from about the seventeenth century, subsequently becoming world-wide (Giddens 1990: 1). Modernity entailed dynamic technological and social transformations, leading to a ruthless break with all preceding historical conditions, and a 'never-ending process of internal ruptures and fragmentation within itself' (Harvey 1994: 12). The circumstances of its emergence have inscribed into sociology a set of antinomies on which sociological theories will tend, implicitly or explicitly, to take a position. By contrast with much earlier philosophy, sociology was historical in the sense that it was concerned less with timeless attributes of human life and more with their historical emergence. The following broad themes will inform discussion throughout the book.

### Emancipation and Enlightenment

Sociology arrived with enormous promise – to resolve the crisis of industrial society through the application of reason to social organization. The idea of a social science, as it developed at the end of the eighteenth century, reflected the belief that unlike traditional, classical and literary pursuits, knowledge should be socially beneficial. The emergent modernist project of social engineering enabled intellectuals to understand themselves as agents of change and as bearers of enlightenment rationality. This conception provided the basis of an **ideology**-critique common to many social theories, such as **positivism**, Marxism, Critical Theory, structuralism and feminism, although it was understood differently in each case. Sociology was a critical project and a great deal of sociological theory has offered itself as an unmasking of ideology in the name of a higher rationality or other source of validity.

## Nature and gender

The growth of capitalism transformed gender relations, something of which classical sociologists were aware, but which they generally misunderstood. Rather, ideas about gender were often constructed around a dichotomy of nature and society. The natural was characteristically coded as feminine, thus the polarities man/nature, mind/body, male/female began to coalesce. 'Nature' could thus serve several purposes: it became a source of nostalgia and romanticism; a criterion of authenticity; a symbol of otherness; an object to be redeemed from domination. But once sexualized in terms of the divide between male/female, 'naturalized women' become (in some theories) the object of nostalgically loaded anti-modernism. Constructions of women in social theory were often a vehicle for nostalgia for the supposedly more natural and authentic world of pre-industrial society. Further, several theorists claimed that since pre-industrial societies were more communal and solidaristic than impersonal industrialism, the latter represented a triumph of masculine over feminine principles (for better or worse).

## Science and methods

The Enlightenment vision of progress through science opened up the possibility of a scientific analysis of society, which was encouraged by the development of new sciences, especially evolutionary biology. This occurred in the context of a decline in religious belief and observance and more generally, the 'crisis of industrial society', which was often understood as a crisis of morality. Sociology often promised not only to provide a scientific analysis of society that would guide future practice, but also to offer a scientifically based morality and thus resolve problems of social disorganization and conflict. On the other hand, this scientistic vision was challenged by an alternative, hermeneutic conception, which emphasized the essential difference between scientific and cultural knowledge. Both approaches though were situated within an evolutionary view of social development that informed much of the framework for classical theory. The debate between these approaches, **naturalism** and **hermeneutics**, became one of the major thematic issues of subsequent sociological theory.

## Social system and social action

We perceive ourselves as agents whose actions have effects. Yet viewed as a whole, society appears to be a system of interrelated institutions and practices that have unintended consequences. This duality has perhaps become more apparent in modern, complex societies in which impersonal systems of organization coexist with an individualistic culture and ethics. A central rationale for sociology was that the increasing complexity of social organization, combined with markets and bureaucratic organizations, meant that social processes escaped everyday understanding and became susceptible to the specialist understanding of the social sciences. Although society could be understood as a self-regulating system, it was apparent that modernity expanded capacities for action within fluid social structures. Sociology claimed to be capable of guiding rational (and therefore willed) interventions in the social system. Thus the duality of action and system became one of the central problems of sociological theory, with some theories opting for system *or* action (e.g. structuralism, symbolic interactionism) and others attempting to reconcile the dilemma (e.g. Parsons and Giddens).

## Cultural habit versus reason

The conception of human action as rationalized and instrumental, represented for example in political economy, has been in tension with conceptions that stress the importance of cultural values in shaping human behaviour. In opposition to *laissez-faire* political economists, for example, early sociologists such as Saint-Simon, Auguste Comte, and later Emile Durkheim, emphasized the moral, rather than purely instrumental, foundations of social integration. They did not accept the claim of political economists, that the pursuit of individual interests produces the greatest good of all. The uneasy relations between these schools of thought in nineteenth century social theory erupted in the 1880s in the *Methodenstreit* (dispute over method), which resulted in the split between economics and sociology. However, within sociology the tension remains and is illustrated for example in Parsons' emphasis of the central value system, against Weber's concept of **rationalization**, or more recently in accounts of market behaviour as 'embedded' in social values.

## Community, society and nostalgia

The development of modern systems of social organization (such as industrial capitalism) and politics (democratic rights and formal freedoms) were from their early days accompanied by a Romantic critique of lost communal and authentic social relations. This ambivalence within the modern worldview was reproduced within sociology and informed debates about the destiny and value of modern industrial society. Many classical sociological theories sought to rediscover community as a counterbalance to mass society. Further, the self-critique of the Enlightenment, and more generally the self-critique of modernity, accompanied industrial society from the beginning. There are divergent but often interrelated themes here. There was the Romantic rejection of, or ambivalence towards, modernity that we shall find for example in Comtean positivism. Yet disenchantment with the consequences of modernity also underlay the growth of hermeneutic methods and wider resistance to positivism which was viewed as an inappropriate application of scientific methods to cultural phenomena. This view was evident in early twentieth century German sociology and in more recent approaches such as Critical Theory and post-structuralism. Critical Theory took the critique of capitalism back to the origins of modern Enlightenment in the ancient world and rejected much of the Enlightenment project as dominating and destructive (e.g. Adorno and Horkheimer 1973). Although this was a rather extreme view, in Marx too we find the paradoxical combination of an enthusiastic endorsement of modernity (e.g. *Manifesto of the Communist Party*: Marx and Engels [1848] 1967) with his expectation that post-capitalist society would overcome **alienation** and re-establish communal regulation and social solidarity. Some contemporary alternative visions, such as deep ecology or ecofeminism, or postmodernist aesthetics, also perhaps draw on anti-modernist cultural traditions. Part of the culture of industrial society is the notion of a rupture with a traditional, communal past, which remains central to sociological theorizing.

## DIMENSIONS OF THE SOCIAL

The object of sociology is 'society', a concept relatively recently formulated and often attributed to intellectual movements in the late eighteenth century (e.g. Collins and Makowsky 1984). There are good grounds for this, although one should bear in mind that its antecedents can be found much earlier. Greek philosophy reflected on the origins of society and the state. Plato's (471–399 BC) *Republic* described an organic social division of labour and envisaged a social utopia based on the rule of a wise elite. Aristotle (384–322 BC) claimed that 'man' was a political animal (*zoon politikon*) whose natural habitat was the city state (polis). Greek concepts of the social were incorporated into some medieval thinking, such as Thomas Aquinas (1225–74), but most importantly into Renaissance thought in the fourteenth and fifteenth centuries (Toulmin 1990; Rengger 1995). However, these were largely reflections on the state. Theorizing the social was closely associated with the birth of modernity, as the emerging concept of society broadened from its earlier meaning, referring to the leading social circles of Paris and Versailles ('high society'), to the idea of an association or organized group, then to social groups in general. This took place in the context where the growth of commercial ethics challenged traditional orders and increased the status of technical knowledge. For some (e.g. political economists), the emerging commercial system had a remarkable facility – it appeared to regulate itself autonomously, without any need for a controlling centre. For critics of early capitalism (including socialists and many sociologists) commercialism undermined social cohesion and posed crucial questions about how societies were and could be integrated. Either way though, the basis of social cohesion then had to be sought in a broader location than personal rulers and the state.

Thus sociology offered a critical diagnosis of the process of modernization of which it was a part. Important to this was a historical understanding of the social as a progressive emergence of higher forms of social organization. Critique of existing conditions was often undertaken in the name of better social arrangements that were not merely desirable but historically emergent. This linear sense of historical movement was apparent in both social and natural evolutionary theories. This perspective had many consequences, one of which was that ethical questions that had previously been regarded as timeless and universal, became relative to particular historical and social circumstances. A further consequence was that knowledge of social development could be used to hasten desired outcomes, so that sociology could contribute to the emergence of a more rational, harmonious, just and regulated society.

In addition to autonomy, differentiation was an important concept, which reflected the depersonalization of political power, separated from the familial rights of monarchs, barons and landlords. The idea of the state as the personal property of the sovereign and benefice of officials slowly gave way to the idea of impersonal rule bound by rules, such as the 1689 Bill of Rights in England. In the process, sovereignty was transferred from the figure of the monarch to the state, which also underwent a process of differentiation, into administrative, judicial, representative functions. Further, the development of trade, commerce and markets increased the complexity of economic organization while establishing the dual notion of social activity, divided into political and civil roles. This is captured in the eighteenth century concept of civil society, which described a realm of contractual and voluntary relationships independent of the state, which thereby became merely one area of social activity among others. At the same time, there was a separation between the public arena of the economy (governed by egoistic passions) and the private sphere of the family (governed by altruistic ones), within which new gender divisions were institutionalized. Thus in eighteenth century thought, overlapping distinctions begin to appear between state/society; economy/domesticity; masculinity/femininity; **egoism**/altruism.

In these dichotomies 'nature' was to play an important but ambiguous role. In some respects nature was alien to cultured civilization – societies were after all progressing from original, barbaric states to cultured civilization. Yet centuries of despotism and superstition had distorted our 'true natures' which in an enlightened age could now be expressed – sweeping away traditional morality, for example, in favour of naturalistic ethics. Further, once split off from the social, nature could become an object of Romantic longing – the location of lost authenticity and a rationally harmonious system. Gendered differences were further inscribed into these ideas. This is the context in which, largely excluded from the emerging public sphere, women could become objects invested with nostalgia. Regarded as more 'natural' than masculinity, 'femininity' could be associated with qualities alienated from the rationalistic, male ego. We shall find in Comte, for example, the idea of a future age based on the rule of the 'feminine principle', embodying qualities of pacifism, sympathy, love and altruism, excluded from industrial society.

However, nostalgia was often present in these constructions of the social. In the face of an increasingly impersonal, commercial and by the end of the eighteenth century, industrial order, social theorists began to mourn the loss of 'community'. Tönnies famously contrasted 'society' with 'community' although the distinction between an impersonal, differentiated society and a pre-industrial community was implicit in earlier debates. Sociology was in some ways caught between the opposing inclinations of celebrating a new industrial order within which it defined its mission while seeking to recreate and rediscover 'community' as a source of authenticity and belonging. The recent emergence of 'communitarian' thinking, associated particularly with Amati Etzioni (1997), illustrates the continuing pull of the latter inclination. Sociology in some ways has been a long search for community.

More specifically, classical theory constructed the social in various ways, around poles of attributes, each of which defined a core component of the social, and created a field of play in which fundamental theoretical debates could take shape. Bringing the above themes together, I shall argue that society has been understood in terms of polar elements, which have been central to major theoretical traditions, of Marxism, Positivism, hermeneutics and Weberianism. But they have also left the way open to synthesis and combination of the different elements. I shall argue in the following chapters that as competing fields of reflection on sociality crystallized, 'society' became a terrain of theoretical dispute and innovation. Following the Enlightenment, the social was constructed around the play of four polar dimensions (see Figure 1.1). These are materiality, morality and habit, culture and rationality. By materiality, I mean the view (for example in classical political economy) that society is constituted primarily by forms of production, distribution and consumption. By morality and habit, I mean the view (found in counter-Enlightenment and Comte) that society is primarily a moral and organic entity integrated through shared values. By culture, I mean symbolic and linguistic practices transmitted through socialization but knowable

**Figure 1.1** Society as multidimensional concept

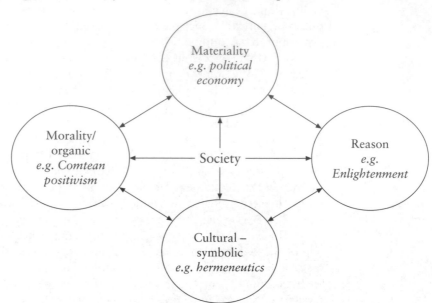

through techniques of understanding and decoding. By reason, I mean the view that the social is constituted through calculated and goal-directed action, a view found in Max Weber among many others. It would be hard to find social theorists who entirely neglected any of these dimensions, though most approaches emphasize one more than the others – which has opened up powerful terrains of dispute in theoretical analysis. It has also created the potential for syntheses.

This model will be developed in the course of this book. The various polarities of theorizing the social is developed particularly in Chapter 2, on the Enlightenment, but is then referred to frequently in subsequent discussion. Chapter 3 addresses the appearance of sociology and the crisis of industrialism through the works of Saint-Simon and Auguste Comte. Marxism and the dilemmas of later Marxists dealing with problems of theory and practice are discussed in Chapter 4, which also addresses their attempts to theorize the 'woman question'. Evolutionary theory and the application of biological concepts to sociology are discussed in Chapter 5, which suggests that Durkheim in particular insisted on the autonomy of sociology in the context of an evolutionary approach. While French classical sociology worked within the post-Enlightenment, positivist tradition, the hermeneutic approach offered a competing conception of cultural science, which is discussed in Chapter 6. Hermeneutics signalled disaffection not only with positivist methods but also, at a deeper level, with modernity itself. This becomes apparent in the later nineteenth century German sociological critiques of capitalism, such as Tönnies and Simmel, who are the subject of Chapter 7. Finally,

Chapter 8 is devoted to Weberian sociology, which attempts to resolve, ultimately incompletely, the dilemmas of classical sociology. Each chapter ends with a list of core concepts rising from the theoretical tradition in question.

Sociology is a theoretical discipline. Whether or not we are specialists in 'theory' the categories that sociologists use are theoretically derived and do not inhere in our data. The concept of 'society' was a theoretical construct that was always fragile in that it was from the beginning caught in dilemmas that do not admit of solution. This indeed is their allure. Theoretical dilemmas open a field of play in which sociological approaches are situated and which they can creatively decompose or synthesize. *Theorizing Classical Sociology* attempts to capture the reflexive nature of this process in which society is a theoretical construct and sociology theorizes the social.

---

### Core concepts in social theory

- Concept of society as an autonomous realm, requiring specialist knowledge.
- Differentiated institutional spheres of the religious, ethical, political and social.
- Differentiation of nature/society and traditional/modern, which are gendered dichotomies.
- Part of the emergence of modernity and projects of technical control.
- Critique and diagnosis of modernity.
- Multiple poles of material, moral, cultural and rational.

---

## FURTHER READING

Randall Collins and Michael Makowsky (1984, 5th edn 1993) *The Discovery of Society* (Random House) is a comprehensive and accessible survey of the emergence of the concept of society through a range of theorists, each of which is discussed in social and historical context. Tim May (1996) *Situating Social Theory* (Open University Press) examines social theory in the context of its traditions and historical development while clearly summarizing the main schools of thought. Stephen P. Turner (ed.) (1996) *Social Theory and Sociology* (Blackwell) combines a wide range of social theorists who consider the present state of social theory and new directions opposed to the classical tradition. George Ritzer (1994) *Sociological Beginnings* (McGraw-Hill) is an introductory account of the development of major sociological theories, biographies of the major founders and the emergence of some major sociological research methods.

# CHAPTER 2

# Enlightenment, reason and science

Sociological theory was shaped through a debate with the Enlightenment in ways that have defined some of the central contours of sociological reasoning. This chapter therefore outlines some key issues in the eighteenth century Enlightenment. In Chapter 1 I argued that social thought began to distinguish itself from earlier social philosophy in several ways, and 'society' emerged as a concept distinct from both nature and the state. Although society was separated from nature in many ways, it was also 'naturalized' in that it developed as a system that could be known through rational, scientific procedures. This meant that unlike philosophical reflection, social theory would address social research, which together would guide intervention in social development based on scientific understanding. Although this was not (I shall argue) a *direct* legacy of the Enlightenment, it was an elaboration of some of its themes and gave rise to one of the most persistent debates in sociology – whether and to what extent, it could be 'scientific'. So the Enlightenment was to pose a number of issues that provided a context for subsequent social theory, which included

- the critique of religious thought in the name of scientific validity
- the idea of progress
- knowledge as practical intervention in the world, as opposed to speculation and contemplation
- the expansion of reasoned debate within open public spheres, which challenged clerical, despotic and aristocratic forms of rule.

These themes took shape gradually and among the work of various writers, in ways that will be explored in the following chapters. This chapter examines the formation of social science through the work of contract theories, such as Hobbes and Rousseau; Scottish political economy; the French Enlightenment, especially Montesquieu and Condorcet; and conservative reactions to the French Revolution. The Comtean synthesis and critique, through which sociology first appeared, is discussed in Chapter 3.

## ENLIGHTENMENT, NATURE AND SOCIETY

What was the Enlightenment? No answer to this question gains general consent and many features of the 'movement' took shape in retrospect, in the reflections of later commentators. For some, such as Porter and Teich (1981), to speak of the Enlightenment at all is to wrongly assume that something links disparate and often contradictory writings of figures in eighteenth century Europe. For others, such as Peter Gay (1996) and Paul Hazard (1965), the Enlightenment represented a unified body of thought developed around themes of autonomy and rationality as the basis of a good society, the rights and welfare of 'man' as an abstract subject and progress through scientific advance. Again, for Zeitlin (1968: 5) the Enlightenment was about the advancement of 'reason' and 'science' through which people could achieve ever-greater degrees of freedom.

The idea that the whole of eighteenth century thought was a reaction against ignorance and superstition was given impetus by Immanual Kant's (1724–1804) famous essay, 'An Answer to the Question: "What is Enlightenment?"' ([1784] 1970), to which he answered, somewhat ambiguously, 'man's emergence from self-inured immaturity' (p. 54). That is, 'the inability to use one's own understanding without guidance of another'. Anticipating to some extent psychoanalytical theories of attachments to childhood, he argues that 'it is so convenient to be immature', therefore 'the largest part of mankind (including the entire fair sex) should consider the step to maturity difficult and dangerous' (p. 55). So 'Enlightenment' is understood here in terms of acquiring the maturity to exercise moral autonomy. Emancipation can occur, if the 'guardians of the common mass will throw off the yolk of immaturity and disseminate the spirit of rational respect' for the principle that everyone should think for themselves. The role assigned here to 'guardians' is ambiguous in that they bring Enlightenment to people whose 'immaturity' consists in part in their 'dependence on spiritual guardians' (p. 56). Indeed, this paradox highlights the role of intellectuals in this process. Gay (1996: 499ff) suggests that it was not always clear whether Enlightenment could extend to *le canaille* (the rabble or mob) who were often regarded as too idiotic to educate themselves. Some eighteenth century thinkers (including Kant) looked to so-called 'enlightened despots' such as Frederick II of Prussia (1712–86) as bearers of progress (Hazard 1965: 350–60; Gay 1996: 397ff). Some *philosophes* (French intellectual exponents of Enlightenment) regarded themselves as a morally and privileged cognoscenti who could, for example, manage without religion themselves, so long as the untutored masses were restrained by the hope of salvation and fear of damnation. The role envisaged for elites could be educative rather than despotic ('men of learning addressing a reading public' as Kant put it) and the 'public use of reason in all matters' was essential to extending moral autonomy (p. 57). However, the role that is specified here for intellectuals, as public educators, was to find echoes in nineteenth century conceptions of emancipatory practice, especially socialism.

There were, however, other sides of the Enlightenment. Kant was writing to some extent in retrospect and reflecting particularly on the German Enlightenment.[1] As well as the serious business of enhancing moral autonomy, there was also frivolous irony and lampooning of hallowed institutions. The Enlightenment, if it was in any sense a cohesive movement, extended beyond philosophy, across literature, the arts, science, theology and politics. In Jonathan Swift's *Gulliver's Travels* (1726) for example, ordinary conditions of life are completely reversed. Revered beliefs, including scientific ones, are satirized, as in the Lagrado Academy, which was trying to extract sunlight from cucumbers and bottle it up for winter use. Similarly, in John Gay's *Beggar's Opera* (1728) every typical operatic situation is parodied, as a gang of thieves, prostitutes and highwaymen take the place of traditional aristocratic subjects, accompanied by popular ballads rather than swelling phrases. The parody nonetheless had a serious intent, to suggest that there was no essential difference between criminal gangs and government ministers who distributed among their followers wealth taken from the public purse. Again, Voltaire (1694–1778), the philosopher often thought to epitomize the Enlightenment, subjected abstractions and metaphysical beliefs to such ruthless parody and exaggeration that he was known as 'the genius of Hate' (Hazard 1965: 438).[2] Later, for both conservative and sociological critics, this style was viewed as epitomizing the 'negative', that is destructive and nihilistic, philosophy of the Enlightenment.

The Enlightenment, then, could assume many forms. For the purposes of this discussion, however, those aspects that are of most interest point towards the birth of sociology. Four issues are of particular importance here.

First, there was the critique of religious systems of thought. Kant echoed the generally negative view of institutional religion among Enlightenment writers, suggesting that 'religious immaturity is the most pernicious and dishonorable variety of all' ([1784] 1970: 55). For many Enlightenment figures, progress could occur only once the institutional power of the Church had been broken. For Diderot, editor of *l'Encyclopédie*, to which all leading eighteenth century French intellectuals contributed, humans would progress in peace only if the idea of God were obliterated (Hazard 1965: 407). Diderot and other *philosophes* followed the seventeenth-century English philosopher Francis Bacon, believing that empirical knowledge could improve the human condition. Indeed, *l'Encyclopédie* aimed to provide an organized synopsis of available knowledge in order that 'our descendants . . . may become . . . happier and more virtuous' (quoted in Hazard 1965: 228). Many contributors were materialists who denied that mind was distinct from matter, thereby denying too religious notions of the soul. Benoît de Mailler and La Mettrie for example regarded the 'soul as an appendage of the body' and thought as merely a product of organic matter, like electricity (La Mettrie, *L'Homme Machine*, 1747).

Such explicit atheism was controversial though, and we should anyway be wary of regarding this period as one universally critical of religion. John Locke, an influence on many Enlightenment writers, had renounced knowledge that was not knowable to the senses, but nevertheless resisted atheism, basing his argument for Natural Rights (to life, liberty and property) on Divine Law. Again, the school of natural jurisprudence founded by Christian Wolff claimed that morality was an affair of reason, and that faith could be rationally justified.[3] More common than atheism was Deism, the belief that God existed, but that his nature and purpose were unknowable. Then there were natural theologians for whom knowledge of order and symmetry in nature could establish rational knowledge of God. Others, such as Rousseau, distinguished between religious belief, which was false, and the social functions of religion, which contributed to social order. In this context Rousseau (1968: 186) advocated a civil religion that would prohibit intolerance and inculcate ideas of the sanctity of the **social contract**. However, even if the Enlightenment was not consistently hostile to religion, the widespread insistence on reason and mistrust of abstract speculation opened the way to understand society as a human product, which was crucial to the sociological imagination. It further raised issues that sociologists were to address, from different points of view of course, including the dichotomies between empirical knowledge and metaphysical belief; society and nature; the bases of social order in a secular age; the critique of ideology and the basis of validity.

Second, there was the question of progress itself. Enlightenment writers did not generally have a theory of historical progress (which would be developed by Hegel, Comte and Marx, among others) although one did begin to take shape in Adam Smith, Condorcet and Turgot. Nonetheless, the idea of linear expansion of reason did begin to become popular during this period, as philosophy broke from cyclical theories of the rise and decline of civilizations, which had roots in classical historiography.[4] For the classical historian Polybius, for example, all civilizations passed through six phases of progress and regression, a claim that was rejected by *philosophes* in part on the empirical grounds that a model derived from the history of Rome could not exhaust all possible historical narratives (McClelland 1996: 307). Anyway, notions of inevitable regression were not conducive to the Age of Reason, which looked with disdain on the Middle Ages as an era of despotism, superstition and clerical domination to which people would never return. In his *Discourses on the Successive Progress of the Human Mind* ([1750] 1913) Turgot argued that we can break the cycle of nature through reason and language, permitting us to grasp knowledge firmly and transmit it to others. He further suggested that history passed through three phases, later echoed by Saint-Simon and Auguste Comte:

1 the religious stage in which rulers were deified and nature anthromorphized
2 the metaphysical stage in which philosophers attacked religious fables but explained the world through abstract idea of 'essences' and 'faculties'
3 the scientific, positive age where people observe mechanical actions of bodies and make hypotheses.

(Gay 1996: 109)

In the latter period progress is inevitable as moral restraints grow milder, the mind is enlightened, nations cooperate and commerce unites the globe.

Similarly, Condorcet (1743–94), a former student of Turgot, developed a ten-stage progressive history in *Sketch for the Historical Picture of the Progress of the Human Mind* (1794). As with Turgot's *Discourses*, this *Sketch* was a history of the mind, that is of culture, beliefs and philosophies, on the basis of which Condorcet divided history into epochs (see Figure 2.1). He identified an alternation between critical and superstitious periods, in which the latter could stimulate the former. Obscurantist, Medieval Scholasticism, for example, had sharpened minds sufficiently

Figure 2.1 Condorcet's Progress of Human Mind

Stage 1    Hordes. Hunting, fishing, gathering.

Stage 2    Pastoral economy. Appearance of property, inequality, slavery.

Stage 3    Mixed agriculture. Leisure time increases, division of labour, literacy. Knowledge of nature grows, but is used only to ensure rule of the powerful.

Stage 4    Hellenistic culture. Flowering of philosophy. But death of Socrates opened war between philosophy and superstition.

Stage 5    Roman Empire. Continued scientific culture. But the spread of Christianity marked the return of superstition and reaction.

Stage 6    Feudal order up to the Crusades. Rule of priests which demoted intellect and secured tyranny.

Stage 7    Later feudalism up to the invention of printing. Sciences begin to restore themselves. Out of scholastic obscurantism scientific method develops.

Stage 8    Critical philosophy (sixteenth and seventeenth centuries). Church weaker, but can still wage terrible persecutions.

Stage 9    Scientific knowledge and continuous reconstruction of society. Battle for progress and science against reaction.

Stage 10   Future society. The elimination of inequalities; human rights; equality of men and women; scientific civilization.

to stimulate the subsequent development of scientific method and systems of classification. The critical age that had flourished in the eighteenth century, in battle with clerical repression, was finally to bring human affairs to a new age:

> The time will therefore come when the sun will shine only on free men who know no other master but their reason; when tyrants and slaves, priests and their stupid or hypocritical instruments will exist only in works of history and on the stage; and when we shall think of them only to pity their victims . . . to recognise and to destroy by force of reason, the first seeds of tyranny and superstition should they ever dare to reappear amongst us.
>
> (Condorcet [1794] 1976: 262–3)

However, contrary to some accounts (e.g. Szacki 1979) eighteenth-century thought did not express unalloyed enthusiasm about the process of 'civilization',[5] and ambivalence was a more typical pose. In *Le Mondain* (1736) and in somewhat uncharacteristic mood, Voltaire had extolled the virtues of luxury and the new 'iron age', in which progress in knowledge and material living were undeniable; governments were restrained by guarantees to citizens; social life was becoming more reasonable and humane. Yet most *philosophes* and, indeed, Voltaire himself in more sombre vein, feared luxury and abundance as a 'dark shadow following the growth of cultivation' (Gay 1996: 100). Rousseau challenged the widespread enthusiasm for civilization by claiming that progress was an illusion and that civilization had made life neither happy nor virtuous. Happiness (in the sense of a life unimpeded by longing for something better) belonged in the state of nature and virtue in simple societies. Yet writers generally sympathetic to the idea of progress too had reservations. Adam Smith, a central figure in the Scottish Enlightenment and the birth of political economy, identified a gradual increase in moral sense, sympathy and self-command among 'civilized nations' and regarded the new commercial society as having advanced civilization to a new historical stage (A. Smith 1976a: 468). But even such a 'cosmic optimist' (Gay 1996: 361) saw negative as well as positive consequences arising from the division of labour. The former arose from dehumanization resulting from overspecialization, which results in mental torpor, loss of ability to engage in rational conversation, express tender sentiment or form just judgements. Similarly, Adam Ferguson's *Essay on the History of Civil Society* (1767) noted how the expansion of commerce and manufacturing extended liberty and abundance yet lead to social disintegration and dehumanization. Ferguson's analysis of conflict endemic in personal and social development in the division of labour intimated tensions that set the scene in some ways for the Marxist critique of alienation. That eighteenth century writers frequently expressed ambivalence about progress is important in that (as we shall see) the idea of the modern is often tinged with nostalgia for a culture that has been lost.

Third, there was the enthusiasm for scientific and socially useful knowledge, based on empirical research, which underpinned the critique of speculative thinking. The 'scientific revolution' of the seventeenth century was widely viewed as a critical turning point in human history, and Newton was widely celebrated as the hero of Enlightenment (Gay 1996: 128ff). Newtonian physics had reduced the complex behaviour of the universe to simple, harmonious, principles of gravity and mathematical laws of motion. Perhaps there were a few principles fundamental to human life too, which once known could provide the basis for rational government? The implications of quest for the social sciences though were varied. For some such as La Mettrie, this required making a knowledge of the mind a physical science following naturalistic methods (R. Smith 1997: 233ff). But this kind of scientism, the belief that the natural sciences offered a model for all knowledge, was atypical of the *philosophes* and the comparisons between physics and human governance was by analogy. Indeed, for much of the eighteenth century, there was no sense of a conflict between admiration for science and the salon culture which emphasized literary modes of expression judged in terms of their *esprit*, of elegance and eloquence. The divide between literary and scientific modes of expression was to crystallize later, influenced on the one hand by post-revolutionary developments in life-sciences and on the other, by the literary Romanticism of Chateaubriand, de Staël and other writers in *Mercure de France* in the 1800s.

The status of natural science did rise during the Napoleonic period (1799–1816) partly because of its applicability to military technology and partly because of developments in physiology and biology. The development of physiological classifications and systematic comparisons of species conducted by Curvier, Cabanis and Lamark not only represented new forms of comparative method but also signalled the differentiation of the sciences into various branches. These developments did offer models for early sociology but this was less a continuation of Enlightenment approaches, so much as a departure from the idea of a harmonic unity of nature, now fragmented into disciplines engaged in boundary disputes. Further, sociologists influenced by these post-revolutionary conceptions of science, notably August Comte, offered a differentiated concept of scientific method and did not attempt to found sociology simply as a copy of existing natural sciences. We shall see in Chapter 3 that Comte argued for a unity of science, in the sense that all branches of knowledge formed an integrated methodological hierarchy, while not claiming that all sciences pursued identical methods.

Scien*tism* then, was not the principal legacy of the Enlightenment, although, the idea that knowledge should be useful and contribute to human happiness was important. Peasants needed to be instructed in the use of new implements, merchants and manufacturers in new technologies, and public servants in new tasks (Gay 1996: 499). This required a break with traditional religious and classical conceptions of education, for which

John Locke had set the scene in his *Some Thoughts Concerning Education*
in 1699 ([1699] 1884). Here he denounced traditional methods of rote
learning and corporal punishment, calling for education that was relevant to students' careers. Diderot likewise advocated secular education,
that Latin should give way to modern languages, teachers paying attention to stages in childhood development, to produce scientists, agricul-
turists and economists, who would 'render useful service' (Hazard 1965:
407). Among educational philosophers there was a celebration of machines and mechanical arts and for Encyclopedists, the status of workers
and craftsmen should be raised 'to the centre around which everything
revolves' (Hazard 1965: 227).

Not only was this about changing the content of education, but also
it involved new theories of personal and social development, in particular the role of environment in shaping moral individuals. What was
controversial about these pedagogical optimists was less their specific
recommendations so much as the implicit challenge to status quo contained in their insistence on the importance of environmental influences.
If, as Locke had claimed, people's character was formed through the
effect of sensations on centres of passion, then as Helvétius argued in
*De l'ésprit* (1758) and *De l'homme* (1772), the 'art of forming man'
is determined by the general environment, including forms of government (R. Smith 1997: 286). Further, the idea that people's character
and disposition were formed by their environment introduced moral
relativism and weakened notions of sin and guilt. Traditional religious
injunctions were of less use to the lawgiver than knowledge of psychology, on which basis people's passions could be adjusted to encourage
them to act justly towards one another (Hazard 1965: 215). The influence of these ideas (and controversies arising from them) can be seen
in the following two centuries in debates over equality and difference,
socialism, nature and nurture, and the potential as well as risks of social
engineering.

Fourth, there was the rule of reason. In the place of government based
on superstition and fear, enlightened rule would be founded on natural
rights, the social equivalent perhaps to Newtonian principles of gravitation. These claims, however, had various implications. Most *philosophes*
were opposed to slavery, despotism and racial discrimination on natural
rights grounds that 'man' possessed universal rights to liberty of body
and mind. But the concept of natural rights did not imply any particular
form of government and until the late eighteenth century (with the
exception of Rousseau) there was little enthusiasm for a republic.[6] Few
*philosophes* were democrats in a contemporary sense, since democracy
retained Roman connotations of 'rule by the mob'. The rule of reason by
contrast would ideally achieve Plato's dream of the 'philosopher king',
or at any rate, power would be concentrated in a sovereign centre from
whence it could become an instrument of reform. Some (like Voltaire)
believed they had found this quality in 'enlightened despots' such as

Frederick II or Catherine of Russia with whom they engaged in admiring correspondence and trotted off to the courts of Berlin and St Petersburg. There was of course a contradiction in such adulation of despotism by advocates of freedom and tolerance, but this was a contradiction that remained unresolved in post-Enlightenment political and intellectual developments.[7]

The emancipatory force of Reason in eighteenth century thought was not confined to statecraft. Beccaria's *On Crime and Punishment* ([1764] 1963) developed an influential programme of penal reform. He argued that laws are social and that judgements should be delivered only with the welfare of society in mind. Similarly, in 1806 Phillipe Pinel announced new techniques for treating 'insanity' based on his work at two Paris asylums, the Bicêtre and Salpétrière, where he had dramatically struck chains from the inmates. His philosophy of 'moral management' was based on principles of creating an educative milieu that stimulated self-respect, thereby enabling patients to control wayward passions. Pinel reflected the Enlightenment's self-understanding as an age of humane rationality in that heavy hand of external restraint (chains, straps, etc.) would be replaced by the rational consent of self-regulating subjects, combined with 'minute observation and classification of insanity' (Pinel [1806] 1962: 45). The reformed asylums of the early nineteenth century, then, were in some ways microcosms of the ideal of the bourgeois polity – public policy based on reason would reform physical and social environments in order to produce autonomous subjects.

The potential force of reason as self-emancipation is further illustrated by Mary Wollstonecraft (1759–97). In *Vindication of the Rights of Woman* ([1792] 1975) she argued that excluded from reason and education, women are confined within the arbitrary power of beauty and sensual experience. Men constitute women as 'the fair sex' through rituals of gallantry and courtesy, thereby separating women from the male world of reason. Once trapped within the sensual world of beauty, women are forced into both financial and emotional dependence on men, and a life of 'listless inactivity'. But women are not passive in this process because they gain power from the game of gallantry and coquetry, while playing on male weakness – the sensual homage to beauty. However, this is a double enslavement because what appears to give women power, male adoration really enslaves them within a 'pleasure-power' prison, by reinforcing their exclusion from respect as equals and rational beings. Women's emancipation therefore lies in education and the development of rational faculties combined with an ascetic life in which both men and women 'submit only to reason and virtue, transforming our inner selves' in 'a revolution in manners and compassion' (S. Alexander 1990: 26; Gane 1993: 59–82).

Concepts of human rights, universalism and constitutional rule then, challenged traditional notions of governance. The Enlightenment's legacy was to insist that

1 constitutions were not given by God or tradition, but as human conventions were subject to change
2 progress in human organization was possible and desirable
3 such reform could be based on reason and knowledge of human needs
4 intellectuals had a crucial role to play in the process of reform.

## INVENTING 'SOCIETY'

The following discussion examines the emergence of concepts of the social around four dimensions that have become central themes of sociological controversy. Theories of social contract were based on an individualistic notion of covenant between subjects and the state, from which civil society could develop. Materiality and morality refers to the idea of the social as embedded in economic processes and their interaction with moral development. Society as a system refers to the concept of society as an organic, functionally integrated whole. Habit and order refers to the view, associated particularly with counter-Enlightenment thought but influential in sociology, that society is constituted through non-rational bonds of solidarity.

### Theories of social contract

Theories of social contract, which were widespread from the Renaissance through to the nineteenth century, were primarily concerned with explaining the existence of the state, and suggested that there had been an original contract, in which people surrendered powers and freedoms to social and political institutions for their mutual benefit. However, in their deliberations on the state, leading theorists of contract – Hobbes, Locke and Rousseau – increasingly presupposed a theory of social life, as the state was positioned within a more general context. Theories of governmental contract have a long history – an early example is the description in Genesis of the Covenant between God and Abraham, which was cited in medieval doctrines of governmental compact (McClelland 1996: 172–3). Later influences were the seventeenth-century Mayflower Compact and the Association of the English Commonwealth, which assumed that every citizen must be party to the contract (Barnes 1969: 33). Despite the religious roots of contract theory, however, three, secular, implications followed from later versions.[8] First, temporal power and social organization could be founded rationally through inquiry into the basis of the social order. Second, political, and by extension general social arrangements are artificial and conventional, rather than naturally or divinely determined. As such they are subject to change by common agreement in the light of rational knowledge. Third, contract arguments introduce a procedural criterion of whether or not the law and social conventions are good. The law becomes good not primarily because of its content but because it was made by the right people in the right way. Although it is implicit that law made according to the correct procedures should be in the collective interests of society, one aim of this theorizing was to justify disobedience, in the event of rulers breaking the contract.

Thomas Hobbes (1588–1679) was in some ways atypical of social contract theorists – his analysis was to show why people should *obey* the state – but he has become a central figure in these debates. Auguste Comte described him as the 'principal precursor of scientific politics'. He was the 'first to apply scientific method to society', and to emphasize the importance of material interests, social contract and the warlike nature of primitive society (Comte [1830] 1975, vol. 2: 445). Hobbes imagined what life would have been like in a presocial state of nature, although he claimed neither that such a state had existed historically nor that it could exist in the future.[9] It was a depiction of essential human tendencies that were an ever-present threat to social peace, which could be guaranteed only through the Agreement. In the state of nature 'the life of man was solitary, poore, nasty, brutish and short' (Hobbes [1651] 1994: 71). This is because without a Common Power, or state, people live in a 'condition which is called Warre, . . . as is every man against every man' (p. 71). Rationality and mutual self-interest, however, persuade people to combine in agreement, to seek peace and be contented with only so much liberty as they would allow against themselves. Thus a Common Power is established by covenant to constrain those who would otherwise violate the social peace, which requires that people surrender their sovereignty to the state in return for protection. The Sovereign Power, as the judge of what is necessary for the Peace, has sole responsibility for making laws, the right of judicature, and the right to make war. Its subjects can challenge sovereignty only when it is no longer able to protect them and otherwise should be obeyed (Hobbes [1651] 1994: 130).

With the social contract comes a separation between political and civil society, which he describes as two systems, that is 'numbers of men joyned in one Interest' as parts of the body (p. 131). The political system is constituted by the Sovereign Power and civil society by subjects 'among themselves'. However, the political system is clearly the dominant part. In entering the social contract people agree to surrender the freedom of the state of nature *to* a Sovereign Power which is not itself a party to the Agreement, but stands above it. Sovereignty is indivisible and irrevocable – it cannot be removed, accused, punished or lawfully executed by its subjects. This is an argument conducted at a high level of generality (Hobbes wanted to avoid being seen to justify either Cromwell's Commonwealth or the Royalist Restoration) and does not imply support for any particular form of government. Whether sovereignty is conferred 'upon one Man, or upon one Assembly of men' what is important is that 'all their Wills' are reduced into one (Hobbes [1651] 1994: 99). People were naturally atomistic and aggressive, yet were possessed of the capacity of reason, which leads them out of the state of nature, to a precarious peace. Being artificial and conventional, the state cannot be derived from human nature although it is necessitated by it, thus society was impossible without the state.

Nonetheless, we see here the formation of a concept of society that was to be developed by subsequent theorists, often in the course of disputing Hobbes' thesis. The separation of civil and political life as mutually sustaining systems was an essential step towards conceptualizing 'the social' as a sphere of activity in itself. Moreover, the realm of private activity, while governed by sovereign laws, was otherwise bound only by conscience (*in foro interno*) and the rules of civic association. That is some aspects of social life at least are self-regulating rather than constrained only by the external power of the sovereign.

One problem with Hobbes' depiction of the state of nature is that he says relatively little about it, but assumes that in this hypothetical scenario people would submit to the Covenant because this was what interest in peace demanded. As an account of the state it is teleological – it explains its existence in terms of the need for its existence. Moreover, since life in the state of nature was one of continuous war, it is unclear what would have prompted people to have suspended their rivalry and sacrificed their sovereignty to a Common Power, even it was 'rational' to do so.

An important counter to Hobbes came from Locke's *Second Treatise on Civil Government* ([1681–3] 1980),[10] where he developed another version of the social contract, based on natural rights and the free consent of the governed. For Locke the state of nature was not terrifying but naturally sociable, in which people enjoyed liberty and recognized one another's rights. Obeying God's law involves a corresponding set of rights – to life, liberty and property. Reason, he argues, tells us that all others have the same rights as ourselves, which includes the right of judgment if one's rights are violated. The evidence for this, Locke believed, could be found in language and in gold as media of exchange, both of which predated state societies. Language demonstrates people's capacity for conventional agreements – to name objects, form rules of grammar etc., while gold as a symbol of value demonstrates the capacity to agree on conventions in the absence of a state. In the natural state, property, competitive commercial relationships and a tendency to harmony were already present. Thus societies arise spontaneously whereas states do not; government exists as a result of a contract to protect rights to life, liberty and property in return for which subjects give their loyalty and the state forfeits its right to rule should it threaten natural rights. Indeed, entering into such a contract is risky, since states have a tendency towards despotism and usurpation of power and should be constrained by constitutional contracts based on natural rights.

Unlike Hobbes' unified sovereignty that stands above civil society, Locke's concept of the contract involves the subordination of the state to society, in which the latter restrains the former. People in Locke's state thus have the right of rebellion (such as that of the English Parliament against James II in 1688), unlike those under Hobbes' *Leviathan*. However, if there is a problem with Hobbes, that it is unclear how such warlike people would ever agree to the contract, there is perhaps the reverse problem in Locke. Why, since the state of nature is so agreeable and covenanting to government so risky, should people have done so in the first place? This problem was endemic in theories that attempted to conceptualize an original moment at which the state or society was born.

With Jean-Jacques Rousseau (1712–78) the balance between civil society and the state moved further in the favour of society. Rousseau did not set out to explain the existence of society at all, but regarded it as a natural, material outcome of agrarian organization. The division of labour had come with the partition of land and hence the emergence of private property. This in turn had created new desires and competition, and the ensuing conflict necessitates the development of government and law. Thus unlike Hobbes (but similar to Ferguson and subsequently Marx) conflict for Rousseau was not the result of human nature, but of the social institution of property (*Discourse on Inequality*, [1754] 1992). Indeed, in the state of nature that may have preceded society, 'man' was a 'stupid and unimaginative animal', without language and unable to imagine any different state. For Rousseau there was no Hobbesian choice between government and freedom, nor was it fear that drove people together, but rather sympathy – 'common miseries which carry our hearts towards humanity' ([1762] 1974: 249). The famous statement with which *The Social Contract* opens, 'Man is born free and is everywhere in chains', was not a call to return to natural freedom, but (as he continues to say) the basis of an inquiry into how political rule can be made legitimate (Rousseau [1762] 1968: 49).

The state of nature is not to be revisited then, but the original state of equality does remain the yardstick by which existing institutions may be evaluated. Moreover, even if the state of nature never existed, as Rousseau suggested in his *Preface to Discourse on Origin of Inequality*, and even if, like Locke, sociability is spontaneous, what has followed has been artificial and corrupting. Two examples should illustrate this. First, inequality breeds dependence so, because of their mutual dependence, both master and slave are unfree – a point that Hegel was later to argue too. An ideal social state would be one in which people become 'equal by covenant and right', where material inequalities are not extreme (Rousseau [1762] 1968: 63) and where people rule themselves as equal parties to a social contract. So far so good. But second, centuries of customs and prejudices inimical to the idea of a democratic republic have first to be destroyed. To be freed from dependence, people are 'obliged to subordinate their will to their reason . . . they must be taught to recognize what they desire' ([1762] 1968: 83). Indeed people must be 'forced to be free' ([1762] 1968: 64). This educative task requires a lawgiver ('the engineer who invents the machine') whose authority can compel people to accept a constitution suited to their needs. The lawgiver is not the sovereign power, which is the people themselves, and must educate, not use violence. Nonetheless, there is here a sense of a return to a way of life more authentic and austere than that in the eighteenth century.

So, although Rousseau presupposes the social, it is also liable to become corrupt, in comparison with a more 'natural' ideal. This can be seen too in his account of the general will in the democratic republic. Sovereign power creates a new kind of public interest, the general will, that transcends private interests (particular wills) and establishes a moral duty among citizens to subordinate private to public interests. The republic can continue to exercise popular sovereignty only so long as an objective harmony of interests is expressed through public opinion. Otherwise Rousseau would have difficulty arguing (as he does) that the minority should be forced to accede to the will of the majority. But eventually the general will tends to degenerate in the face of particular wills because

- there is a tendency for governments to usurp sovereign power and become tyrannies
- the bustle of commerce and crafts reduces public virtue
- the development of paid deputies entail consequent loss of popular sovereignty
- social ties weaken as particular wills make themselves felt.

The general will can be corrupted, but society does not thereby disintegrate. In Rousseau the social has a resilience that was unknown to Hobbes, because it is not merely a collection of atomized individuals, but governed by 'morals, customs and beliefs' on which the success of the law depends (Rousseau [1762] 1968: 99). Even so, his account of the tendency of the general will to degenerate reveals something anachronistic about Rousseau's thought. The division of labour ('bustle of commerce and crafts') is viewed as a threat to unified sovereignty at a point when society was undergoing rapid social differentiation. The social contract was modelled on an idealized view of ancient city states and in this sense his work displays a longing for community – the small society of equals in which each is known to the other. The idea of the lawgiver, moreover, replays an origin myth, which refuses to accept the diffuse and organic nature of social institutions and conventions. With the development of sociology in the nineteenth century, speculation as to the origins of society along with the individualistic notions of contract gives way to a more organic view.

## MATERIALITY AND MORALITY

During the eighteenth century commerce and the market became increasingly visible and important aspects of social life. This had a number of consequences. One was that society could no longer be viewed as organized from a political centre, but appeared rather to be a diffuse collection of voluntary associations operating in civil society. Another consequence was that a potential value conflict arose between the self-interested nature of commercial activity and the interests of public good. One way of reconciling this problem was to argue that private, egotistical vices of commerce, paradoxically perhaps, gave rise to public good. In the *Fable of the Bees, Or Private Vices, Public Benefits* ([1729] 1924) Bernard Mandeville (1670–1733) argued precisely that. There was no match, he claimed, between individual intentions, which may be selfish, and social outcomes, which may be beneficial. The unintended and unpredictable outcome of private vice was the generation of wealth *and* increased social integration, as society becomes a harmonious interplay of different kinds of activities, without dissolving into chaos. Two ideas are particularly important here. First, the consequences of individual actions are detached from their intentions, which gives birth to the theory of unintended consequences. Second, social difference and the division of labour were integrative, not destructive, through what Adam Smith famously called the 'hidden hand' of the market, bringing order out of apparent chaos.

With Adam Smith (1723–90) there is a decisive move from individualistic contract theories. Here society is an always existing set of networks of association that are not derived from individual reason but from human sentiments, such as the sexual impulse, property, sympathy and prejudice. He found in political economy a self-regulating harmony comparable to that of the Newtonian universe.[11] There was no need for a hypothetical state of nature or social contract, because 'society . . . appears like a great immense machine, whose regular and harmonious movements produce a thousand agreeable effects' (A. Smith 1976a: 463). Hobbes' 'odious doctrine', he says, provided no criterion for distinguishing right from wrong, and anyway purely selfish sentiments could not provide the basis for social solidarity (1976a: 467). Nor though, do natural ethics, which can be used to argue contradictory cases. For example, was it lawful to commit suicide? Yes, because Nature permitted it. But then no, because Nature was concerned with the survival of the species and whoever destroys themselves contravenes Nature's law.

On what then does the harmony of society depend? Commercial societies (like Britain) seemed to be miracles of voluntary social cooperation through the use of labour, one consequence of which is that the militaristic state, which was central to seventeenth century politics, was of diminishing significance. Societies appeared to divide naturally into different economic and social functions in ways that supplemented one another. But Smith did not claim that the division of labour was self-sufficient, producing a spontaneous order, rather social integration was achieved because of the human faculty of sympathy. This is not innate but derived from experience as we learn to 'place ourselves in the circumstances of another', and it is pleasant to know that others share our emotions because when we share it we approve it too. This capacity for sympathy enables us to regulate our conduct by anticipating the effects of our actions on others who then serve as a mirror to ourselves. Smith describes this self-reflection as the 'impartial spectator' who stands apart from and modifying interaction, giving rise to 'self-command' of conduct in 'civilized nations'. This is contrasted with the 'self-denial' of 'rude and barbarous peoples', who follow strict codes of conduct but are insensible to the torment of others. Here Smith articulates the contrast noted above, between social control operating through external restraint (fear of punishment) and that arising from what sociologists later called internalization of cultural values. Smith further developed a materialistic account of stages of social development organized around the progress of productive systems. These passed through hunting, pastoral, agricultural and commercial forms, which introduced the important idea that progress is governed by innovations in production.

For Smith, though, markets tended to create harmony, while power and conflict play relatively minor parts in his theory. This is less the case with Adam Ferguson (1723–1816) who placed the development of civil society at the centre of analysis (Ferguson [1767] 1966: 8). We never 'leave' the state of nature, he says, because we are continually in creative interaction with the environment. However, social development arises from the institution of property, which brings with it inequalities of rank, the subordination of women and slaves, and warring communities, as people unite into clans and fraternities. But foreign wars establish national boundaries, and within the areas of domestic peace thus created develop trade and commerce, the division of labour, civil society, the rule of law and liberal sentiments. Like Smith, Ferguson ([1767] 1966: 273) views state power with suspicion, since it threatens to subvert the independence of civil society. But Ferguson is troubled also by the negative consequences of commercial society – that communities may 'lose the sense of every connection . . . and have no common affairs but those of trade' (p. 219). Ferguson was not a critic of capitalism, but raised questions about the social consequences of economic organization that have been replayed in sociology in various ways.

The Scottish Enlightenment, in which the development of political economy was central, made a range of important contributions to the theory of society. Placed in the forefront of analysis were

- the division of labour as a principle of regulation and its implications for social solidarity
- continual progress linked to changes in forms of economic life
- the gradual domination of industry over the military state
- the study of society rather than the individual and rejection of the ahistoricial individualism of social contract theories.

**Figure 2.2** Montesquieu's theory of government

| Governments | Spirit | Sovereignty | Example |
|---|---|---|---|
| **Republic** | Virtue | Citizen-voter | Athens |
| **Monarchy** | Honour | Monarch with constitutional law | England |
| **Despotism** | Fear | Individual power unlimited | Asiatic states |

## SOCIETY AS A SYSTEM

It used to be said (e.g. Aron 1970) that Montesquieu (1689–1755) founded sociology. This was probably an exaggeration, since his theory was not specifically social in focus but contained speculations on the influence of climate on national character, as well as displaying some residual theological concerns. However, his comparative analysis of forms of government, in *Spirit of the Laws* ([1748] 1949), was acknowledged as an influence by many theorists, including Rousseau, Ferguson, Comte and Durkheim. Whereas the theory of social contract had envisaged civil society emerging through an agreement between people and a lawgiver, Montesquieu dispensed with the idea of a presocial state. 'Man', he said, 'is born into society and there he stays' (Durkheim 1965: 64). He rejected Hobbes' concept of atomized, warring individuals on the grounds that the war of all could never bring social peace, which required virtue enforced by the law. Further he noted that forms of the law varied between countries and seemed to express a relationship with an ensemble of natural and social factors particular to each region of the world. In *Spirit of the Laws* he set out to develop a comparative analysis of forms of government.

Each form of government had three aspects: its nature, spirit and object. By nature, he meant its formal constitutional structure; by spirit, its tendency to act in a particular way; by object, its ultimate purpose, such as 'liberty' or 'honour'. Following the history of ancient Rome, which he argued had experienced all forms of government, Montesquieu identi-fied three types (see Figure 2.2). First, there were republics (e.g. Athens) founded on the spirit of virtue or civic ethics. By virtue he meant thirst for glory, self-denial and sacrifice of what one hold dearest for heroic values. Republics would require (as for Rousseau) communities small enough for face-to-face contact and democratic assemblies. Second, there were monarchies (e.g. England) founded on honour or status, by which he meant the ambition for preferment and titles. This was his favoured type, which embodied the principle of separation of powers between the legislature, executive and juridical branches of government. Here the monarch, though sovereign, was subject to checks and balances of the law, parliament, and 'the intermediate powers', such as guilds, the church, communities and professional bodies. Both these types, however, were in danger of degenerating into the third, despotism (e.g. Asian societies) founded on fear and the will of an individual. By fear, he meant the caprice of the prince in the face of which the population are passive. Montesquieu was not suggesting that societies such as China and Russia were literally ruled by one despot, but that lacking a system of balances, power was devolved to 'petty tyrants' who were unanswerable to the law and used their positions for self-enrichment. His description of despotism, further, was part of his answer to Hobbes. Absolute state power neither worked well nor brought social peace, and was therefore unlikely to survive long among the self-assertive people that Hobbes depicts in the state of nature.

In explaining these variations he looked at the interaction of the natural environment with social factors. He considered geography (climate and soil), the way of life (were people ploughmen, hunters, herdsmen, etc.?), forms of trade and currency, population, religion, mores and manners. The type of government that develops is that best suited to these conditions. Thus laws are embedded in the wider system of relationships within the society and in particular adapt to material nature. In some respects Montesquieu was a crude materialist, to the point of claiming that climate affects the 'fibres' of the body – so that people in northern, cold climates were flexible and open in their manners, while southerners rigid and resistant to work! But the principle that climate, topography and soil interact with social and political systems was an attempt to offer a holistic and synthetic approach to social analysis. He did also suggest that as societies became more complex, social factors become more determinate and act back to shape the environment.

An important legacy of Montesquieu's was to view society as a system of interrelated elements working for mutual benefit, which had been suggested in part of course by the existence of a functionally integrated division of labour. Thus in Montesquieu's social theory the individualistic idea of contract gave way to a systemic and organic view of the social that has to be understood through comparative analysis. Montesquieu further developed a notion of social differentiation of society into subsystems. Thus laws regulate subjects; manners regulate private lives; customs regulate external behaviour. Implicit in this is a cultural relativism which suggests that traditions reflect particular conditions and cannot therefore be judged good or bad in themselves.

## HABIT AND ORDER

The industrial revolution was accompanied from its outset by a Romantic critique that was to be influential in sociology in significant respects.

Two figures who were important in the counter-revolutionary reaction and in the development of sociology were Louis de Bonald (1754–1840) and Joseph de Maistre (1754–1821). For the conservative counter-Enlightenment, the French Revolution and emerging capitalism had broken the old moral order based on church, family, community and the essential system of status. The Enlightenment's critical stance, they believed, combined with the **Jacobins**' assault on the 'immobile' society and polity of the *ancien régime* destroyed the bases of social order (Reedy 1994). For de Bonald (1864, vol. 3: 956) the Revolution was a 'horrifying, moral, political historical phenomenon which . . . displays the effectiveness of human perversity in its decomposition of the social body'. Democracy, he claimed, represented anti-natural government derogating royal and ministerial functions.

A central issue here was the nature and basis of the social order. In different ways, Enlightenment thinkers had supposed that society could be based on rational consent, a claim that for its critics was a dangerous conceit. For de Maistre and de Bonald constitutions could be devised neither by social contract nor revolution, but were the slow, invisible work of history. De Maistre ([1796] 1974) claimed that they were a divine creation and, without the dogma of God the Lawgiver, all moral obligations were an illusion. People, he claimed, are fit to live in civic liberty only to the extent that it is led by Christian principles. Human nature is irreducible to rational will and the bases of the social order are organic and non-rational. Thus in the Republic of Virtue (1793–4) the Jacobins attempted to substitute Christianity with the Cult of the Supreme Being, introducing a new calendar, festivals and rituals. But Christian culture had thrived and people remained attached to the 'commemoration of half-forgotten deeds of local saints' (Milbank 1993: 55).

Moreover, the Enlightenment could not explain why unreason dominated human history. Take for example the practice of sacrifice, which (De Maistre claimed) is found in all cultures. Rationalist philosophers have no way of accounting for this except as an offering to placate or influence the gods – that is, as a kind of instrumental exchange. But they cannot understand sacrifice as a symbolic substitute for the offence against the power of the sacred. In Christianity the Fall is an offence against this power for which mere repentance is insufficient, and expiation demands blood to replenish itself (Milbank 1993: 56). For de Bonald, Christian society could dispense with actual sacrifice because of the infinite and all-sufficient sacrifice offered to the Father by the Son. The major public events of the Catholic Church though are symbolic sacrifices – of the crucifixion and repeated immolations of the Mass. Thus sacrifice does not have a rational explanation, and for de Maistre and de Bonald can be understood only if one understands the social itself as a sacred order. This idea was to be particularly important in Durkheim's theory of ritual and, more generally, in his understanding of the non-rational bases of social order.

For the conservatives moreover, medieval society, which was rejected by the *philosophes* as an era of tyranny and superstition, had actually solved problems of social integration. This view was shared by conservatives such as de Staël, Lamartine and Chateaubriand, who hoped for a return of faith and glorified the past. For de Bonald this order was based in the rituals (rather than specifically the beliefs) of Catholicism, the power of the monarchy and the multiple intermediate associations of feudal society, such as nobility, guilds, communities and professional bodies. Medieval society embodied the natural order of relations between monarch, nobility and people which expressed three functions of power, ministership and subservience respectively.

This was not simply a reaction against modernity, but 'traditionalism that had become conscious of itself', in that their critique took account of social and intellectual changes in the eighteenth century and attempted to meet them head on (Heilbron 1995: 162). This was a challenge to Kant's celebration of individual judgement, and a defence of dogma and authority. It was against Rousseau's vision of radical democracy, in the name of natural hierarchy and organic constitutions. It was against Montesquieu's 'division of powers' in favour of a theory of the unity of power, safeguarded by religious conscience. For de Bonald the social changes of the eighteenth century – commerce, industry and large cities – were as subversive as the Jacobins of organic social bonds. Increased social distance between individuals had seen the triumph of the moneyed character of all life (Nisbet 1986: 65). This was, moreover, an assault on the universalistic language of rights. Critical philosophy, said de Bonald, had seen the triumph of 'I' over 'we', of selfish egoism over altruism and community. 'I have met', said de Maistre, 'Russians, Frenchmen, Englishmen, but 'I have never met man in general' (Menczer 1952: 34).

Further, writers like de Maistre and de Bonald mounted their deeply reactionary assault on the rights and universalism of Enlightenment through the language of social science. 'Society' remained for them a central category and they thought of themselves as social scientists, though not pursuing the methods of the natural sciences, which they regarded as inappropriate to moral life (Heilbron 1995: 159). De Bonald's theory of society, which need not concern us in detail, was a complex elaboration of the Trinitarian principle: each facet of society could be understood in terms of three elements, such as 'I/you/he' in grammar, 'father/mother/child', 'sovereign/executive/subject' and so on. But it was nonetheless a theory of *society* as an organic entity. De Maistre further retained the Enlightenment's concept of progress. When he said that 'only Christian society has known progress; non-Christian empires . . . only knew stability, so that the Muslim East presents a picture of arrested progress' (Menczer 1952: 45), he was voicing an ethnocentrism that was shared by most nineteenth century theorists of social evolution.

We shall see in Chapter 3 how sociology was in some ways a blend of Enlightenment themes, with these writers' emphasis on community, the organic nature of society and the centrality of ritual and the sacred in social order. Despite their critique of established religion, many Enlightenment writers had continued to address theological issues in their social theory. Paradoxically, the secularization of social thought in Saint-Simon, Comte and Durkheim came about via the absorption of arch-conservative social theology. Perhaps what these writers did was to make explicit a nostalgia for habit and community that had been latent in much eighteenth century thinking. Perhaps too, their emphasis on the social functions of religion, rather than on its core beliefs, enabled subsequent secular theorists to seek substitute practices appropriate for a secular, industrial society. This was to become the project of positivist sociology.

---

**Core concepts in Enlightenment and social theory**

- Birth of 'society' as distinct concept.
- Theory becomes historical, progressive and evolutionary.
- Loss of community in commercial society.
- Detraditionalization (decline of the sacred and hierarchy) poses problems of defining the basis of social orders.
- Science and technology contribute to progress.
- Conditions of freedom and equality are possible through reason.
- Revolution may be a rational solution to human degradation, resulting in emancipation.

---

**FURTHER READING**

Peter Gay (1996) *Enlightenment* (Norton) is a classical and comprehensive study that avoids attempts to depict the process within a single trajectory. Written in an accessible and lively style. Roger Smith (1997) *Fontana History of the Human Sciences* (Fontana) is of breathtaking scope and thoroughness. Good on Enlightenment and reactions to the French Revolution against a background of developments in the life sciences. Theodor Adorno and Max Horkheimer (1973) *Dialectic of Enlightenment* (Verso) were writing in the dark days of 1944 when Europe was threatened by Nazism; they get beyond rationalist defences and conservative critiques of Enlightenment to identify two contradictory processes of emancipation and repression, the latter linked to the domination of nature. Difficult but challenging.

**NOTES**

1 The German Enlightenment (*Aufklärung*) took a different character from that in France, England and Scotland, in that the former occurred later, had

no clear cultural centre, showed little enthusiasm for Locke, did not look so clearly to the natural sciences as a model of knowledge in general, and was less confident in its materialism (R. Smith 1997: 125–17).

2 Voltaire's antisemitism is an example of this. In his entry 'Juifs' in his *Dictionnaire philosophique* he described Jews as 'an ignorant and barbarous people' uniting 'sordid avarice' with 'detestable superstition' (1994: 181).

3 Again, differences between the western European and German Enlightenments are relevant. An object of the German *Aufklärung* was to establish a rational knowledge of God (see Chapter 6) rather than atheism.

4 Parallel to this was the development of biological systems of classification such as Linnaeus' *Systema natural* (1735) and Buffon's *Histoire Naturelle* (1750) together with Maupertuis's theory of the transmutation of species. These all contributed to a sense of linear historical time.

5 During the eighteenth century the idea 'civilization' was extended from a juridical concept (the process whereby a criminal case is transferred to civil courts) to refer to the idea of society coming to be governed by legal process (Hazard 1965: 391).

6 The American Revolution (1777–8) changed this to some extent, because it was possible to interpret this as indicating the failure of monarchical constitutionalism and, if people freely choosing a form of rule had opted for a republic, then perhaps people were republican by nature.

7 David Caute (1988: 264ff) sees a continuity between the *philosophes*' admiration of Enlightened Despotism as the rule of reason and the enthusiasm for Stalin's Soviet Union widespread among western intellectuals in the 1930s.

8 Theories of contract did not immediately lose links with theology. Hobbes for example devoted a third of his *Leviathan* to consideration of 'A Christian Common-Wealth', although the secular implications of contract theory were apparent and in 1666 he was threatened with prosecution for heterodoxy.

9 This is a point on which most commentators on Hobbes agree, although it should be noted that the colonization of America and encounter with Native Americans led some seventeenth- and eighteenth-century theorists to believe that here were people still in a 'state of nature' similar to that in which Europeans must once have lived. Although this view was very bad anthropology it was remarkably persistent, being repeated for example by Engels in *Origin of Family, Private Property, and the State* (1884).

10 Locke's *First Treatise* ([1680] 1960) was an attack on Filmer's doctrine of Divine Right (in *Patriarchia*) according to which the king ruled as the father of the nation, just as the patriarchal father ruled the household in accordance with natural law. Since God was the author of nature, what was in accordance with nature must be divinely intended. It is interesting that both Filmer's argument and Locke's counter, that principles of popular government could be derived from natural rights, both looked to 'nature' to derive arguments about legitimate government.

11 Smith's *Wealth of Nations* ([1784] 1976b) was partly a refutation of mercantilism that advocated state regulation of imports and exports and accumulation of gold. Smith aimed to show that the economy contained its own dynamism and self-regulating principles, therefore government intervention should be minimized, though not abolished entirely.

# CHAPTER 3

# Comtean positivism and sociology

This chapter outlines the formation of sociology by its founder, Auguste Comte (1798–1857) for whom society was a moral order. In histories of the discipline, however, Comte is often passed over without detailed discussion, almost as though we are embarrassed by this somewhat eccentric ancestor. While other classical theorists have contemporary followers – Marxists, Durkheimians and Weberians for example – there are now virtually no Comteans. This neglect and embarrassment arises perhaps from his later work, after 1844, when this advocate of the dawning of science and reason founded a secular 'Religion of Humanity', proposed society as the 'Great Being' and devised a calendar of 'saints' of Positivism. Nonetheless, the neglect of Comte is unfortunate, since his writing is revealing as to the early theoretical and political project of scientific sociology. Comte's Religion of Humanity, if bizarre, followed in some ways from his diagnosis of the crisis of industrial society, as a moral crisis arising from the loss of spiritual authority in a secular age, and followed the precedent of earlier secular religions, such as Saint-Simon's 'New Christianity'. Moreover, Comte developed a systematic theory of the growth of knowledge that was to remain influential for much of the nineteenth century, and set out central methodological principles of the discipline, some of which are now widely accepted. In order to understand Comte's role in the formation of sociology, it would be useful first to examine the general context of his work in the early nineteenth century.

## REVOLUTIONS, CRISES AND IDEOLOGUES

Was the organic conception of society as a moral entity a response to revolutionary upheaval? Certainly, the Enlightenment and the birth of sociology are separated by the watershed of the 1789 French Revolution.

Many participating in this believed that they were living through the most momentous event in human history, the effects of which were not confined to France, but in many respects were global (see Wallerstein 1990). The revolution had a demonstration effect that stimulated uprisings elsewhere, such as the 1791 slave revolt in Santo Domingo, as ideas of republican government and constitutional rights spread across Europe. The Jacobin Republic of Virtue, though short lived (1793–4), became a point of reference for revolutionary politics during the following century. This 'unprecedented social experiment', according to Ferenc Fehér (1990: 11), 'created a new economic and cultural regime' that became a blueprint for later revolutionary movements. No nineteenth-century politician or thinker, whether radical or conservative, could forget that deliberate human action had resulted in profound social and political changes. Some proponents of the revolution described their practice as *l'art social*, the reorganization of society along lines dictated by rational knowledge (Smith 1997: 423). This was a vision that was to recur in the following two centuries, notably, for its intellectual admirers, in the Soviet Union during the 1930s (Caute 1988: 264–81).

According to some accounts sociology was a response to a perceived crisis arising from political and industrial revolution. Indeed, it was for a long time standard practice among historians to conceive of the French Revolution and the industrial revolution as different moments in the same general process of modernization (e.g. Cameron 1966). Sociology then offered a scientific diagnosis of the crisis of European society, combining the promise of reform with the conservative emphasis on organic social integration through institutions of guilds, community, religious ritual and monarchy (e.g. Nisbet 1967). These were discussed in Chapter 2. It is often suggested that Comtean sociology was a blend of the Enlightenment belief in progress with organic and theocratic ideas of the conservatives (Collins and Makowsky 1984: 28; Seidman 1994: 26ff). Early sociologists attempted to provide an answer to the problem of social order without accepting the whole of the conservative critique, retaining in particular the progressive impetus of the Enlightenment, the idea of the inevitability of industrial society and the centrality of scientific knowledge in this process. J. C. Alexander (1989: 69–70) suggests that sociology developed as a 'search for meaning within a secular world' following the dislocations brought about by the growth of science, the Enlightenment, secular revolutions such as 1789 and industrialization, which created new problems of social cohesion and reform.[1]

Others, however, have questioned these accounts, arguing that the origins of sociology lie deep in European thought and that anyway the two 'revolutions' were very different in nature (Kaiser 1980). Giddens (1979: 208–34) has taken issue with Nisbet's thesis that sociology was a conservative reaction to modernity, describing this as one of the four 'myths' about the origins of sociology.[2] Houlton (1996) similarly argues that such views are 'superficial', since many themes in social theory originate in the Renaissance. In any event, sociology was more than just a blend of Enlightenment and counter-Enlightenment theories. Both approaches had already been synthesized, and thereby transformed, by the Ideologues. They were French intellectuals in the post-revolutionary period who, while not successful in their political ambitions, had assimilated their experience of the revolution into a programme for the social sciences. They were influential in the work of Saint-Simon, Comte and, less directly, Marx.[3]

The Ideologues included Georges Cabanis, a physician; Destutt de Tracy, philosopher; Pierre-Simon de Laplace, mathematician; Philippe Pinel, psychiatrist; Jean-Baptiste Say, political economist; Emmanuel abbé Sieyès, politician; Germaine de Staël, philosopher. They were organized initially in Condorcet's *Société de 1789* and subsequently in the *Société des observateurs de l'homme*. They were involved with the development of physiology, which promised to provide a scientific account of variations in human behaviour and many hoped that this would lead to a science of morality and politics, offering the key to rational social 'organization' (a concept derived from the physiological term 'organ'). They hoped to fulfil Condorcet's dream of creating a social science in which the laws of social organization could be derived from the study of human nature (Pickering 1993: 62ff) and rejected (as did Saint-Simon and Comte) 'metaphysical' standpoints that obscured the development of true social theory. This was to become a persuasive claim – if one could clear away cognitive distortions, arising from metaphysics (for positivists) or class interests (for Marxists) then the truth of social reality would be apprehended (Gouldner 1976: 11ff).

The Ideologues took a scientistic approach to human affairs further than the Enlightenment, which (as we saw in Chapter 2) was more literary in style. Comparative anatomy offered a new system of classification, of both humans and animals, which developed a functional view of the integration of species that was later to influence both evolutionary theory and anthropology (Heilbron 1995: 137; Smith 1997: 275). The new discipline of biology (increasingly a point of reference for the social sciences) pointed towards a historical view of the natural world. In 1802 Lamarck proposed what would become an influential theory of evolution, arguing that species were not fixed units but changed over time. The popularity of natural chronologies encouraged a historical approach in the social sciences, which was apparent in, for example, Jean-Baptiste Say's *Treatise on Political Economy* (1821), in which the economy was viewed as an organic, complex and evolving totality.

The idea of organic growth through gradual evolution provided an apt analogy for the Ideologues' political experiences. Initially supporters of the revolution, they became more critical after the Terror and latterly opposed to revolution itself, emphasizing the need for organic and gradual social change. In particular, Say argued that the revolutionary transfer of power was meaningless without a corresponding moral change. Thus 'what happens when a moral revolution does not follow the first? Nothing, or almost nothing. Authority changes hands but the nation remains the same' (Kaiser 1980: 145). This critique of political revolution shifted attention from the state to society as a moral-organic process. The Ideologues came to regard political institutions as secondary to society and government as 'only part of the social organization', so that for Destutt de Tracy it was not the form but the function of the state, whether it served the common interest, that was important to human well-being.

Further, the democratic ideal of a republic of equals, expressed by Rousseau, gave way to a more differentiated view of society. The Terror had persuaded the Ideologues that egalitarian democracy was risky because people could not be trusted to act rationally. This view was given further credence by the physiologist, Cabanis, who, in contrast with Enlightenment universalism, emphasized innate differences among human temperaments and the need for society to repress vicious habits and passions (Smith 1997: 241). Thus state power had to be entrusted to an enlightened few (Kaiser 1980), a view that reflected an elitist tendency in Enlightenment thought (discussed in Chapter 2). The Ideologues hoped to establish a new aristocracy of enlightened people on the grounds that the public good was best served when those who dominated society were its most enlightened members. In contrast to the radical egalitarianism of Jacobins like Saint-Juste, who claimed Rousseau as a mentor, the Ideologues regarded social class differences as both necessary and inevitable. Social antagonisms and chaos arose in the absence of integrating institutions of the monarchy, state church and community, which provided bases for consensus and stability.

Clearly here was an echo of de Bonald and de Maistre. However, the Ideologues' programme for recreating social order did not involve a return to the values and institutions of the past. Rather, they embraced the industrial age as containing the solution to the crisis of post-revolutionary society. For Say, again, society would be properly constituted once it was organized for the purpose of economic production and social hierarchy was meritocratic, so that labour and initiative were rewarded accordingly. This new moral integration would be facilitated by consensus and an interdependent division of labour. Thus society would be founded not on the rearrangement of political power, which preoccupied revolutionaries, but on the organization of material production. The social recognition of distinctions among productive sectors, each with its own function, would not drive wedges between social classes, but would provide the social glue necessary to restore social harmony. Though performing different functions, each sector would have a common interest in promoting production through an ethic of work and cooperation. For Say the advantages of social cooperation were most clear in the market where the prosperity of one industry is favourable to the prosperity of all the others.

Two consequences of this thinking are worth noting. First, Ideologues moved social thought further from social contract theories, in which the good society was that best adjusted to a hypothetical state of natural necessity. If social organization was organically evolving as a structured and differentiated whole, then the ideas of the lawgiver and original contract were inappropriate. The social thought of the Ideologues and their successors was historical and tried to understand how specific societies had developed as a whole. Second, although physiology was regarded as the proper basis for philosophy and moral science, such views were opposed by Romantics, who waged 'open warfare' on the sciences. Those around the *Journal des débates* for example challenged the growing claims of scientific approaches to human life, and echoed de Bonald's claim that 'every sensible person' ought to prefer moral to natural science (Heilbron 1995: 159).[4] This divide, between the scientific and literary cultures, was to become central to debates about modern culture and fuelled anxieties over the dehumanizing effects of science, a debate that has been of central importance to sociological methods. The 1810s had transformed the debate between defenders and critics of the Enlightenment, especially by the Ideologues' application of physiological methods to the study of society. Saint-Simon and Comte further developed this response to the crisis of modernity.

## SAINT-SIMON AND 'SOCIALISM'

The philosophy of the last century was revolutionary; that of the nineteenth century must be organizational.

(Saint-Simon 1966: 158)

Henri Saint-Simon (1760–1825) is an ambiguous figure in the history of social thought. Although his thinking was unsystematic, he gave rise to an influential form of socialism and is often credited with most of the ideas later developed by Comte (Markham 1964). In what was later to become characteristic nineteenth-century style, Saint-Simon blended social analysis with what might now be called 'futurology'. That is, the idea that the present could be understood from the standpoint of the future, since there was a discernible historical movement within which social science was situated and to which it contributed. Abandoning ideas of original social contract as ahistorical, Saint-Simon placed 'social organization' at the centre of analysis. This new science was initially to be a branch of physiology (Saint-Simon 1975: 75) although he later regarded that approach as too reductionist (Pickering 1993: 99).

Like Comte, Saint-Simon's immediate concern was with the crisis in European (especially French) societies that arose from the transition from a feudal-theological to industrial-scientific system. The 1789 Revolution had swept away the remnants of the former, but the latter had yet to become stabilized in new cultural and institutional forms. In his 1805 essay *Introduction to the Scientific Work of the Nineteenth Century* (1975) Saint-Simon argued that the moral crisis threatening Europe could be resolved by immediate construction of a theoretical system unifying all knowledge. Some of his proposals, such as the application of scientific method to the study of society, the organization of a new scientific age in which the state would assume responsibility for social welfare, institutional cooperation in a unified Europe, were later to become widely shared. In the early nineteenth century though, these ideas appeared radical, and to many, bizarre.

Extending the ideas of the Ideologues, Saint-Simon and Auguste Comte developed a system of 'positive philosophy' which conceived of society as a natural system, subject to objective forces that could be managed by social scientists. Though influenced by the Ideologues, Saint-Simon complained of the narrowness of their conception of social integration through industry and attempted to expand their ideas into a more comprehensive doctrine (Kaiser 1980: 159). Nonetheless, their elitist ideas of a regime dominated by entrepreneurs and scientists, devoted to economic expansion, who would use their expertise and authority to maximize production and minimize disorder, appear in both Saint-Simon and Comte. Both proceeded from the same understanding as the Ideologues, that the solution to social fragmentation lay in the advance of industrialization, rather than the redrafting of constitutions. In this context, the role of religion and the non-rational bases of social order were issues of central concern to both writers.

Saint-Simon's work linked the Ideologues with eighteenth-century Enlightenment and the new scientific and industrial ethos of the early nineteenth century. 'Society', understood as 'a mass and union of men devoted to useful works', bound by a 'community of ideas' (Pickering 1993: 92), obeyed to law-like principles. Saint-Simon developed a theory of social change which suggested that all societies carry the seeds of their own decay, as their institutional structure and beliefs fail to address the needs of the newly emerging economically and socially dominant classes. Thus post-medieval Europe saw the rise of independent producers and merchants who entered into conflict with the established feudal powers, a conflict that resulted in class struggle and uneasy resolution. Like the Ideologues, Saint-Simon argued that industrial society was an inescapable form of modern organization which would need to resolve its own problems. There was no possibility of returning, in the way that Fourier, for example, advocated, to some rural, pre-industrial communal way of life.[5] Since political change results from the instruments of production, contemporary technology as a new social order, calls for corresponding political change.

History, for Saint-Simon was a history of class conflict (class defined in terms of functional-occupational groups) between productive and idle classes. Those who do not produce are immoral because they consume at the expense of producers (*les industriels*) who are suppressed by force

(Saint-Simon 1975: 158, 187). The ensuing class conflict between these groups is the means by which social transformation between forms of social organization occurs. The 'feudal-theocratic order' was dominated by priests, nobles and the military who robbed the producers, the serfs (Saint-Simon 1975: 177). In later feudalism, from the fifteenth century, this order was challenged by classes who were derived from the old system yet were independent of it, classes which because of their political situation had to challenge and break free from feudalism. These were the lawyers and metaphysicians. In temporal affairs, lawyers undermined arbitrary and oppressive feudal justice by developing a systematic and fairer system of jurisprudence. In spiritual matters, the metaphysicians were responsible for the Reformation which undermined the hold of Catholicism in Europe and established the principle of freedom of conscience (Saint-Simon 1975: 177).

Thus a new social system emerged 'within the bosom of the old', during which time new classes appear. However, the crisis of medieval feudalism was but an intermediate phase, a prelude to the 'scientific-industrial' society that was taking shape in the early nineteenth century. The lawyers and metaphysicians who served the historical purpose of undermining feudalism themselves became an incipient dominating class, especially after the French Revolution when they replaced the old nobility and priesthood that had been decisively defeated. The legal-metaphysical worldview, though, was inadequate for the needs of the industrial system in which the newly emerging class of producers were merchants, industrialists, artists and proletarians. Poverty and crises, caused by the anarchy of production and exchange, impeded the full development of this system. Producers were moreover subject to the authority of incompetents – nobles, rentiers and speculators – who produced nothing, but dominated the proletariat and constrained industry. Saint-Simon saw his theory of social organization as providing the intellectual means for *les industriels* to challenge the existing order and institute a harmonious form of organization.

If some of this sounds familiar, it is perhaps because aspects of Saint-Simon's analysis reappear in Marx's theory of history, as we shall see in Chapter 4.[6] Both Marx and Saint-Simon had a vision of the future towards which their analysis of the present was orientated. They differed in other respects though. A great deal of Saint-Simon's work contains plans for future social organization, including draft constitutions, parliaments, professional and scientific associations and a new religion. Marx eschewed this kind of utopian thinking and preferred not to 'write the cook books for the socialist kitchens of the future'. Unlike Marx moreover, Saint-Simon identified no central class conflict within *capitalism*, but more a conflict between representatives of the decaying and rising social systems. The class that represented the new industrial order, *les industriels,* combined both workers and entrepreneurs.[7] Again, unlike Marx, Saint-Simon's aim was to forestall conflict and create an organically integrated society. In common with the conservatives and Ideologues, Saint-Simon argued that to be durable, social change should be anchored in custom and tradition. To improve society one had to work with, not against, the movement of history. So by contrast with the conservatives' nostalgia for medieval order, this meant that there could be no return to the past, since the transition to industrial society was inevitable. Again this view was shared by Marx, although for him the direction of historical evolution pointed towards the kind of revolutionary cataclysm that Saint-Simon hoped to avoid.

He offered, in a rather unsystematic way, a sense of historical development that he claimed was missing from the Enlightenment. Societies pass through critical and organic periods, a process that reflects a physiological tendency for living systems to alternate between habit and the desire for new sensations. Critical periods, such as that beginning with the Reformation, are marked by disharmony and disunity, loss of community and breaking the bonds of the social. Thus since the fifteenth century Europe had been in revolution, a process that culminated in the Encyclopedists' efforts to overthrow old systems of belief. This was reflected in social organization, as the growth of industry brought increasing centralization and fundamental changes in the organization of production. In organic periods by contrast, principles of thought are widely accepted; there is a clearly defined hierarchy and unity of faith. The close of the eighteenth century, Saint-Simon hoped, would bring to an end this critical period which would be replaced by one of organic industrialism. This system would become universal as industrial societies converged around optimal forms of functional integration based on the division of labour.

In his 1821 essay *Industrial System* Saint-Simon (1975) developed an organic conception of society, in which functional and spontaneous integration would arise from commerce only if regulated by a moral centre. This would be provided by an artistic and scientific elite of professional leaders. 'These men', he said, are 'the most central producers, those who make the most important products, those who direct the enterprises most useful to the nation [which] would become a lifeless corpse as soon as it lost them' (Saint-Simon 1964: 72–3).[8] Under the guidance of an elite of *savants*, society was to become self-regulating, rather like an academic community. It will be a happy age for the human race, he said, when functions of rulers will be reduced until they are no more than supervisors in colleges, who have only one task: to maintain order. It is the teachers who are responsible for directing the pupils' work and it should be the same in the state. Scientists, artists and artisans should direct the nation's work and the ruler's concern is only with ensuring that the work is not hindered (Saint-Simon 1975: 200).

Saint-Simon is often described as a founder of socialism, although the term was coined by one of his followers, Pierre Leroux in *Le Globe* in 1832 (Kolakowski 1989: 187ff). In so far as Saint-Simon's ideas were 'socialist' they were orientated to 'social' projects of capital investment such as canals, railways and steamship lines organized through central planning which would establish social harmony. His 1825 essay *On Social Organization* (1975) recommended that priority be given to state expenditure that ensured work for all 'fit men' to secure their physical existence. Combined with other measures (the spread of knowledge of positive science, provision of recreation and interests to develop the intelligence) the proletarian class would become committed to the new industrial order (Saint-Simon 1975: 265). Once the proletariat were integrated into the new order, there would be no need to spend large sums of money on police and armies. The 'government machine' would be subordinate to administration, which would be organized by those most suited to manage, that is, 'scientists, artists, industrialists and heads of industrial concerns'. Society would retain a hierarchical structure, but one based on ability rather than dominated by nobles, which would therefore command widespread acceptance. Saint-Simon's socialism, then, was a project for a scientific intelligentsia, who would have a key role in the process of social administration of society. This would be an industrial society moreover, in which the legitimation of hierarchy was a reflection of the values of intellectuals – reward (both status and material) based on ability and achievement. Inheritance would be abolished and competition give way to emulation as the motive for progress.

However, another essay in 1825, *New Christianity*, (Saint-Simon 1975) suggests that just reward in itself would be insufficient to ensure social integration. As a 'community of ideas', society was (as for de Bonald) religious in nature. However, eighteenth-century 'anti-theology' had disorganized the theological system and a new 'terrestrial' (secular) morality was the 'only link which can unify men in society' (Saint-Simon 1975: 171). He proposed a secular religion that would have its own 'morality, worship, dogma, clergy and hierarchy', which would be particularly important to instil the appropriate values among the new cultural and scientific elite, in order to 'make them the managing directors of the human race' (Saint-Simon 1825: 105). Moral doctrine would be most important in the 'new Christianity', which would preach brotherhood, charity, 'gentleness, kindness, clarity, honesty', and the need to work for the improvement of humanity.

Saint-Simon's ideas, like those of early nineteenth century socialism, reflect enthusiasm for the new industrial age combined with a critique of unregulated capitalism that draws in part on a Romantic evocation of the pre-capitalist life. There were many sources to be drawn upon, such as Plato's *Republic*, the communist ideas of medieval sectarians and Renaissance utopians, for example Thomas More, whose *Utopia* (1516) reflected on the early effects of capitalist accumulation. However, Saint-Simon differed from these pre-modern antecedents in that he did not seek a return to a pre-industrial idyll, but sought functional substitutes for the major components of social integration. Thus the rule of warriors would be replaced by industrialists, theologians by a technocracy, hierarchy based on birth by a meritocracy, a theological worldview by a secular religion. Two central sociological concepts then became established – the concept of society as a functionally integrated moral whole, and the importance of a common value system in maintaining social order. These were to find systematic expression in Comte's sociology.

## POSITIVISM

> It cannot be necessary to prove to anybody reading this book that Ideas govern the world, or throw it into chaos. In other words, that all social mechanism rests upon Opinions.
>
> (Comte 1976: 48)

It is with Comte that the idea of the social, exhibiting complexity and specificity distinct from other forms of organic life is clearly articulated, along with the new science, sociology, which will complete the evolution of human knowledge. Comtean positivism was a product of the managerial ethos widely held by graduates from the *écoles polytechniques* of the 1820s, which also included Saint-Simon. Although Comte himself did not finish his course he was imbued with their ethos of social reform that could be accomplished through the application of scientific principles to social problems (Pickering 1993: 29–30). These graduates were disaffected with post-revolutionary society and the limited occupational opportunities it provided for the employment of their skills, a situation which fuelled many socialist and radical movements in Paris during the 1820s and 1830s. These often generated utopian and technocratic schemes for a new rational society in which technically trained graduates would find their rightful place (Ben-David 1962–3). Comte blended these technocratic ideas with those of the conservatives, who won increased prominence after the accession of Charles X in 1824. He offered a programme that aimed to transcend party politics, in a way that might now be described as 'beyond left and right' (Giddens 1994).

Comte's programme for a science of the social was tentative and recognized that the endeavour is in its infancy – its present condition being analogous to that of astrology in relation to astronomy and alchemy to chemistry (Comte 1976: 88). Like Saint-Simon, for whom he worked as a secretary between 1817 and 1824, Comte built on the Ideologues' synthesis of Enlightenment rationalism and the counter-Enlightenment critique, though perhaps with more sympathy for the latter.[9] The 'great de Maistre', he said, 'was of material assistance in preparing the true theory of progress' and although 'animated by the retrograde spirit . . . will always be ranked among the necessary antecedents of the Positive system' (Comte 1976: 83). For Comte, both the revolution and the reaction that followed were necessary antecedents of the Positive System. Comte offered an explanation of the crisis of modernity to which sociology was the solution, offering guidance in social reconstruction that would work with the direction of historical evolution.[10] An understanding of this process would show that the revolution was not an aberration but the outcome of a crisis in European culture dating back to the thirteenth century (Gane 1996). European society was in the last phase of this transformation, although revolution had failed to establish unity or a rational basis for social organization.

Positivism was an intellectual and political movement, in which sociology was only one aspect. Though originating in Comte's *System of Positive Politics* (1824) 'positivism' acquired varied meanings, and during the nineteenth and twentieth centuries became a major issue of controversy in sociology and philosophy. These are summarized in Figure 3.1. The general features of positivism in the *Positive Philosophy* (vol. 1: 1–35) were as follows:

- Reflecting the influence of Bacon and Hume, positivism was anti-metaphysical. Science deals with statements that can be tested against observable phenomena, not hidden essences.
- Hypotheses are derived from theories and the only purpose of conducting observations is to address theoretical questions. The validity of knowledge moreover is relative to its social and historical context.
- All phenomena are subject to 'invariable natural laws' of covariance. These are not *causal* laws, since causes are unseen and are therefore metaphysical. Newton's law of gravitation exemplifies appropriate method, since it refers to observable relations of force among moving bodies. The objective of scientific method is to develop the simplest formulations and smallest numbers of laws, ideally expressed mathematically.
- Positivism aimed to combine sciences in a hierarchy (see pp. 49–52) while retaining what we might now call their 'relative autonomy'. That is, each science has its specific methods, concepts, and level of development – so unlike some later versions of positivism, Comte's was non-reductionist. The laws of more general sciences presupposed those of more specific ones, but not vice versa. Thus sociology, for example, presupposed humans as biological organisms but this did not mean that human social behaviour could be explained with reference to biology.
- Society, knowledge and individuals pass through three phases of evolution (theological, metaphysical and positive) but they do not do this simultaneously. Evolution takes place at different rates in different parts of society. See the 'Law of Three States' (pp. 44–9).
- Positivism addressed the 'great political and moral crisis' of modernity, which originated in intellectual incoherence. Positivism offered the basis for new consensus on 'general ideas', although Comte implies that agreement over procedures for resolving disputes is more important than over substantive issues. People would not always agree, but disputes would be resolved through scientific procedures and guided by a common methodology.[11]

**Figure 3.1** Positivism

**Comtean positivism**
- Described the history of human thought evolving through three states: theological, metaphysical, positive.
- Claimed there was a unity and hierarchy of sciences, moving from the most abstract and mathematical to the most complex and organic.
- General scientific method involves observation, comparison and experiment, but methods should be discipline-specific.
- Science proceeds from theories which are tested against observation (i.e. deductive, not inductive).
- Aim of science is to develop laws which can assist prediction and intervention.

**Later nineteenth century positivism**
- E.g. Mach, Poincaré, Duhem.
- Like the Comtean version, anti-metaphysical, but focused on scientific methods and the status of theories and concepts. Offered no grand theory of human development.
- Claimed that scientific concepts are conventions, useful for organizing observation, not real entities.
- The test of a theory's explanatory power is successful prediction.

**Logical positivism**
- In the twentieth century 'positivism' often referred to logical positivism of the Vienna Circle in the 1920s (Carnap, Ayre, Neurath).
- Proposed a unity of sciences that could be expressed in theory-neutral language.
- Rigorous rejection of metaphysics which applied to all statements not susceptible to observable justification. E.g. 'God exists' 'God does not exist' are neither true nor false but, because they have no observable referent, are equally meaningless.
- Logical positivism thus rejected a great deal of philosophy (including most of Comte) as meaningless.

**Later positivism**
By the 1970s positivism had become a term of abuse and there were very few self-proclaimed 'positivists'. Karl Popper (1902–94) for example was one of the foremost critics of logical positivism yet was frequently accused by critics of being a 'positivist' himself. By the 1990s debate over positivism had faded although many of the issues were subsumed into debates between realist and anti-realist epistemologies.

- Unlike the negative philosophy of the eighteenth century, positivism would generate ideas that contribute to social reconstruction. An important aim of science, then, is the prevision of applied knowledge (hence *savoir pour prévoir, prévoir pour pouvoir*),[12] although Comte stressed that science's ultimate goal is 'to know the laws of phenomena'. That is, knowledge is an end in itself.

Comtean positivism differentiated itself from two other major political and intellectual movements of the nineteenth century, liberalism and socialism, although Comte had some sympathy for both. Liberalism's focus on individual rights and action gave too little attention to the 'community of interest' in society, while its language of popular sovereignty and contract was demagogic (Pickering 1993: 111–12). Moreover liberalism was too closely allied to political economy and Comte doubted whether *laissez faire* would promote prosperity (Pickering 1993: 196). Comte, who was influenced by Say, did not dispute with political economy the importance of economic factors in social life, and agreed on the centrality of the division of labour in modern societies. However 'strangely enough our modern economists claim the discovery of [the division of labour] whilst narrowing it, with metaphysical empiricism, to a mere law of industry' (Comte 1976: 129). For Comte, division and differentiation of roles was a social (not merely economic) evolutionary trend and, in opposition to liberals and political economists, the proper functioning of a complex society would require central coordination by government (Pickering 1993: 196). The economy was anyway not self-sufficient or self-equilibrating but the source of social pathologies, such as poverty and class conflict.

Socialists too of course argued this, but Comte opposed socialism on several grounds. Like Saint-Simon, Comte held that there was no necessary conflict between capital and labour; that the concentration of wealth was inevitable, but should be distributed according to merit; inequality was necessary for social order; social democracy threatened to destroy individuality and reduce everyone to the same level. However, Comte disputed the 'anti-social theory' of the liberals that property conferred absolute right on its possessor. He argued (like the socialists) that property was a social institution in need of regulation and that positivism accepted the 'fundamental principle of communism' that all powers (including wealth) should be devoted to the service of the community (Comte 1976: 181). But the question of whether property was privately or socially owned was less important than how it was used. Owners and managers had a social duty to use property to the best advantage of society, something that would be ensured by new moral codes (Comte 1976: 183). Positivism he said was the 'party of construction' that would satisfy the poor while restoring the confidence of the rich (Comte 1976: 181). In common with the socialists, Comte regarded industrial workers as a likely constituency for his ideas, and hoped that the 'action of the proletariat would realize the final breakthrough to a Positive state' (Pickering 1993: 705; Gane 1996: 19). Some central ideas in Comte's sociology will now be examined in more detail.

### Law of Three States

The Law of Three States is one of Comte's most famous and central propositions. It claims that the evolution of societies, individuals and

**Figure 3.2** Comte's Law of Three States

| statics | dynamics Theological | Metaphysical | Positive |
|---|---|---|---|
| **Intellect** | supernatural | occult | natural |
| **Secular powers** | warriors | lawyers and metaphysicians | industrialists |
| **Spiritual powers** | priests | clergy | intellectuals |
| **Basis of government** | divine right | popular sovereignty | scientific politics |
| **Basis of solidarity** | attachment | veneration | benevolence |
| **Acitvity** | military | commercial | industrial society |
| **Social unit** | kinship | nation | human race |

forms of knowledge occurs in a necessary sequence, that will be replicated by each society, but at different times (Comte 1976: 39). Material
and moral conditions interact with one another, but the importance of
the latter increases with the progress of civilization, which is summarized in Figure 3.2. The names of the states, theological, metaphysical and
positive, were taken from Turgot and Saint-Simon's schemes of world
history, although Comte developed his own conception of these and
filled them out in considerably more detail. The process operates at the
level both of social systems and of individuals, including individual
development. We are, Comte says, 'theologians in childhood, metaphysicians in youth, and natural philosophers in virility' (1976: 41). Thus the
law applied to all aspects of society but (as with Saint-Simon) was
expressed in terms of the development of ideas and knowledge. It could
thus be regarded as a kind of collective learning process through which
the whole of humanity was destined to pass. The law was intended to be
'an abstract expression of a general reality' although its operation was as
inescapable 'as the original impulse which causes our planet to revolve
around the sun' (Comte 1974: 100).

In each society there are elemental forces – material, intellectual and
moral – which correspond to the form of social organization, knowledge
and moral codes, respectively. In outline, Comte's schematic view of
history claimed that progress entailed a transition from military to
industrial social organization, from fetishism to positivism in systems
of knowledge and competitive egoism to cooperative altruism in moral
codes.[13] A guiding principle of the law was that 'a new system of thought
could not be constituted until the old one had exhausted its potential'
and social conditions were conducive to its establishment (Comte 1976:

13). Further, each new idea has an initially progressive function in social evolution: 'institutions and doctrines reached at every period, the greatest perfection compatible with the corresponding civilization . . . During their greatest vigour, they always manifested a progressive and never a retrograde character' (Comte 1974: 165). However, the three states could coexist despite the domination of one: 'In our day three different systems coexist in the heart of society: the theological-feudal system, the scientific-industrial system and lastly the . . . transitional system of metaphysicians and lawyers' (Comte 1974: 152). Indeed, each state carries within itself embryonic forms of future states. There are similarities, at a methodological level, here to Marx. He too claimed that an epoch would not perish until all the potential forces within it had been developed, that ideas could first serve progressive purposes and then become reactionary, and that different modes of production could coexist within a single **social formation**. The substance of Marx's theory, however, differs from Comte's in various ways that will be outlined in Chapter 4.[14] The following discussion outlines Comte's conception of states and their rough periodization.

### Theological state

In the theological or fictitious state, the human mind seeks to know the essential nature of things – first and final causes, origins and purposes – and believes that all phenomena are produced by the action of supernatural beings. Theology was a primitive attempt to understand and control the natural world. Unlike much Enlightenment thought, Comte was not dismissive of theological worldviews; on the contrary he argued that they addressed essential human needs, a view that became more pronounced in his religion of humanity. As societies grew in complexity though, so the nature of theological beliefs changed, and the theological period was itself divided into three states, fetishism, polytheism and monotheism.

### Fetishism

Human vulnerability to nature meant that life in early societies was insecure and threatening. Acknowledging this power, but at the same time attempting to control it, human imagination invested the immediate natural world with supernatural powers. Spirits and gods inhabited trees, rivers, winds, mountains etc., and could be placated through rituals and sacrifices. In this earliest form of religion, the worship of spiritual deities and totemic forces anthropomorphized nature and imbued it with life. This theological spirit in turn sustained a warrior society, which imbued habits of discipline and brought families together in mutual defence. It imposed slavery on subject peoples, which became the dominant form of production in the ancient world. However, fetishist theology lacked unifying social power and as scientific explanations of natural events became available they were adopted as a more effective basis for action. As warrior societies unified into ancient empires with complex social systems, the warrior caste became redundant. Thus, for social and intellectual reasons the transition from a theological to scientific worldview began in this earliest state, although this was merely the beginning of a long voyage of the human mind.

*Polytheism*
Imagination conceived of a cosmos of gods and spirits who are abstract and removed from everyday life but can still be placated through ritual and the conduct of life. An example of this was Ancient Egypt, where speculation on the nature of the cosmos saw the development of complex systems of belief such as astrology. Yet the very process of abstraction that underlay polytheism pointed towards the subsequent state of metaphysics which was already present here in embryonic form (Comte [1830] 1975 vol. 2: 267). In this period, theology was linked to the height of the military regimes in the ancient world, and the military cult became incorporated into the state, which created stability and encouraged monogamy and patriotism. This period saw the development of fine arts, philosophy and the power of the imagination. However, this phase contained tensions that became apparent in Ancient Greece, where weary of disorderly capricious gods, the supernatural assembly was reduced to a monocentric cosmology. At the same time, the split between natural and moral philosophies in Greece ended an original unity of thought and established an antagonism between scientific and moral systems that would remain until positivism re-established unity.

*Monotheism*
Late in the Roman Empire, the polytheistic state give way to Christian monotheism, a simplification of worldviews where various deities were compressed into one god, which became more abstract and removed from the world. While responsible for the universe as a 'First Cause', the explanation of its operations could refer to more immediate mechanical forces, even if these were ultimately attributed to god. Though appearing in the Roman Empire, monotheism reached its fullest expression in medieval feudalism where it was an agent of social change. Economic activity moved from cities into agriculture based in small territorial units, where slavery was replaced by serfdom. European Christendom saw the ascendancy of spiritual over temporal authority, the former being embodied in saintly ideals that provided models for predominant ways of life. Like de Maistre, Comte regarded the moral efficacy of Catholicism as having derived from ritual in binding social integration, rather than the doctrine in itself. The ethos of chivalry encouraged sociability and solidarity in a situation where central political power was weak. Even in the heyday of the Catholic-feudal system though, in the eleventh century, tensions were appearing that would eventually undermine it. Spiritual

authority began to fragment as it was usurped by temporal powers. The Catholic-feudal system was subverted intellectually by Luther and temporally by the subordination of clerical to royal power. Faced with the challenge of Protestantism, Catholic clergy allied themselves with royal power and became instruments of reactionary monarchies, thus weakening its spiritual authority. This instigated the opening of the transitional period between theology and positivism.

### Metaphysical state

The metaphysical or abstract state was one of transition between the theological and positive. The decomposition of medieval theocracy opened a period of heterogeneous transition, in which tendencies from the theological and positive systems converged and clashed. Worldviews were based on natural philosophy and abstract entities of Spirit, Matter, Force and Ultimate Causes. Essences and forms in the world produce all phenomena. However, with speculative thought, theocratic ideas gradually gave way to criticism and argument. As with Saint-Simon, the emergence of a new state is accompanied by the appearance of new social classes – breaking the power of the feudal state was accomplished by the 'enfranchisement of Commons', which began with the emergence of metaphysicians and lawyers between the fourteenth and fifteenth centuries. Metaphysicians were academic scholars in universities who developed a naturalistic approach to phenomena, partly under the influence of the lawyers, who gained power in French parliaments and were hostile to Catholic power. Subsequently, in the sixteenth to eighteenth centuries, their critical doctrine was further stimulated by the Reformation, which established principles of freedom of thought and action and challenged oppressive institutions of slavery and serfdom. However, it too then turned against itself, opposed progress and began to promote religious hatred. The scientific advances of the seventeenth century then prompted widespread loss of faith (among intellectuals) and encouraged Deism, with which the metaphysical system came into its own. This again passed through three phases (!), marked by the work of Hobbes (founding the scientific study of society); the spread of new ideas through universities during the eighteenth-century Enlightenment; and its revolutionary application to politics at the end of the eighteenth century, which saw the triumph of metaphysicians and lawyers. However, scientific and industrial development had rendered these ideas problematic and created the need for precise, scientific, positive knowledge. Thus metaphysical thought in its turn had become a retrogressive constraint on progress.

### Positive age

The goal of positivism was the establishment of a society guided by scientific planning which would rebuild social integration ruptured by revolution and crisis of the old order. This would complete the transition began in the early theological state from a fetishistic to positive worldview and their corresponding forms of social organization. Although positivism would be the final state in human history this did not mean that the pursuit of knowledge would cease. All human knowledge, Comte said, is limited because our organization as a species combined with its cumulative nature, makes final certainty unlikely. The positive age would be peaceful and non-colonialist (Comte 1976: 168), governed by the spiritual power of philosophers and scientists. People would identify with Humanity as a whole, rather than with nation or race.[15] As with Saint-Simon's meritocratic utopia, social integration would be based on mutual recognition of the relative skills and functions of different groups. Thus a hierarchy of consensual mutual responsibilities would develop and be self-sustaining (Comte 1974: 104).

Positive civilization consisted of industry, science and art, embodying the principles of utility, truth and beauty, respectively.[16] In accordance with the law (it may come as no surprise), each of these recapitulated the three states in their own evolution. They each began spontaneously, in the late Middle Ages, when they liberated human creativity – thus industry freed slaves and serfs; science and philosophy posed crucial questions of method and attempted to penetrate the essence of things; the arts reflected human imagination and creativity. During the metaphysical stage each conflicted with the reigning institutions – industry rivalled the military state; natural philosophers such as Galileo, Descartes and Bacon challenged traditional ideas through reason and observation; artists grew increasingly critical and independent, pointing to their future role as 'spiritual chiefs' of modernity (Pickering 1993: 658). In the transition to the positive age each is characterized by conflict – industry has empowered the commons but is driven by egoism and the pursuit of profit to the exclusion of social solidarity; science and philosophy have split and the former is harnessed to the state; the arts meanwhile have become regressive, in so far as artists insist on the incompatibility of science and the arts illustrated by Romantic critiques of science (Heilbron 1995). These crises and conflicts will be resolved though in the positive age. The Law of Three States was thus closely linked to the development of knowledge and intellect, which was its driving force.

## Sociology and the hierarchy of sciences

A considerable amount of Comte's *Positive Philosophy* was devoted to epistemology and the elaboration of a temporal hierarchy of sciences, in which sociology was the last and most complex. Sociology subsumed other disciplines in that it presupposed their laws and offered a reflexive understanding of the progress of the human intellect. This was not, strictly speaking, a chronology of science so much as what might be called a 'genealogy', in that it reconstructed their emergence and specified the conceptual conditions necessary for each new science to emerge. The emergence of sciences followed the principles of the Law of Three States, so each science had itself to pass through each of the phases, and was dependent on the conceptual innovations of the one preceding. Each discipline was defined by the way in which it constituted its object – it sought laws of a particular kind which could not be explained in terms of already existing sciences. Biology for example studied 'man the animal' but not the cumulative growth of institutions and traditions of social life, which was left to sociology (Fletcher 1971: 177). Thus the 'same' subject matter could be appropriated by different sciences, which was an important (and often overlooked) contribution of Comte to historical epistemology.

The Law of Three States specified a progression from simple to complex organizational forms and a corresponding decrease in the generality of laws. Those of physics, for example, applied to all bodies in the universe, the laws of biology only to organic ones, and those of sociology only to institutional and cultural life. Thus the sciences to emerge first were the most abstract and inorganic disciplines of mathematics (on which all others were dependent), then astronomy, physics and chemistry, which addressed increasingly complex and specific objects. Only then could emerge sciences of organic and complex forms of existence – physiology, biology and sociology. Thus sociology was dependent on core concepts of biology, such as functional differentiation, division of labour, normality and pathology, and organic complexity.

This did not, however, mean that social life was reducible to biology. Quite the reverse, it was an error 'of so-called philosophers who pretend to be authorities in sociology' but claim that social variations are explicable in terms of (biological categories such as) 'race' (Comte 1976 139). The real basis of variation, he says, is the law of the increase in complexity of society in which two components of the social (statics and dynamics) interact. Laws of succession (dynamics) derive from the Law of Three States, and describe the process of progress and adaptation towards specialization of functions (Comte 1976: 153ff). However, these are constrained by statics, which could be described as 'functional prerequisites'. That is, conditions of social existence that are present in some form in all societies, even though their character changes in the course of historical development. 'Human nature' for example (see Figure 3.3) is made up of emotions, actions, intellect and understanding. But with the emergence of industrial-scientific civilization, altruism rather than egoism, intellect and concrete and deductive understanding, all become predominant. Social statics are fundamental principles of social integration, although again, their character will change in the course of social evolution. These are religion (as the unifying principle), property (the product of traditions), family (the site of affective bonds, sensibility and intellect), language (the medium of cultural transmission) and division

**Figure 3.3** Statics and dynamics

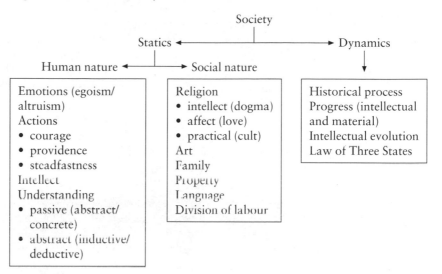

of labour (social organization) (Comte 1976: 117–48). Although the concept of social statics passed out of use in twentieth-century sociology, the idea still informs many theoretical approaches, in addition to functionalism, which is its most obvious successor.

Sociology thus defines a specific object of study, society, distinct from other sciences, which requires methods appropriate to its particular nature. The first three of these (observation, experiment and comparison) sociology shared with other sciences, while a fourth (historical method) was specific to sciences dealing with process and change (Comte 1976: 102ff). Each, however, took account of the organic complexity of society. Without observation science was impossible, although social inquiry posed particular difficulties. For one thing, society is a phenomenon 'forever proceeding before our eyes in which we are a part' (Comte 1976: 121). Thus the sociologist needed to approach society 'as if an outsider, viewing from afar'. Further, observation did not entail empiricism: 'no real observation of any kind', he said, 'is possible, except in as far as it is first directed, and finally interpreted by some theory . . . all isolated, empirical observation is idle' (Comte 1976: 102). Similarly, experiment, while central to sciences, was clearly difficult in sociology. But one could follow the practice in biology, where any 'artificial disturbance of any social element must affect the rest'. That is, analysis of pathological cases (such as revolutionary times) would show how normal social functioning is disturbed, thereby revealing the principles of normal functioning (e.g. the bases of social integration).

The very dynamic nature of society facilitated comparative methods. However, Comte's understanding of comparison revealed some typically nineteenth-century Eurocentric presuppositions, which reappear in theorists as diverse as Spencer, Durkheim, Marx and Engels. Sociology would compare 'higher' (complex) and 'lower' (simple) levels of development which corresponded to European and non-European societies respectively. It would further compare both consecutive and coexisting states of society, which was possible since different societies and spheres within them progressed at different rates. Finally, comparison would be developed into a historical method, applicable only to the most complex phenomena and was feasible only because people learned from previous generations. The historical method would trace the progress of the 'most advanced' societies through the three states, thus providing guidance for the less advanced (Comte [1830] 1975, vol. 2: 1–6).

### Asexual love and the religion of humanity

In his later work, especially the *Catechism of Positive Religion* (1858), Comte developed the idea of a secular cult, the Religion of Humanity, which would provide the moral cohesion necessary to 'cement' the positive age. Moral integration, which was the ultimate goal of positivism, would be weak without the organization of a creed to develop human sentiments to the highest degree (Pickering 1993: 620). Now, the idea of a secular religion was not in itself exceptional. We have seen that Saint-Simon proposed a 'new Christianity' and many *philosophes* had been preoccupied with problems of religion and social order.[17] Underlying this, at one level, was the 'problem of order', that is, what are the basic conditions for social integration, especially in an age where secularization has robbed authority of its sacred aura? However, the positivist religion reveals more than this, in that it makes explicit the gendering of the social space that was occurring in the early nineteenth century, which is then inscribed into sociological concepts.

At the centre of the Religion of Humanity was a cult of 'the feminine principle' which would be the basis of morality in the positive age. The *Catechism of Positive Religion*, which proposed a deification of the 'Virgin Mother' and sanctification of 'feminine' qualities, was a response to early century feminism with which Comte had initially been sympathetic.[18] The cult was to incorporate women in the 'western revolution', but on terms that preserved their subordinate status to men. Women would be 'released from the necessity to work outside the home' and 'elevated to the status of angels', but their intellect would be 'subordinated to the heart'. Reason, which governed the public sphere, was masculine and required guidance from the moral and emotional superiority of feminine principle (Gane 1993: 120–7; 1996). This would be institutionalized into rituals and beliefs that recreated the medieval cult of the Virgin Mother. However, this was not only a proposal for institutionalizing differences between men and women, but also prescribed an ideal concept of femininity, just as the medieval cult of the Madonna was defined against the figure of Eve, the source of evil.

Comte proposed asexual love as the ideal of positivist personal relationships, which would transcend the sexual 'debasement' of love in existing society. This goal, Comte suggested, could become a reality once people were freed from the sexual act as a requirement for reproduction. Comte advanced what he called the 'daring hypothesis' that in the future the 'male stimulus' to biological reproduction might be replaced by an alternative stimulus, at women's free disposal (Gane 1993: 126–7). With domestic life desexualized, intimate relations between men and women could pursue a higher, purified ideal. However, a strict (if consensual) division of roles and attributes would govern gender relations, and Comte did not consider the possibility that such a biotechnical revolution might undermine, rather than consolidate the institutions of patriarchy.

The ideal of liberating women from sexuality reflects the devil/saint dichotomy that inhabited the Victorian imagination. Indeed, it reflects and is reflected in Comte's personal life. After her death from tuberculosis in 1844, Comte elevated Clothilde de Vaux, with whom he had had an asexual relationship, into a saint of the positive age – the ideal for positivist woman. This contrasted with his claim that his first wife, Caroline Massin, had been a prostitute, a claim, made after the marriage had ended, which is disputed among his biographers (Pickering 1993; Gane 1993; 1996). Whatever the truth of his claim, though, Comte's juxtaposition of these women illustrates the Victorian dichotomy between women as 'angels' (meekly self-sacrificial) or (sexualized) 'demons', poised like women in Bram Stoker's *Dracula* (1897) between angelic service and vampiristic mutation (Auerbach 1982: 25). Women would thus be 'liberated' into a romanticized asexual space defined by the intersecting dichotomies between society and nature, public and private, egoism and altruism, intellect and emotion, desire and purity.

In this way Comte attempted to codify, and inscribe within sociology, gendered categories that emerged with the process of social differentiation. The goal of positivism was harmony and consensus within a functionally hierarchical society, and that of science to demonstrate which social changes were possible and which were not. Comte thus attempted to persuade his colleagues that segregated gender institutions would create social harmony dictated by scientific knowledge. Yet his overall view of social evolution suggested that it led away from dependence on physiology towards expansion of the intellect and morality. The domestic sphere to which women would be confined, however, remained dependent on the contrasting physiological dispositions of men and women. Biology, he claimed, had given us a solid basis to the hierarchy of the sexes, and industrial society should not attempt to override these. Anatomy had determined that women lack the capacity for abstraction and argument, although their passions are more generous than men's

(Comte 1976: 203). Thus Comte was unable to apply to gender analysis the sociological imagination that enabled him to dismiss biological explanations of 'racial' difference. Indeed, his attempt to bring gender relations, a social institution, into line with alleged 'natural' dispositions seems to give up on one of his central methodological claims – the autonomy of the social from biology.

## Comte and sociological theory

Comte's work is clearly open to considerable criticism. His analysis of gender relations recycled prevailing cultural stereotypes rather than subjecting them to critical scrutiny. Although he claimed the Law of Three States was tentative, he considered no data that would have contested it, nor even opened up complexities in his schema. His historical account is, to say the least, schematic and deterministic. His account of modern society vastly overestimated the decline of religion while (paradoxically perhaps) assuming that it required a secular substitute. He drew attention (as had Saint-Simon) to the importance of functional differentiation in industrial society, yet saw no bases for social cohesion other than common values and a cult modelled on medieval rituals. Comte further overestimated the decline of militarism in modern societies, while missing completely the integral role of colonialism in nineteenth century capitalism. Indeed, much of his description of the positive society was wishful thinking about a scientifically guided harmonious moral future. He naively assumed that positivism would end class and gender conflict by demonstrating natural relations of subordination arising from functional differentiation.

So why concern ourselves with Comte? I noted at the beginning of this chapter that, compared with other classical sociologists, Comte is rarely read. Yet this conceals the ways in which, despite bizarre aspects, many of his ideas have been influential. Most important perhaps, is the centrality of the social, that is, his insistence that people are significant only as social beings, that society is an organic necessity which 'commands all times and places' (Comte 1976: 121). But there are other themes too in Comtean social theory that are deeply inscribed into sociological thinking. These include the idea of society as decentralized and functionally integrated; the binding nature of culture and the importance of language; the problem of social integration in secular and complex societies; phases of development and the problem of modernization; historical and comparative methods; theory-guided research. He also, along with Saint-Simon and the Ideologues, drew attention to the importance of scientific intellectuals in industrial social systems. There was in addition Comte's historical epistemology that would influence Gaston Bachelard (1884–1962) and George Canguilhem (b. 1904) and hence, perhaps indirectly, theorists such as Althusser, Foucault and Bourdieu. Comte popularized an influential model of evolution through increasing complexity and differentiation that was to be developed by Spencer and others. This is not to say that subsequent sociologists agreed with Comte; many such as Durkheim, who acknowledged his influence, were highly critical. But Comte was significant in mapping the conceptual terrain for sociology even among theorists who would never consider themselves 'Comteans'.

This chapter has addressed two aspects of the 'debate with the Enlightenment' that began after 1789. First, the conservative counter-revolution proposed the organic concept of society, based on tradition, sacred rituals and intermediate institutions such as family, community, property and church. I have suggested that these ideas were influential, via the Ideologues, among those, such as Saint-Simon and Comte, who did not share the retrogressive conclusions of de Bonald and de Maistre. Second, I have shown how the development of positivist sociology was a synthesis of Enlightenment commitments to reason and progress through social engineering, with the idea of society an organic entity bound together by non-rational, spiritual, sentiments. Society became constituted as a reality *sui generis* and social science as a means of devising appropriate interventions. The following chapters will examine further aspects of this debate, each of which inhabit an intellectual terrain defined by poles of reason and irrationality; individualism and collectivism; atomistic and organic concepts of society.

---

### Core concepts in moral-organic theories

- Crisis of modernity, loss of consensus and community.
- Secularization and problem of authority.
- Social policy to guide orderly progress vs. revolution.
- Scientific accounts of human behaviour vs. Romantic critiques of scientism.
- Class differentiation – cohesion or conflict?
- History as progressive evolutionary narrative, which defines the meaning of ideas and movements.
- Social differentiation into discrete spheres (e.g. material, scientific, aesthetic).
- Evolutionary schema replicated in each sphere of society.

---

### FURTHER READING

The most comprehensive study of Comte is Mary Pickering (1993) *Auguste Comte: An Intellectual Biography* (Cambridge University Press), which is well written and provides a good balance of biographical and intellectual details. On positivism in general Leszek Kolakowski (1972) *Positivist Philosophy* (Penguin) is a classical summary and discussion. Johan Heilbron (1995) *The Rise of Social Theory* (Polity) rescues Comte from obscurity and places him in the context of eighteenth- and nineteenth-century social thought. Mike Gane (1993) *Harmless Lovers* (Routledge) has an excellent chapter on Comte, whom he treats with sympathetic criticism.

## NOTES

1 Alexander continues by arguing that in assimilating Judaeo-Christian themes of progress and rationality in history, nineteenth-century social theory managed to avoid the 'problem of meaning' until the end of the century. Weber, however, aware that modernity threatened a 'polar night of icy darkness', expressed pessimistic loss of earlier certainties. (This is discussed in Chapter 8.)

2 Giddens' argument is made largely in relation to Durkheim, rather than sociology in general. The other three 'myths' were that sociology was preoccupied with the Hobbesian problem of order (a view propagated by Parsons); that sometime between the 1860s and 1920 sociology rejected grandiose theory in favour of scientific methods (Giddens claims there was a continuity of concerns); and that there has been a persistent debate between 'consensus' and 'conflict' approaches (theorists like Marx and Durkheim were aware of both). But he did not dispute that classical sociology had taken up the problem of the 'roots of the modern crisis' in post-revolutionary Europe.

3 The term 'ideology', coined by Destrutt de Tracy (1754–1836), comes from the Ideologues, although in this original sense ideology was to be the science of ideas, their elements and relations. Later, particularly in Marx, ideology came to refer to ideas and beliefs that were distorted by class interest. Subsequently the term came to have many meanings, including the realm of ideas as opposed to material structures.

4 This aspect of the counter-Enlightenment, their hostility to scientific approaches to life, was not accepted by Comte although he shared their aims – to reintegrate society and resolve the crisis of modernity.

5 Charles Fourier (1772–1837) attacked the new capitalist civilization for its atomism and corruption of natural passions, while seeking to restore organic communities (*phalanstères*) as cells of the new society. In the socialist future women would be fully equal with men, families abolished and children raised communally.

6 Marx began to study Saint-Simon even before he read Hegel and as a student attended lectures given by Ludwig Gall, a leading Saint-Simonian (Bottomore and Rubel 1970: 25).

7 Saint-Simon did not rule out conflict between 'directing industrials' (capitalists and managers) and 'executive industrials' (workers) but believed that this could be avoided if society was organized to benefit the moral and physical needs of the whole population (Saint-Simon 1975: 265). After 1830 some Saint-Simonians, like Pierre Leroux (1797–1871), began referring to conflict between the bourgeoisie and proletariat (Szacki 1979: 130).

8 He went on to say that were France to lose 'all the great officers of the royal household, ministers of state', other officials and ten thousand proprietors who live like nobles, this would result in no political evil.

9  One of the many sources of Comte's disagreement with Saint-Simon (ironic-
   ally as it turned out) was the latter's proposal for a secular religion (Pickering
   1993: 237).

10 Contrary to some accounts, Comte proposed neither a 'government of scientists' nor of sociologists, but regarded such ideas as dangerous utopias. In his
   positive society, spiritual, advisory authority would be located among educated
   generalists with an understanding of science (Pickering 1993: 702).

11 The implicit (and undeveloped) distinction here between substantive agreement, and consensus over procedures for resolving disputes, was significant
   and is often overlooked. Procedural agreement as a goal for industrial societies
   that would retain diversity in substantive beliefs appeared again in Durkheim,
   in Weber and, more recently, Habermas.

12 'Knowledge for foresight, foresight for action' (*pouvoir* in the sense of 'making possible') is an often-quoted slogan of positivism (*Positive Philosophy*
   1830–4: 12).

13 In characteristic nineteenth-century fashion, Comte's sketch of history, offered
   in support of the law, refers only to western Europe. One of the conditions
   for the destruction of feudalism, emancipation of commons did not occur in
   Russia and China, where intellectual and social conditions were different
   (Comte 1974: 88). But all societies would in due course pass through the
   three states, and again parallels could be sought and found with Marx's
   sketch of history. Comte did not address the question of what effect knowledge of the process might have on the operation of the law, a problem that
   arose too in Marx's later work (see Chapter 4).

14 Since Marx had little familiarity with Comte's work until 1866, these similarities probably come from their common antecedent, Saint-Simon.

15 This internationalism reflected one mood of Enlightenment. Voltaire contrasted the 'good patriot' who is 'the enemy of the rest of humanity' with the
   'citizen of the universe' who would wish his country never greater or richer
   than any other. Condorcet looked forward to universal peace, civil liberties
   and international order. Schiller claimed to have traded his fatherland to the
   world and similarly, Kant believed that humanity's potential could be fulfilled
   only through world citizenship (Heater 1990: 53–4).

16 The similarity between these and Kant's three orders of judgement (theoretical,
   practical and aesthetic) is striking. For discussion of Comte's reception of
   Kant see Pickering (1993: 289–96).

17 Montesquieu and Gibbon noted that the Romans had manufactured religious
   ideas to keep plebeians in check. Rousseau (1968: 186) advocated a civil
   religion, breach of which being punished by death. The Jacobins institutionalized the Cult of the Supreme Being in the Republic of Virtue (1793–4).

18 Comte's early writing on women was influenced by Mary Wollstonecraft. In
   a letter in 1818 he said that 'women in general and collectively have suffered so
   much from [men] that I believe that I am particularly obliged to compensate
   . . . for the general offenses of my sex'. Men 'used the horrible law of the
   strongest to dominate women' which would cease in a civilized society.
   However, in correspondence with J. S. Mill in the 1840s, Comte admitted
   that, despite its early impression on him, he had set his mind against
   Wollstonecraft's 'curious doctrine' (Comte 1976: 198ff).

# CHAPTER 4

# Reason's revolt thunders

For reason in revolt now thunders; And at last ends the age of cant.
Away with all your superstitions; Servile masses arise, arise[1]

Karl Marx (1818–83) and Frederick Engels (1820–95) developed one of
the most important social theories of the nineteenth century, which was
situated in the nineteenth century genre of grand evolutionary theorizing.
Their work was a synthesis, particularly of German Hegelian philosophy,
political economy and French radicalism. The importance of Hegelianism
for Marx (which is outlined briefly on pp. 59–61) should not obscure the
significance of the French intellectual context, which connects Marx to
the development of some key sociological ideas. At around the same time
as Comte's later work, Marx was developing a theory of **society** existing
*sui generis*, though one which emphasized the importance of the material
conditions in shaping human history. Like Comte and Saint-Simon, Marx
viewed history as passing through stages of evolution, although this was
an idea to which he arguably became less committed in later life. Marx
claimed to be applying scientific methods to social development, in order
to provide a rational basis for political intervention, while demonstrating
which kinds of social changes were possible and which were not. Marx
and Saint-Simon insisted on the inevitability of the emergence of industrial
society, yet expected that a future society would restore harmony and
consensus within a technologically sophisticated order. Again like Saint-
Simon, Marx regarded social classes as representing emergent social forces
that initially have a progressive, but subsequently a retrogressive historical role. There were crucial differences too, of course. Whereas Comte
and Saint-Simon regarded a hierarchical society based on functionally
differentiated class divisions as both necessary and desirable, Marx looked
towards an egalitarian and de-differentiated future society.

This chapter presents a critical account of the central themes in Marx's
thought with particular reference to the ways in which unresolved problems
opened up subsequent dispute and diversity in Marxist theory. These
problems were compounded by the unfinished and fragmentary nature
of Marx's work which left considerable scope for subsequent additions

and reinterpretations. In the *Grundrisse* (a collection of notebooks written during 1857–8) Marx drafted several plans for his *Critique of Political Economy*. The whole opus was to involve the following books: (1) *Capital*, comprising capital in general (value, money, capital), competition, credit, share capital and communism; (2) Landed property; (3) Wage labour; (4) The state; (5) International trade; (6) World market. Yet the three volumes of *Capital* actually written (of which only the first was published in Marx's lifetime, in 1867) corresponded to merely the first part of the original design.

## CRITIQUE OF THE HEGELIANS

When Marx was a student in the 1830s, Georg Frederich Hegel (1770–1831) was the dominant philosophical figure in Europe. Hegel's work was of awe inspiring monumental ambition, aiming to incorporate the history of all previous philosophies. He conceived of this entire history as a process of completion, as all existence evolved to full self-consciousness. Hegel and his followers, the 'Young Hegelians', developed one of the most influential philosophical doctrines of the nineteenth century, Idealism, which saw the fundamental task of philosophy as understanding human existence through knowledge of abstract categories of Being, Reason, History and Spirit. This could be seen as an elaboration of the Enlightenment innovation of 'historicizing' philosophy, so that thinking and criticizing do not take place in a timeless social vacuum, but within the **dialectics** of history itself.

Hegel's *Phenomenology of Mind* (1805) was completed in Jena during Napoleon's invasion, an event which he felt lent immediacy to his philosophy. The *Phenomenology* attempted to trace the progress of Mind through a journey of experience through which Mind would recognize itself as the agent of history. In the process, apparently static oppositions within philosophy, such as the Cartesian distinction between subject and object, would be reconciled.[2] Thought, for Hegel, developed historically, moving dialectically through opposition, mutual criticism and transformation, and the *Phenomenology* reconstructed the phases through which humanity had struggled to become aware of itself as the self-conscious subject of history. Although the successive stages of consciousness do not always correspond with actual history, some major events (e.g. the Reformation and Napoleon's conquests) and philosophical movements (e.g. Kantianism) are presented as steps up the ladder of intellectual discovery. This is a journey in which Mind struggles to progress from mere consciousness to self-consciousness of itself thereby overcoming the static distinctions between subject and object. The split between ego (subject) and the world (object) arises from an 'unhappy consciousness' in that the first sense of self is awareness of a lack, of desire frustrated by the presence of other egos in the world. There then begins a search for unity and reconciliation that will be fulfilled only at the end of the journey, and only within philosophy, when Mind reaches a state of absolute knowledge (see Taylor 1979; Solomon 1983; Kolakowski 1989: 56–80).[3]

This is all quite abstract and one perhaps gets more sense of the socio-logical implications of dialectical thinking from Hegel's account of the master–slave encounter in the *Phenomenology* (Hegel [1805] 1949: 229–40). This has found resonance for example, among Marxists, feminists and the Black Consciousness movement.[4] This is an encounter between two primeval egos, who confront each other as obstructions to their own possession of the world. This could be a fight to the death, but one self submits and is enslaved, which results in a struggle for *recognition*. The labour of the slave signifies abstention from enjoyment, repression of desire and perpetual fear of the master. But the slave, whose labour gives form to objects, gradually comes to see the world as an exterioration of his own consciousness, while the master paradoxically remains in a state of dependence, and therefore unfreedom, on the slave. This is only the beginning of a struggle for recognition though, to overcome aliena-tion, and apprehend the world, and its oppressive conditions, as human products.

Hegel gave further sociological form to his philosophy in his account of the family, civil society and the state, in the *Philosophy of Right* (1821). Spirit achieves self-knowledge through differentiation into dis-crete spheres, which nonetheless together form a totality. In the family, socialization towards moral autonomy transforms biological and psycho-logical needs into individual desires. But families are not self-sufficient and in complex societies associate through civil society, the sphere of production, distribution and consumption, which meets a system of needs that are modified and multiplied in the process. It has its own regulatory institutions (Justice, Public Authority, Corporations) but these are instruments for achieving personal, egotistical ends. Indeed, Hegel's view of civil society anticipated Marx's critique of class polarization and dehumanization, as 'the conflict between vast wealth and vast poverty steps forth, a poverty unable to improve its condition [which] turns into the utmost dismemberment of will, inner rebellion and hatred' (Hegel [1821] 1967: 149–51).

However, this will be overcome if the constitutional-legal state (*Rechtstaat*) synthesizes the ethical life of the family with the public domain of civil society. Rather than view the state as a threat to free-dom, for Hegel it is an embodiment of ethical autonomy and universalism, against the particularism of private interests. Because the civil service was recruited by public examination, it stood above particular inter-ests of 'birth, rank and occupation', and was therefore a 'universal class' that realized the convergence of rationality with reality. Although this characterization of a legal state was far removed from the Prussian state in the 1830s, Hegelianism became for a while its official ideology.

According to one interpretation, Hegel's claim that the state embodied the synthesis of reason and ethics was a justification for the status quo. This, combined with the theological language of Hegel's later work, prompted the radical group of 'Young Hegelians' to subject his philosophy to critique. These 'left' Hegelians, whose Berlin *Doktorklub* Marx joined in 1836, included:

- Moses Hess (1812–75), who linked Hegelian ideas to the communist movement
- Bruno Bauer (1809–82), former theologian, who saw his philosophy as a negation of Christianity, and history as a permanent antagonism of Is and Ought
- Arnold Ruge (1802–80), who argued that Hegel had turned his system into an apologia for conformism, whereas there was an inevitable disharmony between the demands of reason and reality
- Ludwig Feuerbach (1804–72), whose materialist critique of religious alienation (*Essence of Christianity*, 1841) was the starting point for Marx's concept.

### Emancipation and proletariat

Human emancipation and the historical role of the proletariat is a central theme in Marx. The centrality of the proletariat was a claim Marx arrived at through theoretical rather than empirical reasoning, which in due course was to pose problems for Marxist theory. But what was Marx's concept of emancipation?

#### Critique of Judaism

Marx's break with Idealism was signalled in his contributions to the debate about Jewish emancipation. He sought to show that even if the state could stand above the particular interests of civil society (birth, rank and occupation), this would not emancipate society from their influence, but on the contrary would allow each free reign. Human emancipation required a radical challenge to the very differentiation between the civil and political society central to Hegelian theory. Marx's *On the Jewish Question* and *The Capacity for Present-Day Jews and Christians to Become Free* (1844) distinguished political from human emancipation, arguing that 'genuine human emancipation' would require the democratic control of society over production and the abolition of private property. However, his argument was curious in two respects. First, his call for the abolition of the boundary between political and civil society rejected Hegel's insistence (shared by many nineteenth-century social theorists) that modern societies develop through increasingly complex and differentiated organizational forms. Marx's underlying vision of a communist

society was a radically de-differentiated one, in which boundaries between the civil and political spheres wither away. Second, this is not the
only kind of difference to be eliminated as a condition of emancipation.
Deploying a characteristically dialectical method, Marx turns the problem of religious tolerance on its head. It is not a question, he suggests, of
the emancipation of the Jews, but rather, the emancipation of society
*from Judaism*. In these essays, Marx (like Bauer and Feuerbach) regarded
Judaism both as a religion and as a metaphor for modern commercial
society and his argument deploys a crude racial stereotype of Jewishness
as 'huckstering' and the embodiment of commercial degeneracy (Greenfeld
1992: 384).

These essays are open to various interpretations, not least that they
express Marx's ambivalence about his own Jewishness (Carlebach 1978).
But Marx's argument amounts to saying that genuine emancipation
requires social homogeneity (cf. Rousseau and the radical Jacobins) and
the elimination of difference. Indeed, in the *Communist Manifesto* (1848)
Marx and Engels credited capitalism with preparing the ground for communism by dissolving differences of gender, town and country, skilled
and unskilled, nationalities and religion 'in the icy water of egotistical
calculation'. However, this view is in conflict with the tendency of modern
societies to fragment life into increasingly differentiated cultural, social
and economic spheres. I shall suggest later in this chapter that this issue
came back to haunt Marxism at the end of the nineteenth century, in the
revisionist controversy and the dispute over the 'woman question'.

### Revolution as philosophical necessity

> Philosophy can be realized only by the abolition of the proletariat, and
> the proletariat can be abolished only by the realization of philosophy.
>                                           (Marx [1844] 1964)

True emancipation is accomplished only by social practice and in his
*Critique of Hegel's Philosophy of Right*, Marx identified an agent, the
class with 'radical chains' which alone can accomplish emancipation.
The proletariat resists not only its particular oppression, but also 'injustice in general' and it cannot emancipate itself without emancipating all
other spheres of humanity (Marx 1978: 73). This was his central claim,
which meant that proletarianization of intermediate social groups – craft
workers, smallholders, colonized peoples – was a necessary precondition
for their emancipation. The historical role of the proletariat arose objectively from its dispossession. Owning no private property, with only its
labour to sell, the proletariat was organized in factories where it was
immiserated and dehumanized by repetitive work. Yet, this collective
organization created the potential for mass organization and consciousness that eluded earlier exploited classes, like peasants and outworkers.[5]
These sociological attributes predisposed the proletariat to express the

general interests of humanity. However, in the 1840s, the concept of the proletariat as the agent of emancipation was arrived at through philosophical deduction of its necessary conditions of existence. In this sense it was perhaps a substitute for Hegel's universal class – the product of historical evolution that it was fated to rise above, unifying subject and object, freedom and necessity; the triumph of reason in history.

Three issues here were subsequently to become important in disputes about Marxist theory. First, since the proletariat's historical role had been logically derived, there was the problem of accounting for the divergence between the empirical proletariat (with diverse interests, internal stratification, attachment to various political ideas) and the ideal proletariat of Marxist theory. This was to be one of the central tensions within Marxism over the following century. Second, Marx equated 'interest' with ownership of property, and gave short shrift to suggestions that interests may derive from other sources, such as political privilege (e.g. Marx 1978: 563), differential market position, gender or ethnicity.[6] Third, the critique of injustice is an ethical position, and Marx's work is infused with moral outrage at hypocrisy and cynical exploitation in capitalism. Yet there is little discussion of ethics as such in Marx and Engels for at least two reasons. First, only the practical actions of the proletariat, and no amount of moralizing, would advance the cause of socialism and anyway ethical protestations were suspected of being covert expressions of class interests. Second, Marxism derived its moral authority from the historical process of proletarian class formation and did not speak from any ahistorical, ethical domain (Crook 1991: 85). But this left Marxism open to two objections. First that it fails to acknowledge its own ethical dimension, and second, that substituting historical necessity for ethics left the way open for justifications of Stalinism as 'regrettable but necessary' (but see Wood 1996 for a defence of Marx's concept of ethics).

## Materialist concept of alienation

The concept of 'alienation' in Marx's early works has given rise to an enormous literature, in part because of its relevance to the 'early–late' debate.[7] The most immediate influence for Marx was Feuerbach's *Essence of Christianity*, which argued that in making religion, people unwittingly project their human essence onto God, whose image represents perfection. This image becomes the source of rules which are reimposed on people's lives as regulations and self-denial. The attributes of deities (creative, merciful, loving etc.) are really alienated human powers that, once recognized as such, can promote human welfare on earth. Marx accepted much of Feuerbach's critique, but took issue with the notion of a human essence projected onto God. Human self-alienation is not psychological, but social and historical, and specifically arises from the system of production.

In the *Economic and Philosophical Manuscripts* (EPM 1844) Marx (1964) discussed four types of alienation:

1  Alienation from the product, where the means of production are owned by capitalists who appropriate and exchange the products of labour. These then take on a life of their own separate from the needs and wishes of the producers, thus workers 'build palaces but live in hovels'.
2  Alienation from productive activity, where work becomes external to the lives of workers, who 'feel freely active' only when eating, drinking and procreating – activities that humans share with animals.
3  Alienation from 'species-being' (our humanity). Marx suggests that creativity, satisfaction in objectifying ourselves through work is an essentially human attribute which is degraded in systems of production that are exploitative where work becomes a drudge.
4  Alienation of 'man from man' – community is dislocated, all social relations become dominated by economics and hostile classes are formed. There was perhaps here a hint of the nostalgia for a more communal kind of society that was noted in Saint-Simon and Comte.

The fundamental injustice of capitalism is that it denigrates precisely what differentiates humans from other animals, namely our capacity for productive creativity which will be fulfilled in a future emancipated society. This expectation, that justice will triumph and humanity will regain its species existence through the proletarian revolution, reflects a combination of Hegelian historical philosophy with Saint-Simonean utopianism.

## HISTORICAL MATERIALISM

Marx's materialism is founded on the claim that production involves cooperation, in the course of which emerge class relations, of ownership and non-ownership of the means of production. Several consequences follow from this: non-owners work for others; their livelihoods depend on their relations with superiors; dominant classes have direct rights over the economic product; owners extract a surplus from the process; the class system is inscribed into political, cultural and legal forms (Cohen 1987: 69). Material relations constitute 'the economic structure of society, the real foundation on which arises the legal and political super-structure' (Cohen 1987: 389–90). These relationships are conceptualized by the **mode of production**, which in each epoch extends its dominance over all aspects of society. Thus the capitalist mode of production (CMP) subordinates pre-capitalist forms of production, such as rural smallholders and hand craft workers, to the logic of capital accumulation.[8] The mode of production has two elements – the forces and social **relations of production**. The former are the technical instruments of production (such as land, labour and skills) which are organized through the latter, the sum total of class relations, techniques of control, political and legal systems.

Technologies themselves are subordinate to social relations (though occasionally Marx suggests otherwise)[9] since machinery is utilized according to the requirements of dominant social (class) relations (Marx to Annenkov 1846). However, the mode of production is an analytical concept and does not exhaust the rich complexity of actual societies (social formations) in which will be found both the traces of earlier modes (such as peasant production in capitalism) and the embryonic forms of future societies. Indeed, in Marx's sequential model of the transition from feudalism to capitalism to communism, the earlier social formation carries within itself the prototype of the later – thus capitalism creates socialized labour, technological production and complex organizational forms that presage a socialist system (Marx 1978: 511).

## Historical sequence

Marx shared with other mid-nineteenth-century social theorists a concept of progressive social evolution set against a perceived crisis in European society, which would be resolved through a combination of scientific knowledge and social agency. Each mode of production defines a dynamic class conflict which is a motor of historical change, the stages of which are summarized in Figure 4.1. What follows is a brief overview of Marx's sketch of historical development, which (with the exception of 'Oriental Despotism') was derived entirely from European history – something that was soon to pose difficulties.

The earliest and universal form of human social organization was primitive communism, which was differentiated in terms of kinship and tribes, since property was communal, classes had not yet emerged and there was a simple sexual division of labour. By comparison with later societies, however, primitive communism embodied a considerable degree of gender equality, a view later elaborated by Engels in *Origin of Family Private Property and the State* (1884). Marx and Engels assumed that history began with primitive hordes where property was owned communally. With pastoralism there follows the settlement of clans for the utilization of land in communities, based on blood, language and customs. These evolve into societies where a surplus product is extracted from direct producers, such as slaves and serfs, the potential for which arose from the relationship between the chief and tribe. There is no clear line of social evolution at this point since primitive communism leads in several directions: Orientalism, based on tribute collected from communal villages; the separation of private and state property, as in Rome; Slavonic communes; Germanic feudalism; systems of communal labour such as Mexico and Peru (Marx [1857–8] 1973: 473). Marx devoted relatively little time to analysing pre-capitalist formations though, all of which were understood in retrospect, from the viewpoint of the most advanced form, the CMP (pp. 100–6).

**Figure 4.1** Marx's sketch of historical evolution

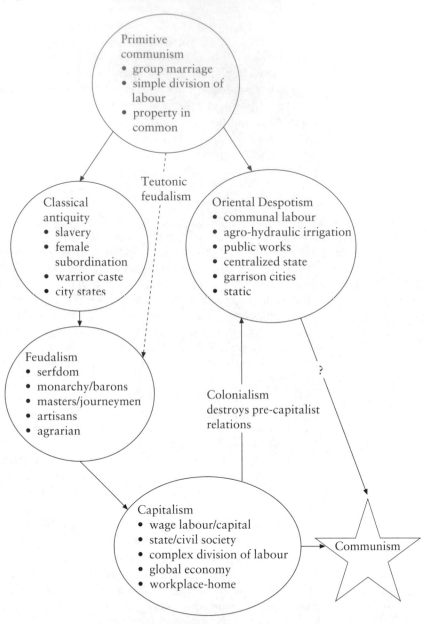

One development from primitive communism was oriental despotism (or the Asiatic mode of production); although the concept was not fully elaborated by Marx, it later assumed increased importance in Wittfogel's (1963) work. In Marx's account, the Asiatic mode retained communal property in villages where production was family based, while cities were undeveloped except as garrisons or trading posts (Marx [1857–8] 1973: 475). Villages produce communally and hand over a surplus (as tribute) to the central state, which undertakes large-scale projects of public works, such as organizing irrigation canals. The absence of productive classes means that these societies lack the dynamic for internally driven change, engender 'stationaryness' and lack imagination. They will be destroyed by colonialism, such as the Opium Wars (1839–42), which will forcibly bring Asiatic societies into the capitalist world system.

The other main line of development from primitive communism were the Ancient societies, such as Greece and Rome, where tribes settled in city states with complex civil and political structures, based on agriculture with rudimentary industry and trade and commerce. Expanding through conquest, Ancient societies were militaristic, with private property emerging as a reward for military service. The money economy (boosted by the wage system in the army) facilitated the expansion of credit and class struggles in the Ancient world appeared between creditors and debtors, coinciding with landowning and indebted landless families (Marx [1867] 1976: 141). The latter became slaves, which remained the basis of the whole productive system, with the slave population being replenished through conquest and enslavement of defeated peoples. The Ancient world further saw the appearance of the state and the subordination of women as chattels, as men occupied the new public civil spheres of society (Engels 1968). However, historical development followed no necessary evolutionary path here, and to explain why in Rome indebted peasants became slaves, while in medieval Europe they became wage-workers, one must examine the specific circumstances of each case (Marx 1978: 572).

A clearer evolutionary trajectory appears in Marx's theory when, after the decline of Rome, world history shifts northwards to Germanic territories. These were the nucleus of a hierarchical system of landownership enforced by armed retainers, from which arose feudal estates, on which serfdom was the axial social relationship. The replacement of slavery by feudalism is not described in detail, nor it is entirely clear why the decline of the former should have led to the latter (Craib 1997: 213). However, whereas slaves were at the disposal of their owner, serfs had access to communal land, but were obliged to pay tithes to the local landowner, on whose estate they were forced to live. Although 'land was the seat of history' (Marx [1857–8] 1973: 471) in that feudalism was predominately rural, towns grew in importance in the later Middle Ages where class relations between masters, journeymen and apprentices mirrored those of the countryside. The need to protect urban property against the 'robber nobility' resulted in the formation of guilds within which developed new social relations and the regulation of economic life by customs, mutual obligations and statutory controls.

Within medieval towns an incipient merchant capitalism began to take shape, increasingly resistant to both aristocratic power and feudal constraints on economic activity – restrictions on trade, labour mobility, interest, rent and so on. The accumulation of wealth by merchants, along with their expanding political power which eradicated the feudal fetters on commercial life, created conditions for the emergence of full-blown capitalism. Initially performing a revolutionary historical role, the bourgeoisie both sweep away pre-modern ways of life and initiate the industrial age, by continually revolutionizing instruments of production (Marx 1978: 223–4). The capitalist mode of production was defined by the relation between formally free labour (in the sense that feudal restraints on labour mobility had gone) and capital, which extracted a surplus through the wage relation. Pre-capitalist forms of production were based on *direct* relations of class domination and servitude, whereas the wage relation is apparently one of reciprocal exchange between capital and labour (Marx [1867] 1976: 350) although this merely conceals the way a surplus is extracted from workers in the form of value (see pp. 72–7). Having emerged in western Europe, capitalism was becoming a global system of production and exchange, spread through colonialism and world trade. It had a highly complex and technical division of labour, with differentiation between public and private, workplace and home, civil and political society. Capitalism is an enormously productive and dynamic system that sweeps away pre-capitalist relations and cultural forms, establishing the dominance of the cash nexus, while a multilayered class system (including intermediate classes) will tend to simplify into a bipolar system of capital and labour. Capitalism was the last antagonistic society and would be replaced by communism.[10]

Was this sequential evolution predetermined so that all societies (as for Comte) had to pass through these phases? Could human agents act to alter the course of historical development? Marx was obliged to confront these questions in the 1870s when, following the wide circulation of *Capital* among Russian radicals, he was criticized for his 'fatal theory of historical inevitability', for example by Nikolai Mikhailovsky (1842–1904). Prior to his exchanges with the Russians, Marx had wavered slightly, but did seem to suggest historical necessity. In the Preface to the first edition of *Capital* (1867) he refers to 'tendencies working with iron necessity towards inevitable results. The country that is more developed industrially only shows to the less developed the image of its own future'. In response to Mikhailovsky, he concedes that Russia may be able to avoid the capitalist stage and build on the collectivism of the traditional village commune (*mir*) but only if a Russian revolution is supported by one in the west. However, in his letter to the Russian revolutionary Vera Zasulich (1881) Marx went further, insisting that 'the historical inevitability' of his thesis 'was expressly limited to western Europe', so the *mir* could regenerate Russian society after a revolution. This implied a rather more voluntaristic conception of history than in his earlier works, which actually had not *expressly* limited the process to western Europe, even if that was what he really meant (Szamuely 1988: 502–25).

## Dual theory of social change

What was the driving force of social change? At first, the answer appears simple, as Marx and Engels say in the *Communist Manifesto*, 'The history of all hitherto existing societies is a history of class struggle', since each mode of production defines a binary axis of conflict. Yet alongside this there is a theory of social change based on conflict between 'old' and 'new' systems of production, that in Saint-Simonian vein, is represented by competing class actors. The implications of these two different positions are not always compatible.

Most of Marx's observations on social change were based on the transition from feudalism to capitalism in western Europe, the most succinct statement of which one finds in the *Preface to a Critique of Political Economy* (1859). Here, echoing Saint-Simon, productive forces developing 'in the womb of bourgeois society' create the material conditions for the final resolution of class antagonisms. However, 'no social order perishes until all the social forces for which there is room in it have developed', at which point, 'the material **forces of production** come into conflict with existing relations of production, that is with property relations', which become fetters on the further development of productive forces.

However, the role of class conflict in this transformation is ambiguous, since it is not clear that struggles defined by a particular mode of production are primarily responsible for the transition from one mode to another. There were slave rebellions in antiquity and peasant rebellions in Medieval feudalism, but neither of these brought about the disintegration of the mode of production, nor did Marx claim they did. In fact, the most significant conflict at the end of feudalism was that between the aristocracy and the incipient bourgeoisie, that is between representatives of the old and new social orders. Here, the serfs and later the peasantry (the 'antagonistic' class within feudalism) were rather marginal historical actors. Feudalism became historically obsolete because it imposed fetters on the further development of productive forces, through feudal land tithes, restricting the mobility of labour, and regulating wages in the guild system. Merchant capitalism was at this stage revolutionary because in order to expand new commercial and productive systems it broke feudal fetters asunder.

Clearly Marx saw here a precedent for the way capitalism in turn will be overtaken by more progressive material forces. The future transition to socialism was prefigured in the productive potential for planning and management and the autonomous 'productive force of science', that capitalism having once promoted, will eventually restrict (Marx [1857–8] 1973: 141). Thus capitalism is doomed for two reasons. First, because of the contradiction between wage-labour and capital, overlaid by its long term crisis tendencies, which are outlined below. Second, capitalism (like feudalism) will eventually impose fetters on its further technological development. In the *Grundrisse*, Marx claims

> Beyond a certain point the development of productive forces becomes a barrier for capital. Thus capitalist relationships become a barrier for the development of the productive force of labour. On arrival at that point, capital . . . enters into the same relationship to the development of social wealth as did the guild system, serfdom, slavery and is necessarily rejected as a fetter.
>
> (Marx [1857–8] 1973: 636)

Its demise is thus demanded not only by the mass of proletarians whom it exploits, but also by the requirement of human progress. Yet it is not clear that the proletariat are the bearers of any new system of production. Indeed, socialist production will still require organization within a complex division of labour which is a 'technical necessity dictated by the instrument of labour itself' (Marx [1867] 1976: 399–400). If the incipient system of production in the nineteenth century was scientific planning and management – its 'bearer' surely was not the mass industrial worker but the professional and managerial stratum, later to become the 'knowledge workers' of post-industrial society – a group closer to Saint-Simon's *les industriels* than Marx's proletariat.

## Ideology and consciousness

After the initial transition from primitive communism to class societies, social organization has an inner logic of which actors have generally been neither aware nor consciously able to control. In unequal societies, differentiated by ownership and non-ownership of productive resources, these relations are essentially conflictual, even if this is at times latent rather than manifest. Potential conflicts may remain latent for many reasons, but Marxists have often claimed that oppressed classes are unable to perceive their real interests because of 'ideological distortions'. Subsequent Marxists have often credited ideology with primary responsibility for maintaining social integration (e.g. Lukács 1968; Adorno 1991) but the concept is problematic, since Marx left an array of possible meanings of ideology, rather than a comprehensive theory.

First, Marx and Engels' only extensive treatment of ideology, *The German Ideology* (1846), was a critique of Hegelian Idealism that offered an alternative, materialist, account of the development of ideas. Idealists wrongly attributed to ideas a determining role in historical development, whereas 'consciousness can never be anything other than conscious existence, and the existence of men is their actual life process'. Two claims are made here. First, ideas cannot have a life independent of practical activity but are produced through labour like other social relations. Second, the types of ideas produced will reflect material conditions, so for example, when the 'separation of powers' is the dominant idea in political philosophy, we find monarchy, aristocracy and bourgeoisie vying for dominance. But Marx did attempt to avoid deterministic materialism (Marx 1978: 156–8) and his primary concern was to demonstrate that ideas were embedded historically in practical activity, which combined consciousness and material relations (Larrain 1979: 54).[11]

A second meaning is that ideologies are distortions involving a kind of imaginary relationship to society. Again in *The German Ideology*, Marx and Engels claim that 'in all ideology men and their circumstances appear upside down as in a camera obscura'. Here ideas are like lenses that, while reflecting material conditions, view them in a distorted way, against which Marx claims to offer true perceptions. Such distortions though may reflect the prevailing level of social development, in which philosophers fail to understand the real nature of the historical conjuncture that has been reached. Marx gives an example of this in his *Critique of Hegel's Philosophy of Right* (1843) where he contrasts English and French political economy with German Idealist philosophy. That Germany produced a speculative philosophy of law, a 'dream history', reflected its failure to establish a constitutional state in reality. German revolutions, such as the Reformation, have taken place in thought, whereas in England and France they have occurred in practical life, leaving no need for speculative fantasies. Yet the Idealists cannot see that the bourgeoisie is too weak and dependent on the aristocracy to bring their *Rechstsaat* into being anyway. Here ideology occludes the impasse in social development, that will be broken only by the revolutionary action of the proletariat (Marx 1978: 68ff).

A third sense of ideology in Marx is similar to what later sociologists call 'legitimation', that is, beliefs that justify the rule of the dominant political class. In the *German Ideology*, Marx says the 'ruling ideas' are the 'ideas of ruling class', because those who control the material means of production also control the ideological means of production. As a result of this, subject classes fail to understand the oppressive nature of the system and their capacity to transform it into a better one. This may be because ideologies obscure the injustice of existing social arrangements, which falsely appear to be natural or inevitable. Marx did *not* use the term 'false consciousness' although he may have implied it. This is probably one of the most heavily worked conceptions of ideology in Marxism, liberally used to explain the proletariat's general lack of enthusiasm for revolution.

A fourth sense of ideology is an inability to penetrate beneath the appearance of things to underlying realities. The exchange of labour for wages has the appearance of being a free and equal exchange between two voluntary parties to a contract (Marx [1867] 1976: 172). In reality though, it is a deeply asymmetrical exchange because the capitalist owns the means of production while workers are forced to sell their labour or starve. Further, the value commodities acquire in the market appears to derive from their own properties, but Marx claims that value arises only through the social relations of production. Thus science shows that the 'products of labour . . . are but material expressions of the human labour spent in their production' but to 'those caught up in the relationship', the value form 'appears as an objective character of products themselves' (Marx [1867] 1976: 79–80). Bourgeois economists and philosophers, however sophisticated their understanding, were prevented by their class position from properly understanding the nature of capitalism. Political economy was 'bourgeois' in that it failed to look beneath the appearance of production, consumption and exchange to the underlying nature of social relations.

These uses of the concept (Idealism, imaginary relation to society, legitimation and class bias) are compatible to some extent, but they do suggest that Marx had not worked through its possible ramifications. Indeed, he suggested in places, such as the *Communist Manifesto* (1848), that unlike earlier societies, capitalism had no need of ideologies and anyway changed at too dynamic a pace ever to allow a 'halo' to form around its activities (see Berman 1985). Further, to critique ideology presupposes that one occupies a non-ideological standpoint, from which true understanding is possible. The importance of offering a foundation for his insights was to generate a great deal of subsequent debate. Marx seemed to suggest two ways of founding a critique of ideology. The first is based on a claim to science, which dispells illusions, a contrast associated particularly with Althusser (1965). However, correct consciousness cannot only be a methodological issue, since researchers with a common epistemology can form quite different conclusions, and anyway it is not clear that Marx used a radically different method from that of other political economists. A second claim to cognitive privilege is located in class position, yet neither Marx nor Engels were proletarians (Engels was a factory owner) so one does not actually have to be in the exploited class to see the truth about capitalism. It is sufficient that one becomes an intellectual advocate of the oppressed and adopts what Georg Lukács ([1923] 1968) later called the 'standpoint of the proletariat'. However, this argument gets rather circular, because 'standpoint epistemologies' amount to grounding truth in a prior set of moral and political commitments, the validity of which still require justification.

## CAPITAL AND EMANCIPATION

### Fetishism of commodities

The greater part of Marx's mature work was devoted to developing a theory of the capitalist mode of production, revealing its exploitative nature and demonstrating that it was doomed. Capitalism was unique among class societies, in that while all modes of production extract a surplus from direct producers, capitalism does so invisibly, in the form of value. With slavery and serfdom the extraction of a surplus (forced labour, the feudal tithe) had been palpable, as was the extraction of tax-rent in Oriental Despotism. But the exchange between capital and labour appears to be a voluntary and mutually beneficial contract in which one commodity, labour power, is exchanged for another, wages. Note that here Marx introduced a concept not present in earlier work (e.g. the EPM) separating labour in general from labour *power*, the capacity to work for a given period of time. With this latter concept, Marx believed he had discovered the secret working of the capitalist economy concealed in bourgeois political economy, which failed to unravel the commodity form and the true origin of profit. Thus Marx began *Capital* with an analysis of the most abstract form of capitalist exchange – the commodity – which has two components, use value and exchange value. **Use value** is a property of things and is often intrinsic to their nature – fuel provides heating, clothes protect against the elements, bread provides food, and so forth. Use values are specific, concrete and ahistorical, in the sense that they exist in all societies. **Exchange value** is specific to societies in which the money form is well developed, and refers to the way a quantity of one commodity, say a kilo of rice, can be expressed in terms of another commodity, say a quarter kilo of coffee. Exchange value, which becomes generalized in capitalism, is made possible by the most abstract of commodities, money, which enables the varied qualities of things (coal, coats, bread etc.) to be reduced to a common quantity – price. More specifically though, in capitalism labour power itself becomes a commodity, measured by an equivalence between the length of the working day (say ten hours) and the wages paid, which is the 'price' of labour. Capitalism thus creates a set of equivalencies among intrinsically different things, in particular, physical goods (cloth, coal, food etc.), time, human labour power and monetary value.

Bourgeois economists treated commodity exchange as an essential and natural feature of all but the simplest societies. However, commodity exchange is the outcome of a historical evolution first to 'simple' then 'complex' circulation. The development of monetary exchange is at first simple reproduction in which products are sold in order to purchase more commodities, where money is essentially itself a use value. Marx expressed this situation as: C-M-C where one commodity (C) is exchanged via money (M) for new commodities (C). An example of this would be a smallholder who sells produce to buy wood for fuel or fencing. In this case money is simply a substitute for subsistence goods. However, with capitalism, this form of circulation gives way to the purchase of labour power itself as a commodity (M-C-$M^1$) in which an initial sum of money (M) is transformed into a larger sum ($M^1$). This is no longer a simple circulation of use values, but a circulation of capital, in which the objective of exchange for the purchaser (the capitalist) is to accumulate money, a process that becomes an end in itself (Marx 1978: 451). But labour power is a very peculiar commodity, the consumption of which leaves the purchaser with greater value ($M^1$) than prior to the exchange!

From where does this additional value come? Classical economists, Marx felt, could not account for profit because they could not confront the exploitative nature of the system. Adam Smith had explained profit as a return for investment and organization; Jean-Baptiste Say, as reward for risk and entrepreneurship; Marx's contemporary, Nassau Senior (1790–1864) regarded it as reward for abstaining from consumption (Marx 1969: 166). But for Marx, M-M$^1$ was possible because of the peculiar character of labour power. Marx accepted Adam Smith's view that laws of supply and demand produced a tendency for commodities to sell at a price equivalent to their costs of production. So if labour power was a commodity, it too would 'sell' at its reproduction cost, that is the subsistence costs of the worker and dependants (Walker 1978: 128). However, labour had the unique capacity to produce commodities to greater value than its own reproduction costs – to spend part of the day working 'free, gratis and for nothing'. Thus, for Marx the additional value (M$^1$) arose not (as economists claimed) from within the market but in the production process itself.

Now, the availability of labour power as a commodity was no automatic or 'natural' occurrence, but required a particular set of historical conditions: a market in commodities, poor but free labours, accumulation of wealth for investment in industry, a market in labour and the development of productive technologies. This process of primitive accumulation, in which capital and labour were initially created, involved centuries of struggle and suffering, 'merciless vandalism', including the enclosure of common land, the disposition of peasants, the starvation of hand craft workers, colonization and enslavement of aboriginal peoples. Thus, 'capital comes into the world dripping from head to foot from every pore, with blood and dirt' (Marx [1867] 1976: 719). So, the exchange between capital and labour embodies a whole set of historical and social relations, to which economists are blind because they see only a self-equilibrating market governed by the price mechanism. Indeed, capital appears as a thing (money) while social relations take on an illusory *fetishistic* (or reified, *versachlichkeit*) form. Hence Marx writes of a **fetishism of commodities**. As in his critique of ideology, there is a suggestion here that people enter into an imaginary relation with society, which Marx attempts, so to speak, to 'deconstruct'. At first then, a 'commodity is a mysterious thing because in it the social character of men's labour appears to them as an objective character stamped on the product of that labour; because the relation of the producers to the sum total of their own labour is presented to them as a social relation, existing not between themselves, but between the products of their labour' (Marx, 1978: 421ff). But critical analysis will reveal this to be merely the illusory form of social relationships.

To understand the implications of Marx's analysis, we need to look more closely at the exchange between capital and labour and the process by which surplus is extracted. Take, for example, a ten hour working day, in which it takes six hours for a worker to produce sufficient value to meet subsistence needs, such as food, housing, clothes, fuel etc. This is the average **socially necessary labour time** required for production of a given commodity, which will vary considerably in different industries, being dependent in part on the level of mechanization of production and in part on prices of basic necessities produced elsewhere in the system. However, in the remaining four hours the value produced is withheld by the capitalist. This *surplus labour time* (= **surplus value**) is the basis of profit, once overheads (fixed costs) have been deducted. In this example, the rate of surplus value then is thus $4 \div 10$ or 40 per cent. However, capitalism is competitive and capitalists are constantly attempting to gain advantage over their competitors, which can be done in two ways. First, the rate of *absolute surplus* can be increased by, for example, reducing wages, speeding up machinery, forcing wives and children of male workers to work alongside them for no pay, and draconian systems of fines and penalties. These are graphically described in Engels' *Condition of the Working Class in England* (1844). Later though, with the introduction of machinery, capitalism finds it more effective to increase the rate of *relative surplus value*. With more advanced machinery, necessary labour time is further reduced, thereby increasing surplus labour. If necessary labour is reduced to (say) four hours, then in the above example the rate of surplus value rises to 60 per cent ($6 \div 10$). This, however, gives individual enterprises only a temporary advantage because the new ratio of necessary to surplus value gets widely adopted and becomes the norm in the given branch of production. So the pressure to innovate begins again, and the proportion of necessary to surplus labour continues to diminish.

All this makes capitalism highly dynamic, continually increasing the productivity of labour and the technical composition of production. It further generates three tendencies central to capitalist development:

- concentration of capital into fewer hands, as uncompetitive firms go under – 'one capitalist kills many'
- social organization of labour into an increasingly complex division of labour
- creation of a world market, as capital seeks new markets, raw materials and cheap labour.

However, a central objective of *Capital* was to show that despite its dynamic capacities, capitalism was prone to crises that would eventually bring about its collapse.

### Cyclical crises and the falling rate of profit

The belief that capitalism would enter a period of long term stagnation and falling profits was widely held among political economists, including Smith, Ricardo, J. S. Mill and Thomas Malthus (Walker 1978: 152–3).[12]

But Marx developed a more specific theory of its crisis tendencies. First, capitalism is subject to cyclical crises that arise because market conditions change more rapidly than investment and production processes – in particular there is a disjuncture between industries producing equipment, or capital goods ('Department 1') and consumption goods ('Department 2'). As one branch of production becomes more profitable, it attracts further investment, more goods are produced more cheaply, markets expand and growth in Department 2 stimulates growth in Department 1. Unemployed workers (the reserve army of labour) are hired and average wages rise for a while. But capital investments (new equipment) involve long term commitments, respond to present levels demand, and no one firm knows for how long the boom will last. Once markets get saturated, wages, interest rates and prices peak and demand falls off. But orders for new machinery have already been placed by Department 2 firms in Department 1. As demand falls, orders are cancelled, recession in Department 2 triggers recession in Department 1, which snowballs into a crisis in the industry as a whole. But these cyclical crises are not initially terminal for capitalism, because appearing at different times in different parts of the system mitigates their effect. They are actually means through which the system as a whole recuperates and is restructured. Marx implies, nonetheless, that since each crisis is more severe than the preceding one, capitalism will end in stagnation and collapse. Whether the proletarian revolution will have to await this cataclysm, is not clear, but working class political parties will learn that capitalism renders their lives subject to the arbitrary play of market forces that could be brought under rational control in a socialist society.

A more serious crisis will arise from a contradiction between the 'social power of capital' and the actions of individual firms. This gives rise to the *tendency of the rate of profit to fall*, which was the underlying crisis tendency of capitalism. As more machinery is introduced into production, less and less work is necessary to produce the same quantity of goods. But in the process the organic composition of capital rises. That is, fixed costs of raw materials and machinery rise relative to additional value created by the application of new labour. Capitalism reduces the proportion of the day spent on necessary labour time, but increases its overheads – heating, lighting, fuel, depreciation, interest etc. Since profit is the ratio of surplus value to costs of production, and since the latter are rising in relation to the former, the *rate* of profit must fall, eventually. Despite the fact that their labour is more productive, workers spend an increasing part of the day reproducing the fixed costs of capital. Therefore the new value added in each product falls relative to its fixed (or 'dead') component. Paradoxically then, as the productivity of labour increases, the rate of profit falls even though the mass of surplus value rises. For Marx, this is the logical tendency of capitalism, even if it is 'offset' in the short term by factors such as colonialism, state intervention or importing raw materials from economies with low production costs.

Marx appeared to have found a contradiction at the heart of capitalism. What is rational for individual capital (machine investment) is irrational (or self-defeating) for the system in the longer term. Three consequences in particular follow from this tendency:

1 Immiseration and exploitation of the proletariat. This may be offset in the short term as reduced demand for labour in some branches of capital, following mechanization, are compensated by new types of enterprises. But the 'absolute general law of capital accumulation' (Marx [1867] 1976: 644) is to create larger reserves of unemployed and thereby reduce average wages.[13]
2 Technological change and the concentration of ownership. Increases in the minimum of capital necessary to be productive creates a tendency for industries to centralize (Marx [1867] 1976: 626).
3 Breakdown of capitalism. The apparent simplicity of the price mechanism conceals the violent process of class conflict and declining resources, which through the leadership of the proletarian party becomes the focus of mass mobilization.

However, the hypothesis of the falling rate of profit is difficult to test, given the complexity of global capital and the variation of necessary labour time in different parts of the system. It is further based on various assumptions, which are open to question:

- Additional value (and therefore profit) is created only by 'living labour' and nothing else.
- Machines are 'dead' labour because their value was realized when sold to the capitalist, therefore machines themselves cannot create new value (though occasionally Marx hints otherwise).
- Value that appears to be created in other ways (e.g. when a work of art increases in price once the painter is famous) occurs only in the sphere of circulation and its 'real' value is unaffected.
- Thus value inheres in commodities and does not always equal price (exchange value). The difficulties with this claim had already led Ricardo to abandon it and Marx's labour theory of value, soon attracted the criticism of being 'metaphysical' (see pp. 78–9).
- Capitalism will eventually run out of ways of forestalling the tendency of the rate of profit to fall – Marx assumed rather than demonstrated this.

Part of the difficulty here is that Marx deployed the language of science in support of an essentially ethical Romantic critique of commodification and the dehumanization of labour.

## LOSING THE NARRATIVE? REVISIONISM AND THE 'WOMAN QUESTION'

Marx's death in 1883 left much of his planned work undone or unpublished, along with many unresolved theoretical and practical problems, some of which were addressed by Engels. One of these was the relationship between Marxism and feminism, posed partly because of the appearance of the suffrage movement, whose demands extended beyond the vote, to the inclusion of women in public life and professions. The disputes over feminism among late nineteenth-century Marxists, however, became entangled in another issue, the revisionist controversy. Both these disputes posed crucial questions about the ability of Marxism to encompass, theoretically and practically, emerging identities and social movements. Despite these difficulties though, Marxism had become what Lyotard later called a 'grand narrative of historical justification' that is, a claim to transcendent universal truth underpinning history and knowledge (Lyotard 1990) at the centre of which was the notion of the proletariat as a unified subject of emancipation. These debates and the divergent positions they engendered, were perhaps an early indication of cracks in this totality.

### Revisionism

The revisionist controversy, which began at the Frankfurt Congress of the German Social Democratic Party (SPD) in 1894, threw Marxism into crisis and set the terms of European socialist debate for the following 20–30 years at least.[14] A central figure in these disputes was Eduard Bernstein (1850–1932) whose *Evolutionary Socialism* ([1899] 1961) set out a philosophical and practical programme for reformist rather than revolutionary socialism. Within the SPD, the controversy was acrimonious and Bernstein was opposed both by the leadership (Karl Kautsky and August Bebel) and 'left' figures such as Klara Zetkin, Rosa Luxemburg and Karl Liebknecht. The controversy reflected major intellectual developments of the period. New economic theories cast doubt on the Marxist theory of value, on which Eugen von Böhm-Bawerk launched a systematic attack.[15] While being attacked as insufficiently scientific by economists, Marxism was also accused by neo-Kantians of positivism and of disregarding ethical questions.[16] Bernstein incorporated both these critiques arguing that:

- Contrary to Marx's expectations, the middle class does not wither away but grows.[17]
- Rather than increased immiseration, working class incomes are rising, making distribution more equitable, even if relative inequalities remain. Living standards rise where trade unions are strong therefore organization *within* capitalism produces benefits.
- The rate of profit does not fall. The business cycle is evening out and recurrent crises are less severe than the preceding ones.
- The growth of large-scale enterprises does not entail a concentration of ownership; rather ownership gets dispersed through the growth of joint stock companies.

- In rural areas small scale enterprise and family farms are flourishing alongside agricultural giants, thus the peasantry is not disappearing. Therefore the SPD had to make itself attractive to non-proletarian classes opposed to large scale capitalism.
- Human agency and ethical choice affect historical outcomes and socialism was not inevitable, but had to win the ethical arguments. As an ethical ideal, socialism was not the property of the proletariat but would win support through argument and demonstration of its beneficial effects.

The ensuing controversy increasingly divided the party between those supporting an evolutionary, parliamentary route to socialism and those advocating revolution, a split that came to a head after 1917 and the formation of the German Communist Party (Gay 1962). However, the dispute left a theoretical legacy that was to frame debates over Marxism during the following decades. Marx had philosophically derived the idea of the proletariat as the universal class, which subsumed all other forms of oppression within its own struggle for emancipation. But the revisionists implicitly questioned the theoretical centrality of the proletariat and the idea of a universal, revolutionary subject. Thus although on one level the dispute was over 'reform vs. revolution', on another level it signalled the fracture of the theoretical unity of Marxism and reflected underlying and unresolved tensions, which were manifest further in the controversy over the 'woman question'.

### Revisionism and the 'Woman Question'

The late nineteenth century saw widespread feminist activism around the issues of suffrage, temperance (which was related to the issue of male violence), access to professional occupations and 'protective legislation', to remove women from industrial occupations (R. Evans 1976; 1979). The latter was highly controversial, separating socialists who generally favoured protective legislation, from 'bourgeois feminists' who did not. Marx, however, had primarily addressed issues that arose in a masculine public sphere and rarely commented on the position of women in capitalist (or socialist) society. True, in *The German Ideology* Marx and Engels ([1846] 1974: 49) argued that, 'The first class oppression that appears in history coincides with the development of the antagonism between man and woman in monogamous marriage and the first class oppression coincides with that of the female sex by the male'. But by describing this as a class relation, they evade the question of whether gender domination has an existence independent of economic factors. The year following Marx's death, Engels published the classical Marxist analysis of patriarchy, the *Origin of Family, Private Property and the State* (1884). He argued that women's subordination had an economic basis in property relationships, and that material relations included both senses of reproduction, economic production and bearing and rearing of children. The conditions for patriarchy were historical and not natural. Indeed, pre-state societies, Engels claims, were democratic with matrilineal descent and elder women powerful in deposing chiefs. Looking for evidence of original societies, which he regarded as a universal stage in social development, Engels followed Marx's *Ethnological Notebooks*, which in turn were based on Lewis Morgan's *Ancient Society*.[18] In characteristic nineteenth century fashion, they sought evidence of the past of European society in contemporary 'primitive' societies such as the Iroquois. So Marx, and then Engels, believed that they had found evidence here of primitive communism, since Iroquois society was matrilineal, had a simple division of labour, no private property, clan members shared food and land, leaders were elected and the bourgeois family was unknown. People did not have exclusive sexual partners, and children were the common responsibility of the clan.

Gender relations in capitalist societies, then, were the result of a particular set of historic circumstances. The development of pastoralism, the rearing of herds, strengthened the position of men in the family and led to the overthrow of matrilinearity. Gender inequality was established through appearance of the state and private property, as men became dominant in the division of labour, instituted patrilinial descent, while women became concubines, slaves and prostitutes. Propertied men who wanted to know which children were their rightful heirs imposed monogamy on women. This represented a 'world historical defeat for women' who were thereby excluded from the public sphere, politics, religion and culture.

For Engels the conditions for women's emancipation would be prepared by capitalism but achieved only under socialism. The more that proletarian women entered the labour market, the more they would assume proletarian identity and differences among them would diminish. Engels was aware that the household itself was a site of gendered relations but reinterpreted these in class terms, so that the 'proletarian man is a proletarian at work but a bourgeois at home, whereas the proletarian woman is a proletarian at work and at home'. Legal equality within a democratic republic was of limited value because this would not abolish the economic dependence of women on men nor the role of the family in supporting institutions of property. Under socialism though, freed from the constraints of private property, the bourgeois family would decline, monogamy be redundant, and society would take over the financial support of children. Sexual relations would be freed from the hypocrisy and constraints of bourgeois society and partners would be chosen on the basis of romantic love, while state childcare would remove anxieties about unwanted pregnancies.[19]

There were problems with Engels' analysis, which subsumed cultural, moral and emotional relations within the sphere of material production.

Women appeared as passive instruments of the needs of class society within which their destiny was to enter the masculine workplace as superexploited proletarians as a condition of emancipation. Questions of morality and personal responsibility were reduced to economic dependence, reflecting the general exclusion from Marxism of ethical and cultural matters. The analysis was limited to women's economic dependence on husbands, removal of which does not guarantee independence, since discrimination arises from within the paid workplace (M. Evans 1987). Further, in Engels' account of the origins of patriarchy, it was unclear why men controlled the herds, when agricultural subsistence was still within women's sphere. To wrest wealth from women's control men must already have appropriated power through deployment of physical and cultural force (Humphries 1987: 14).

Nonetheless, the views of Engels, Bebel and Zetkin became the central plank of the Party's response to feminism. While the Party's policy was to encourage women to fight for political rights and to mobilize in unions, it insisted theoretically on the centrality of class struggle (Landes 1981). This entailed a refusal to accept any common cause with so-called 'bourgeois feminist' movements, such as the Central Association of Women and Girls of Germany, which was regarded as a 'right deviation' (Thönnessen 1969; Draper and Lipow 1976; Landes 1981). This is not to say that all Marxists avoided issues of gender, sexuality and the family, but the sexual radicalism of Zetkin and Alexandra Kollonti had little theoretical resonance with concepts of public, political and workplace struggle. Marxism inhabited the public social terrain constituted by post-Enlightenment thought in which 'private matters' were largely beyond the scope of the theory. To have acknowledged that women represented an oppressed group that transcended class divisions would have given way on central issue of Revisionist controversy, and acknowledged that there were struggles complementary to and independent of class.

This was not just a local and historically specific dispute, but one with implications for relationship between Marxism and feminism and beyond this, the idea of central loci of conflict in society. Could a theory grounded in modes of economic production address the gender of exploiters and those whose labour is appropriated (Barrett 1988)? As a theory of the public sphere, Marxism had difficulty dealing with movements that subjected patriarchy and private social relations to critical scrutiny. Similarly, the dispute raised the question of whether women represent a subject transcending divisions of class or, as Marxists claimed, polarized like any other social location? Do gender relations have a specific character or are they subordinate to the logic of capitalism? The difficulty that Marxists encountered with these questions points towards the fragmentation of the nineteenth century modernist project of emancipation encapsulated by single theory, and the women's movement foreshadowed the wider issue of fractured identities and interlacing social movements which were to come to the fore of later sociological concerns.

## MARXISM AND SOCIAL THEORY

Marxism is one of the most significant theories of society and has defined the parameters of many subsequent sociological debates, partly because of the vitality of the western Marxist intellectual tradition throughout the twentieth century. Many contemporary debates were foreshadowed in Marxism, including structure vs. action; class and conflict as central engine of social change; certainty and the notion of historical validity; material as opposed to cultural accounts of the social. But the theory, never completed by Marx himself, left many problems. There was an unresolved ambivalence between the structural determinism of *Capital* and the more voluntaristic and action-orientated ideas expressed in the *Eighteenth Brumaire* and Marx's correspondence with the Russians. Marxism constituted the social in terms of materiality defined in his critique of Idealism, but thereby left the area of cultural relations for subsequent theorizing, which often (as for example with Critical Theory) involved looking beyond Marxism for inspiration. There was little attention to normative aspects of social life which meant that the foundation of critical activity was itself unclear. Rather than lay claim to moral justification for the critique of capitalism, Marx and Engels sought justification in the formation of a class that necessarily represented the emancipation of humanity. Meanwhile, in later works, the activity of normative critique was expressed via the language of science which claimed to uncover 'real' social relations from the mist of ideology. Yet little epistemological justification is offered for this undertaking and we are left with an Enlightenment juxtaposition of reason against metaphysics, combined with a theory of historical necessity that promises to make everything transparent in the end. Though offering a theory of the differentiation of capitalist society through the division of labour, it envisaged radical de-differentiation of both institutions and sociocultural forms in the future, for which little sociological justification was offered. Similarly, Marxism had little to say about the bases of social integration and rather more about social crisis and transformation. When Marxists theorized the unexpected survival of capitalism, they often relied on an overworked theory of ideology that had been only partially developed by Marx himself. Lack of attention to the state and political process in general meant that Marxists often derived these from economic structures and overlooked the extent to which political systems could not only follow a separate logic from the economic, but also intervene in class relations to affect their outcomes. Finally, the theory was Eurocentric in its conception of historical development, and had then to deal with the paradox that social revolutions claiming 'Marxist' inspiration occurred in societies on the periphery of capitalism, rather than in its heartland. These criticisms, though, should not detract from the richness of Marx's analysis and its impact on social theorizing. What I am suggesting is that these unresolved issues created wide scope for further theorizing both within and outside the Marxist framework that has shaped our contemporary understanding of social theory.

---

**Core issues in Marxism and social theory**

- Material versus cultural explanations of society.
- Progressive theory of social change – classes as 'bearers' of new organizational forms.
- Ideology and the problem of correct consciousness.
- Class, agency and structure.
- Logics of economic and political crisis – coincide or separate?
- Emancipation and its limits – the universal subject of history. Marxism and feminism.
- History as a necessary process or open to unintended consequences? Single or multiple logic?

---

## FURTHER READING

To experience the passion and vitality of his work, read Marx himself, see for example, Marx (1978, reprinted 1998) *Selected Writings*. Georg Lichtheim (1969) *Marxism* (Routledge) has been around for a while but is rich in detail, clarity and context. Readable and perceptive, Shlomo Avineri (1968) *Social and Political Thought of Karl Marx* (Cambridge University Press) has again lasted well to become a classical exposition and discussion of Marxism. Leszek Kolakowski (1978) *Main Currents of Marxism* (3 vols, Oxford University Press) is comprehensive and detailed especially on the political and intellectual background to Marxism. For discussions of feminism and Marxism see the collection edited by Alice. S. Rossi (1973) *The Feminist Papers* (Columbia University Press) and Michele Barrett (1988) *Women's Oppression Today* (Verso).

## NOTES

1 From *The Internationale*, written to celebrate the 1871 Paris Commune and subsequently an anthem of the international communist movement.
2 'Cartesian' comes from René Descartes (1596–1650), who is generally credited with laying the philosophical foundations of modern thought by arguing that the mind was wholly distinct from matter and from our bodies. In the resulting 'Cartesian dualism' the mind is entirely separate from the external world.
3 Hegel's dialectic is often rendered in terms of 'thesis' (affirmation of a thought which is incomplete or contradictory), 'antithesis' (affirmation of its negation) and 'synthesis' (a higher unity which itself becomes a 'thesis'). This may be a useful schema but was not used by Hegel himself.

4  Hegel's concept of recognition further resonates with the 'cultural turn' in social sciences which has played a politics of recognition (identity, cultural valuation) against a politics of redistribution (economic justice). See for example Fraser (1995) and Ray and Sayer (1999).

5  Marx viewed peasants as a 'sack of potatoes' unable to break free from their individualistic consciousness (Marx 1978: 137–18).

6  Marx did show some awareness of this issue, commenting that national and religious prejudice divides the English proletariat into 'two hostile camps' of Irish and English, similar to that between poor whites and blacks in the southern USA (Marx, letter to Meyer and Vogt, 9 April 1870 in Marx 1978). But its implications for class consciousness were not elaborated.

7  Several of Marx's early works, especially the *Economic and Philosophical Manuscripts*, which show a clearer Hegelian influence than later works like *Capital*, were unknown until 1923, so a Marxist 'orthodoxy' had already developed unaware of their existence. There has periodically been debate over the degree of continuity throughout Marx's oeuvre, in particular, whether the concept of 'alienation' disappears in later work. Althusser (1965) claimed that there was an 'epistemological break' between the humanist and scientific Marx, a view challenged for example by Avineri (1968), Thompson (1978), Israel (1971), Mészáros (1975) and Walton and Gamble (1972). Much of the steam has gone from this debate now and it will not be considered here.

8  'The peasant is destined to become a small capitalist, or suffer the loss of the means of production (which may happen although he remains their nominal owner, as in the case of mortgages) and be transformed into a wage-worker' (Marx 1969: 400ff).

9  In *The Poverty of Philosophy*, 'The hand-mill gives you society with the feudal lord; the steam-mill, society with the industrial capitalist' (Marx 1966: 95).

10  Marx deliberately gave few hints as to his vision of communism, though his *Critique of the Gotha Programme* ([1875] 1968) offers one of the most detailed statements, including his concepts of a lower and higher stage of socalism and the democratic dictatorship of the proletariat.

11  Nonetheless, by the 1880s, Engels felt it necessary to extricate Marxism from charges of materialist determinism, claiming that economic factors were determining 'only in the last instance' (Engels, letter to J. Bloch, 21 September 1890, in Marx and Engels [1884] 1968).

12  Such predictions – including Marx's – were extrapolations based on analysis of formal properties of capitalism. No one had access to data to show whether or not the rate of profit was falling. See discussions in Walker (1978), Barran and Sweezy (1966) and Clarke's (1994) defence of Marx's theory of crisis.

13  Some of those made unemployed because of mechanization could be absorbed into the (in Marx's terms) unproductive service sector. Indeed, Marx notes that as a result of the 'extraordinary productiveness of industry' those employed in textile factories and mines in Britain in 1861 numbered less than those in domestic service (Marx [1867] 1976: 468–70).

14  One example of this was Karl Popper's influential arguments about the unscientificity of Marxism (e.g. Popper 1970) which drew on issues raised by the Revisionists.

15  Böhm-Bawerk's critique and a response by Hilferding are summarized by Kolakowski (1989, vol. 2: 290–7).

16 The Heidelberg school of neo-Kantianism was particularly relevant, where philosophers emphasized the centrality of ethics and differences between natural and social sciences. (This is discussed further in Chapter 6.)

17 Actually, despite his prediction in the *Communist Manifesto* that the 'intermediate classes' would disappear, Marx ([1862] 1969) elsewhere argued that the middle class would grow within capitalism as the latter's administrative requirements expanded, and would form a 'consumption class', offsetting the falling rate of profit. He does not seem to have worked this insight into the corpus of his theory.

18 Morgan's *Ancient Society* (1877) itself became a classic among Marxists because he claimed that cultural evolution is dependent on the evolution of technical control of nature; that civilization tends towards a transcendence of private property; that working men will arise and institute a higher form of liberty, equality and fraternity than that which existed in ancient society (White 1969: 109–25).

19 Prior to Engels' study, August Bebel (1840–1913) had published *Women and Socialism* (1970) but subsequently revised his argument in deference to Engels (Draper and Lipow 1976; R. Evans, 1979). Bebel was more sympathetic than Engels to the distinctiveness of women's issues. Though divided by class antagonism, he said, 'women have a great many more points in common than the men engaged in the class struggle, and though they march in separate armies they may strike a united blow' (Rossi 1973: 497).

# CHAPTER 5

# Durkheim, differentiation and morality

Since the efforts of Enlightenment thinkers to develop a secular system of ethics, 'nature' and 'society' have been placed in ambiguous juxtaposition. For many Enlightenment writers, natural harmony offered a model for potential social integration which, once freed from irrational beliefs and authorities, would allow people to realize their true natures. Thus pre-revolutionary appeals to nature had legitimized the critique of authority and custom in the name of a potentially harmonious rational order. But the more 'nature' was invoked to legitimize a *post*-revolutionary order, the harsher it became and the more fatalistic and inevitable were its laws. Natural laws came to rule with the necessity of scientific ones, awareness of which would bring social policies in line with the process of social evolution. One example of this thinking was Thomas Malthus (1766–1834) whose *Essay on the Principle of Population* ([1798] 1888) was a rejoinder to Condorcet's progressivist optimism. Population increase generated competition for resources, and while food output increased by arithmetical progression, Malthus claimed, human population increased geometrically. Thus a mass of 'surplus population' were condemned to poverty and starvation, which could be offset only by the kind of punitive moral and social discipline embodied in the 1834 English New Poor Law. Nature, then, was harsh and competitive and set an inflexible context within which social development could occur, an idea that both contributed to and was reinforced by the rise of evolutionary thinking in the nineteenth century.

This chapter examines the importance of evolutionary thought in later classical theory, especially that of Emile Durkheim, whose sociology was an ambiguous reaction to main strands of social evolutionism, such as that of Herbert Spencer. In his critique of Spencer, Durkheim emphasized the autonomy of the social from biological and psychological influences, while arguing for a sociological alternative to the individualism of political economy. With Durkheim, the idea of the social as a level of reality available to scientific analysis took shape more concretely than in earlier writers, such as Comte. Whereas Comte had viewed social evolution as leading to homogeneous organizational forms, Durkheim regarded evolution as leading to diverse types of society, albeit arranged on a hierarchy of 'higher' or 'lower' forms. Durkheim did, however, adopt Comte's biological metaphor of normality and pathology as a way of understanding the 'crisis of industrialism', which for him too arose from inadequate social integration. In addressing the problem of social solidarity Durkheim developed a complex theory of individual and society, moral integration and social development, the origins of modern societies, and the symbolic force of religion. To put Durkheim's theory in context, however, I shall briefly examine other evolutionary approaches.

## SOCIAL DIFFERENTIATION AND COMPLEXITY

It is remarkable how Darwin recognizes among beasts and plants his English society with its division of labour, competition, opening-up of new markets.

(Marx 1978: 526)

Social theorists did not so much borrow evolutionary concepts from biology as both natural and social evolutionism had distant roots in Enlightenment notions of linear development. The concept of an increasingly complex division of labour first appeared in the social sciences (especially political economy), from whence it was applied to biological evolution, subsequently being 'borrowed back' by evolutionary sociologists. In *Origin of Species* ([1859] 1964) Charles Darwin (1808–82) had drawn insights from social thought, in particular Malthus' theory of population pressure; political economy's derivation of collective outcomes from individual interactions; the measurement of variation pioneered by the human population statistics of Adolphe Quételet (1796–1874). Then 'Social Darwinists' deployed evolutionary principles such as the 'survival of the fittest' (actually Spencer's, *not* Darwin's notion) in justification of competitive capitalism. Regarding human societies as an extension of nature could justify claims that inequalities between people are natural, and that colonialism was a 'civilizing mission' to 'uncivilized peoples'. This in turn legitimized racist theories of social development in which, according to Spencer, the technical and social 'achievements' of the 'white race' were products of a higher level of biological development. Since social progress improves human nature, 'races' left behind in the struggle for advancement were fossils doomed to extinction (Bowler 1984: 226).

The work of Herbert Spencer (1820–1903) represented the most systematic attempt to develop an evolutionary sociology which included a system of ethics derived from evolutionary laws. Between 1860 and 1896 he produced a massive series of volumes of his *Synthetic Philosophy* (which are now mostly unread) including the *First Principles* (1887),

*Principles of Biology* (1884), *Principles of Psychology* (1881), *Principles of Sociology* (1883 5) and *Principles of Ethics* ([1879] 1978). Like Malthus, Spencer was concerned with differential survival – the mechanism of organic evolution that explained the success or failure of different organizational forms. Thus evolution involved an inherent, not necessarily linear, progress from an incoherent homogeneity, made up of simple organisms, to increasingly organized, complex and differentiated ones. Social forms which survive are those that 'had fitness to conditions which made better arrangements impracticable' (Spencer 1873: 394).

Spencer's sociology is often regarded as being derived from Comte's (e.g. Barnes 1969: 81) although this was a suggestion he strongly resisted, claiming that his own method was objective and naturalistic, whereas Comte's was subjective and ideational (Spencer 1904, vol. 2: 570). But there are undoubtedly important similarities in their approaches. Like Comte, Spencer regarded society as an organism that displayed functional and sustaining relationships similar to those of biological organisms. Spencer shared Comte's distinction between statics and dynamics and they shared a methodology based on empirical observation, comparison and historical deduction. Both were determinists who believed that all societies were ultimately fated to undergo the European path of transformation; they both adhered to a naturalistic epistemology in which sociology was to adopt (albeit with modifications) the methods of the natural sciences. However, two important differences were that, first, for Spencer it was individuals who were the subject of social evolutionary adaptation, rather than societies as a whole; second, Spencer regarded Comte's view of society, as a moral order, conservative and idealistic. For Spencer, social integration was not achieved through shared moral values but through the emergent interdependence of core institutions: ceremonial, familial, political, ecclesiastical, occupational and industrial.

Spencer's social dynamics understood social evolution as gradual and progressive but distinguished between two broad types – the military and industrial. **Military societies** are 'tribal' in organization, dominated by the warrior cast (reflecting its importance in regulating exchanges with other societies), have an undeveloped economy based initially on hunting, later developing pastoralism. Temporary chiefs who appear at times of crisis are replaced by a system of permanent chiefs whose power rests in military control organized through subordination of the community to centralized, despotic government. Military societies allow unlimited control of personal conduct and the forced observance of ritual, belief and obedience to rulers. They are thus in a state of 'compulsory cooperation'. Tracks and rude paths link scattered settlements, so communications are slow, while the predominant form of exchange is barter, which later develops into trade between communities.

Social equilibrium is achieved through a struggle for existence, which is the engine of social change. Spencer's account of this is essentially descriptive and attempts to show that there is a necessary mechanism at work. The habitual conflict between early societies leads to militarism and the dominance of warriors. In simple hunting tribes, specialization of function is only crudely developed (for example, divisions between hunters and warriors) but as militarism achieves social integration, smaller units are combined into nations, which in the process creates areas of peace, within which cultivation and crafts develop, along with rudimentary political institutions. The division of labour is still elementary but as structural differentiation increases, so their functional interdependence grows. The long term outcome of this process is that an **industrial society** emerges with a high degree of complexity, differentiation of structure and function, occupational specialization and complex class hierarchies. As conflict between neighbouring societies diminishes, so the importance of the military decreases in proportion to civil relationships. Thus regulation of the external environment becomes less decisive for the overall nature of the society than internal regulation which is achieved increasingly through competition and voluntary, contractual relationships. The conditions for maximization of cooperation through contract and interdependence (and therefore for further evolution) was a non-interventionist, liberal *laissez-faire* state and continuing increase of civil over military functions.

This is a progressive development, which involved a decline in the irrational and an increase in rational systems of thought and action. Early societies were governed by fear of the living (a hint of a Hobbesian war of all) but increased group size and cooperation generated a 'feeling of community' which was crystallized into custom and tradition. However, the unconscious psychological content of tradition is irrational – fear of the dead comes to replace fear of the living, and is expressed in fear of the gods. Thus at this stage, irrational institutions have functions for social evolution. However, progress involves the development of rational faculties which are evolutionary achievements derived from experience. Like Comte, social evolution is a learning process, although one governed by the need for survival rather than by cognitive systems. Custom as the basis for regulation gives way to laws that are codified and implemented through a system of justice, moral injunctions lose the authority of the sacred and are placed increasingly on a scientific basis. Like Saint-Simon (and Marx), Spencer held a 'fetter theory' of change in that industrial societies will rid themselves of irrationalities 'which be cast aside only when they become hindrances' (Spencer 1873: 169). In much of this work, progress was viewed as a necessary aspect of evolution, since imperfect forms will disappear and he looked towards a new state of nature based on division of labour and minimal state interference (Peel 1971: 92). However, this rationalist utopia was clouded with pessimism in his later years, since he regarded the spread of colonialism and the increasingly interventionist state as regression towards militarism.

Despite the widespread neglect of Spencer's social thought today, he set the scene for a number of subsequent themes and debates in sociology, including:

- complexity and differentiation as dominant processes of social evolution, a view central to structural-functional accounts of society, notably Talcott Parsons and Niklas Luhmann
- individualism and competition as the basis of sociality, an idea influential in various sociological approaches, including the American social evolutionists, such as Graham Sumner (1840–1910) and in a different way, the German sociologist Georg Simmel (see Chapter 7)
- secularization and the extension of rational systems of action as a defining process of modernity
- society as a self-organizing system of functionally integrated parts which increase human freedom as social relationships become increasingly voluntary and contractual.

## EMILE DURKHEIM AND MORAL SOCIALITY

Although writing broadly within the evolutionary paradigm, Emile Durkheim (1858–1917) was important in consolidating a separation of society from biology, which had been proposed earlier by Comte. Durkheim insisted that society was an emergent moral entity in itself, *sui generis*, not reducible to any other explanatory level, thus sociology could be differentiated from other disciplines such as physiology, psychiatry, jurisprudence, philosophy and political economy, even if, as we shall see, these distinctions were not always rigorously maintained. Further, recent changes in the prevailing intellectual-political mood in Europe have opened the way to a re-evaluation of Durkheim's place in sociology. He has often been regarded as a conservative, concerned primarily with the problem of order (e.g. Nisbet 1967; Coser 1977; Lehmann 1994) and sometimes as the weakest of the classical triumvirate. Regarding Durkheim's 'conservatism' – he was certainly not a Marxist, and viewed class conflict as symptomatic of social pathology rather than an inevitable feature of an unequal social order. On the other hand, he identified with the Republican left in the politics of the Third Republic (1875–1940), and hoped that through market regulation and civic associations of employers and workers, the destructive potential of class conflict could be mitigated. Durkheim was similar in some of his views to British Fabians, and was sympathetic to the French reformist socialist, Jean Jaurès (J. A. Hughes *et al.* 1995: 152). However, the political implications of Durkheim's sociology are less clear than either of these views imply, and he *was* 'conservative' in that he shared with many evolutionary theorists the view that existing social institutions were the necessary result of adaptive development. Even so, recent assessments have emphasized the importance of his theories of social solidarity, the moral division of labour and symbolic representations. There is currently evidence of a Durkheim revival, as sociological interest in issues of trust, social integration and the cultural foundations of economic organization has grown (Misztal 1996; Crow forthcoming).

### Society as a moral reality

Durkheim's distinctive approach to social theory can be illustrated by contrast with Marxism on the one hand, and Comtean-Spencerian evolutionism on the other. While Marx and Engels developed a concept of the social that was material in focus, Durkheim insisted not only on the autonomy of the cultural-symbolic realm, but also on its priority in social development. He agreed with Marxists that social evolution 'has causes [of] which the authors of historical events' were unaware, but regarded it as false to derive the source of evolution from industrial technology and view the economic factor as a source of progress, evidence for which was borrowed from the industrial history of England (Durkheim 1972: 159). On the contrary, religion is the most primitive of all social phenomena from which are derived all other manifestations of collective activity, including law, morality, art, science and politics. Thus,

> in the beginning everything is religious . . . No one has yet shown under what economic influences naturalism developed out of totemism, by what series of changes in technology it became in one place the abstract monotheism of Jahwe, and in another Graeco-Latin polytheism . . . it is indisputable that at the outset, the economic factor is rudimentary, while religious life is by contrast, luxuriant and all-pervading.
>
> (Durkheim 1972: 161)

Durkheim wished to avoid claiming either that the economic factor was an epiphenomenon (since once it exists, it exerts influence) or that it is a substratum, since the malaise of European society does not originate only in industry (Durkheim 1972: 102).

However, Durkheim objected to Comte's 'exaggerated intellectualism' (defining stages in terms of dominant worldviews) which undermined his claims to naturalism. Comte's concept of 'humanity' was too abstract and denied the diversity of social types, while his Law of Three States was similarly ahistorical and non-empirical. Particular societies, states and nations interested Comte only in so far as they help him mark successive stages in human progress, his sociology being 'unique among sciences in having as its object an entity of which there is only one type' (Durkheim 1969c: 681). Comte's sociology was not really positive science because it lacked the principle of the accumulation of knowledge, so that regarding his system as complete, he did not progressively expand the number of specialist questions to be investigated.

Durkheim's main objection to Spencer, on the other hand, was the latter's individualism, which viewed industrial societies as integrated through contractual relationships. A contract, Durkheim says, 'is not sufficient unto itself, but is possible only thanks to a regulation of the contract which is originally social' (Durkheim 1933: 196). Developing an argument that has increasing resonance in contemporary discussions of economy and society (e.g. Granovetter and Swedberg 1992) Durkheim sees economic forms and individual agreements as embedded in cultural and institutional arrangements that are *moral*. Society cannot therefore be reduced to the competitions and agreements of individuals since these can be sustained only through shared, regulatory moral frameworks. Contracts depend on trust, which is implicit in any agreement, thus in the labour contract the parties agree not only to exchange labour for wages, but also to uphold the agreement, the latter being implicit and presupposing the existence of pre-contractual solidarity. The kind of social contract envisaged by Hobbes and Rousseau and echoed in Spencer, therefore, was an impossible fiction since contracts presuppose the existence of society.

This further meant that egoistic competition could not be the basis of social integration and the relevance of Darwinian thinking to society was highly limited. Social Darwinists overlook the 'essential element of moral life, that is, the moderating influence that society exercises over its members which tempers . . . the brutal action of the struggle for existence and selection' (Durkheim 1933: 196). Altruism, not competition, is the fundamental basis of sociality. Thus Durkheim understood society as an organic whole that existed prior to and independently of individuals, an emergent reality *sui generis*, that is not reducible to individual states of mind and actions. Differences between individuals result from the groups of which they are part and are shaped by social currents. To those who claim everything in social life is individual because society is made up of individuals, Durkheim replies that 'of course society has no other substratum' (than individuals) but the new phenomena formed by their association are 'produced and react upon individual consciences and in large part produce them' (Durkheim 1933: 350 n. 16). Although this hints at a reciprocal interaction between individual and society in the making of the latter, clear priority is given to socialization of individuals into the moral order.[1] Indeed, it is the accumulated cultural and technological wealth of society which distinguished humans from animals. Further, society is a ritual order, a collective conscience founded on the emotional rhythms of human interaction. His concept of society incorporated the idea of the non-rational foundations of social order while (arguably) avoiding the conservative conclusions of counter-Enlightenment writers like de Maistre and de Bonald while offering an alternative to contract theories.

## Rules of method

In common with Comtean positivism, Durkheim regarded sociology as a science, albeit with distinctive methods appropriate to the study of society. In the *Rules of Sociological Method* (1895) Durkheim contrasted the common-sense, 'ideological' perception of society as the product of individual will with the knowledge that comes from 'long and special' sociological training (Durkheim [1895] 1964: 17). From this standpoint he attempted to show that society has an objective reality external to individual consciousness and will. Individualistic accounts of society (such as J. S. Mill and Jeremy Bentham) ignored how social solidarity and moral regulation must be presupposed by social actors in order for exchanges between individuals to take place at all. Thus the *Rules* set out to achieve three aims:

- to demonstrate the objectivity of the social
- to separate sociology from philosophy and biology
- to define the subject matter of sociology.

To these ends, the *Rules* begins with the famous injunction to 'consider social facts as things' (Durkheim [1895] 1964: 2). That is, we should treat social phenomena as objective, not reducible to individual experience, but identified in collective phenomena such as the legal system and social statistics, which could be known only posteriori, through observation. Social facts are 'ways of acting, thinking and feeling external to individuals', that are endowed with coercion and may take various forms, such as religious, political, familial, literary or artistic. Their key characteristics then are externality and constraint.[2] Not that Durkheim claimed that social facts are material things (the rule was to treat them *as* things) but that social organization as an emergent reality produced effects that could not be adequately explained with reference to other levels such as biology or psychology. A 'thing' is an object of knowledge not controlled by intellect and therefore understood only on condition that the mind goes outside itself through observations and experiments. A social fact then is not available to introspection, it cannot be 'known from within' ([1895] 1964: xiv). Social facts entail obligations and have coercive power, the presence of which is recognized by the threat of sanction or resistance to it which thus exists independently of individuals and not created by them.

The injunction to consider social facts things could involve the relatively uncontentious claim that socialization inculcates within us ways of seeing, feeling and acting that could not have been arrived at spontaneously, since we are confronted by a world already organized into systems of categories, rules, meanings and social relations. Language is an obvious example of this – a prerequisite of communication, a complex set of precoded symbols and rules we are obliged to follow. If we want to operate effectively in the social world we are constrained to follow certain rules, which exist independently of our feelings about them. In this sense, it would be absurd to imagine that social phenomena could be explained with reference simply to individuals and most sociologists, I think, would accept Durkheim's reasoning thus far.

However, other aspects of his concept of social facts are more contentious. First, Durkheim gave scant attention to the complex interactions that occur between individuals and society, in that once people have acquired social skills, they can act on, manipulate and distance themselves from social conventions and expectations. Subsequently, symbolic inter-actionists such as Erving Goffman (e.g. 1959) were to explore the complexities of role taking and distancing. Second, Durkheim envisaged a duality of individual and society, in which the eternality of social obligations (as 'brother, husband, citizen') entails by contrast a self whose perception and orientation is private and discrete. Yet the very concept of the 'self' may be a complex social construction. Third, not only does the social order exist *sui generis* for Durkheim, but also it has functional needs which are trans-individual and non-reducible to the needs of individual people.

Durkheim did, however, explicitly reject functional explanations of the origins of social institutions, a mistake he attributed to Spencer. When explaining social phenomenon 'we must seek separately the efficient cause which produces it, and the function it fulfills' since 'social phenomena do not generally exist for the useful results they produce' ([1895] 1964: 95). Social functions may explain the *persistence* of social customs and institutions but not their *origins*, which must be sought in preceding social facts (p. 110). The functions of an institution or practice can be known only through its effects, so 'to show how a fact is useful is not to explain how it was created or why it is as it is' (pp. 84–5) and a fact can exist without serving any end. Further, practices themselves can change their function without changing their nature, as for example, the religious dogmas of Christianity have different functions now than they did in the Middle Ages.

Durkheim's functional approach to explaining the persistence of social phenomena links up with his distinction between 'normal' and 'pathological' conditions of society. With a degree of tautology, Durkheim described healthy conditions as 'those most widely distributed and occur in other societies' and unhealthy ones as those which 'depart from what is normal and widespread'. To ascertain whether a social fact is normal, we ask:

- whether it is generally disposed through society
- what are the conditions leading to its generality
- whether it has become more or less intense over time
- how the original facts compare with the present and estimate the extent of change.

Often seeking ways of challenging commonsense perceptions of social life, Durkheim uses these criteria to suggest the reverse of what his contemporaries might have assumed. So the *decline* of religion in modern societies does not indicate social pathology, rather its generality confirms that it is a normal process (Durkheim 1933: 49). Similarly, crime is widely regarded as pathological, but is actually necessary since the collective ritual of punishment serves to reaffirm and strengthen collective sentiments

(Durkheim [1895] 1964: 81). Although criminals themselves are atavistic, crime is functional for social integration – an idea that still flies in the face of much conventional wisdom. However, the particular distribution of crime, and sudden fluctuations in its rate, may be indicative of social pathology. The sharp increase in crime rates in certain areas of rapidly expanding nineteenth-century cities indicated a pathological condition associated with urbanization. Durkheim used a similar logic in his analysis of suicide rates – a stable rate reflected a normal condition but sudden fluctuations could be indicative of pathology.

The three types of social facts identified in the *Rules* – legal codes, social statistics and religious dogmas – correspond to the bases of Durkheim's three major studies: *Division of Labour in Society* (1895), *Suicide* (1897) and *Elementary Forms of the Religious Life* (1912) respectively. The significance of each of these for Durkheim's sociology will now be considered.

### Evolution and the moral division of labour

Despite his criticisms of Spencer's sociology, Durkheim shared the latter's view that social evolution proceeds from simple and undifferentiated to complex and differentiated forms of organization. However, rather than see the division of labour as a purely functional set of arrangements sustained by contract, Durkheim drew a distinction between the physical and moral division of labour in which the latter is determinant. Durkheim's evolutionary theory is structured around the major morphological change from mechanical to organic forms of the division of labour, which described a transition from simple, segmented to complex functionally integrated societies (see Figure 5.1). The transformation from **mechanical** to **organic solidarity** was the result of three developments (Durkheim 1972: 150–4).[3] These were:

1 An increase in population density, which stimulated differentiation, in turn reducing competition for resources, because people with different needs can live together in cooperation.
2 Growth of towns and urban life, with a consequent decline in agriculture, increase the proximity and frequency of contact among people.
3 The increasing number and rapidity of the means of communication and transportation increases the moral density of society, that is, the complexity of moral codes, legal rules and mutual obligations.

For Durkheim social adaptation occurs through the realm of moral values, a view that distanced him both from reductive evolutionists (for whom society was an extension of nature) and from political economists. In relation to the latter, he says, 'credit is due to economists for having seen the spontaneous character of social life', but they derive economic behaviour from the individual. Yet the individual actor is social and the product of

**Figure 5.1** Durkheim: mechanical and organic societies

| Mechanical solidarity | Organic solidarity |
| --- | --- |
| Simple occupational structure | Complex occupational structure |
| Segmented, low integration | Interdependent, high integration |
| Agricultural | Urban |
| Low specialization | High specialization |
| Homogeneous (religious) value system | Heterogeneous (secular) values |
| Kinship central unit of affiliation | Organic functional complexity |
| Single hierarchy | Multiple authorities |
| Collectivism | Individualism |
| Decentralized | Centralized state – organ of social thought |
| Repressive law | Restitutive law |

moral regulation, a conquest of society *over* nature. Nonetheless, despite his disavowal of materialist explanations of the social, he did attribute to material forces (population density, urbanization and communications) the power to require adaptive social changes, even though these then emerge as a moral not material reality. This is moreover, as many have commented (e.g. Craib 1997: 188) only a sketchy theory of social change.

### Mechanical and organic societies

The most important theme in the *Division of Labour* is Durkheim's (1933) distinction, which follows from the above discussion, between two main types of society – mechanical and organic. It is through this contrast that Durkheim develops his diagnosis of the pathological condition of modern society. But his concept of 'the general evolution of societies' as a tree on which 'societies are situated lower or higher' (Durkheim 1969c: 246) reflected the widespread evolutionary concept of a scale of organizational forms. Mechanical or segmented societies were homogeneous with a very basic division of labour and therefore, for Durkheim, represented 'social species' lower on the evolutionary tree. For example in simple agricultural societies, many people would have been involved in subsistence production, using similar technologies and living in geographically disparate communities. Within these small communities beliefs and 'sensations' (experiences) were common to all members (Durkheim 1933: 129). The collective conscience was unified and strong, being reinforced periodically through public rituals in which there was powerful pressure to participate and which attached individuals to the group. The common conscience of the group was enforced through extensive and repetitive juridical rules that imposed uniform beliefs and practices on all members (1933: 226). Legal and moral rules were thus 'repressive' in that the range of prohibited behaviours was extensive and included matters such as belief and sexual conduct that in later societies would more probably be treated as matters of personal choice (Durkheim 1969d: 245). Further, punishments were generally severe, since 'death pure and simple does not constitute the supreme punishment; it is aggravated, for crimes considered most heinous, by additional tortures (*supplices*)' (1969d: 250). Kinship was the dominant institution in mechanical societies and domestic production formed the basis of social integration. Hence mechanical societies were decentralized and geographically disparate, by contrast with the centralized systems described by Spencer's concept of 'military society'.

Organic solidarity, on the other hand, is heterogeneous, with a complex and differentiated division of labour, based on specialization, diversification and cooperation. While expanding the scope of individual liberty, the organic division of labour also increases the extent of interdependence among its branches, thus individuals are linked more closely to each other than in mechanical societies. The collective conscience weakens as it fragments into moral codes specific to particular occupations and activities, while religion ceases to be a unifying system of belief. 'If there is one truth that history has settled beyond doubt, it is that religion embraces an ever-diminishing part of social life' (Durkheim 1933: 19). In the place of a unitary collective conscience, organic societies are (as with Spencer) integrated through contractual relationships. However, unlike Spencer, these contracts and economic exchanges generally depend upon moral ties that are deeper and reach 'far beyond the short moments during which exchange is made' (1933: 227). The extent and severity of repressive criminal law diminishes proportionately, as the extent of civil, restitutive law increases. The legal system, further, becomes secularized in that for 'primitive peoples, crime consisted almost entirely of failing to accomplish the practices of the cult, violating ritual prohibitions, deviating from ancestral morality, disobeying authority' whereas for modern peoples 'crime consists essentially in injury to some human interest' (1969d: 265). The modern legal system itself differentiates, reflecting a more complex society, into specialist organs of domestic, commercial, constitutional and administrative law. Kinship declines in significance and occupational functions become the basis of new solidarity that would (Durkheim hoped) become the nucleus of a network of corporate institutions, an argument developed in *Professional Ethics and Civic Morals* ([1950] 1992). These professional guilds would be regulated by codes of ethics that would mitigate the destructive effects of competition and conflicting interests. Finally, the state emerges as the 'organizing centre' of a differentiated society and guarantor of individual liberties since the (republican, democratic) state articulates and mediates divergent and conflicting values of class and occupation.

However, this notion of a harmoniously integrated organic division of labour had not been realized in nineteenth century industrial societies. On the contrary, they were suffering from a pathological, 'anomic' division of labour. **Anomie** (from Greek *anomia*, absence of law) referred to a state of 'normlessness' that arose from a lack of balance between individual expectations (that were potentially limitless) and the constraints of social reality. Normative regulation (transmitted via socialization, or 'moral education') acts as a constraint on desires that cannot all be satisfied within a given social environment. This analysis is further developed in *Suicide* (see pp. 98–103) where Durkheim argues that the needs of animals are defined biologically and adaptively adjusted to their environment. Humans, however, have spiritual, that is non-material, needs that are subject to no necessary limit, indeed even their fulfilment can lead to increased dissatisfaction, as people's horizons of ambition extend.[4] Appetites could not be appeased unless limited by moral bounds, in the absence of which unchecked desires leads to ennui and unhappiness (Durkheim [1897] 1970: 253). Anomie in industrial societies resulted from such things as commercial failure; conflict between capital and labour; weakening of collective sentiments; degrading of the individual into a machine; lack of harmony between individuals and their function; increasing equality and contractual solidarity in the absence of 'more advanced forms of regulation'; insufficiently differentiated or integrated division of labour (Durkheim 1933: 353). This is essentially a control theory which predicts that with the weakening of regulation and integration, unruly passions will break into social disorder. Thus despite Durkheim's insistence on sociological explanations always having reference to antecedent *social* facts, he actually grounds his account in a theory of human psychology, and the comparison between Durkheim's and Freud's notions of individual desires in conflict with the demands of morality has been noted (e.g. Craib 1997: 192).

### Suicide and social currents

Since society was primarily a moral order, social change could be understood through study of the transformation of moral and legal codes, the existence of which could be seen most clearly where the ritual order had been defamed and punishment was invoked to reaffirm the collective conscience. Although Durkheim did not undertake his planned *Criminology* (Lukes 1973: 257) *Suicide* (1897) is perhaps Durkheim's most famous work and contains his only general discussion of social integration. It is a classical piece of sociological reasoning which attempted to demonstrate the applicability of sociological analysis to what was apparently a highly individualistic form of behaviour. If Durkheim could

**Figure 5.2** Durkheim: forms of social solidarity

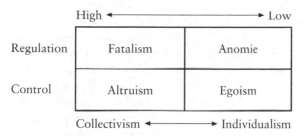

demonstrate that suicidal behaviour was subject to social forces that operated beyond the subjective awareness of the individual, then he had established a strong case for organic social holism. *Suicide* is important too in that it has become a model for the use of empirical analysis to corroborate a general theory, despite the many criticisms to which it is inevitably open after a hundred years (Collins and Makowsky 1984: 112).

While attempting to demonstrate the superiority of sociological over psychological explanation, Durkheim did not claim to account for the behaviour of individuals but only of the statistical rate for a given community. Nineteenth-century moral statistics, such as those accumulated by Quételet, had shown suicide (and rates of births, deaths, marriages and crime) to have a generally stable distribution from year to year. Therefore, Durkheim argued, these must depend upon some regular and predictably distributed phenomena of some kind: geographical, biological or social. Durkheim assumes that possible individual motives for suicide are widely distributed among communities and do not in themselves account for fluctuations in the rate. For example in France between 1856 and 1878 suicides rose by 40 per cent, and by over 100 per cent in Saxony between 1854 and 1880. In both cases the motives for suicide (poverty, family troubles, distress, mental sickness etc.) will have remained relatively constant. So to explain variations in the rate 'we must seek directly the states of the various social environments (religious, domestic, political, occupational etc.) in terms of which the variations of suicide occur' (Durkheim [1897] 1970: 151).

In order to demonstrate the validity of a sociological approach, Durkheim began by considering and refuting the influence of extrasocial factors, such as insanity, race, climate and temperature, on the ground that no statistical correlations could be found between these and the suicide rate. He offered an alternative explanation that the suicide rate was determined by social 'suicidogenic forces', which would show suicide rates to be social phenomena, reflecting the levels of moral integration and regulation. His explanation developed around two axes – integration and control – reflecting different configurations of individual and society, which are shown in Figure 5.2. The left hand of the matrix is typical of **mechanical solidarity** with high levels of collectivism, where regulation and control are high, generating potentially pathological levels of fatalism and altruism, respectively. Conversely, the right of the matrix is typical of individualistic organic solidarity, where regulation and control are lower, generating potentially pathological anomie and egoism, respectively. This enables Durkheim to develop a morphological model, in which these categories are defined by different types of suicidogenic causes, since 'only in so far as the effective causes differ can there be different types of suicide' (Durkheim [1897] 1970: 146). Every proven difference between causes therefore implies a similar difference between effects, thus, we would not classify social phenomena in terms of their described characteristics, but by the causes which produce them.

### The integrative axis: egoism and altruism

Egoism and altruism lie at opposite ends of the social integration axis. Egoism refers to excessive self-reflection on personal matters, a turning away from society, such that the ties binding one individual to another are weakened and people have too little contact with the social fabric. A central proposition is that 'suicide varies inversely with the degree of integration of social groups of which the individual forms a part'. That is, what is crucial for determining whether or not an individual commits suicide is the degree of their social, or moral, integration into society. As a rule, in industrial societies, the lower the level of social integration, the higher the expected rate of suicide. More specifically, Durkheim advanced three lower level generalizations, which will be briefly explained:

1 Suicide varies inversely with the degree of integration of religious society
2 Suicide varies inversely with the degree of integration of domestic society
3 Suicide varies inversely with the degree of integration of political society.

#### Degree of integration of religious society
Religion serves to link individuals to people outside themselves and the stronger the ties, the lower the suicide rate and vice versa. Durkheim noted that the suicide rate in Protestant countries was 20–30 per cent higher than in Catholic ones and sought the explanation for this in the different implications of the two denominations for social integration. Catholic dogma and customs are fixed and require individual subordination to their authority. Ritual has an important role in the church and so binds people together in a way that Protestantism is unable to do. 'The proclivity of Protestantism for suicide must relate to the spirit of free inquiry that animates thus religion . . . the priest has no other sources but himself and his conscience.' The decline of religious tradition leaves people with only their individual reflection and moral consciousness, which encourages a critical attitude and consequently weakens ties to the religious community (Durkheim [1897] 1970: 158). Protestants are

less likely to accept the world as it is, and more likely to disrupt established patterns of thought on which they feel less constrained. It is not primarily the intellectual nature of Protestantism that accounts for this higher suicide risk but rather its weak social cohesion. Thus, Durkheim notes, the suicide rate among Jews is lower still than among Catholics, despite Judaism's tradition of learning and free inquiry. However, Durkheim claims that the degree of religious solidarity among Jews is high, a cohesion that has been reinforced by intolerance shown by the outside community (pp. 160–1).

### Degree of integration of domestic society

Many believed that suicide increased as the conditions of life became more difficult, which meant that, since family life increases one's burdens and responsibilities it must also increase the risk of suicide. This was not so, Durkheim argued, since when adjusted for age, unmarried people take their own lives more frequently than married, and marriage may reduce the risk of suicide by 50 per cent ([1897] 1970: 171). In France 1889–91, among men aged 30–40, there were 627 unmarried suicides and 226 married, per million inhabitants (p. 178). Durkheim's explanation of this is that since moral integration counteracts egoism, the higher the commitments suppressing tendencies to withdraw into oneself, the greater the protection against suicide. Indeed, while the primary family group (of intergenerational blood ties) offers a weaker protection than the conjugal tie (husband and wife, whose commitment is based on mutual interests and romantic attachment) the integrative demands of a combination of types generates the lowest suicide risk (p. 180). Divorce, on the other hand, increases the risk of suicide for men but not for women. For women 'marriage is a profitless yoke' that brings 'low status and exclusion from social life' hence divorce places women at less risk of suicide than it does men.[5]

### Degree of integration of political society

Integration into the national community is a third form of solidarity that reduces egoism, especially during times of crisis. Whereas a commonsense view is that suicides will rise during periods of crisis, Durkheim claims that the reverse is true. Social disruption increases the intensity of collective sentiments and stimulates a partisan spirit drawing people together towards a common end. Crises (such as wars) thus create a moral effect of arousing public feelings and militate against egoism. If egoistic suicide is a result of weak social integration, altruistic suicide is conversely a result of excessive social integration. Where custom and habit govern the individual, altruistic suicides are high. In such situations, the individual sacrifices their own life because of commandments from a higher source of authority, such as religious or political allegiances. Much of Durkheim's evidence for this claim came from mechanical societies. He distinguished three subtypes:

1 obligatory altruistic suicide where society imposes an explicit duty to take one's own life, such as the self immolation of Brahmin widows
2 optional altruistic suicide where death attracts honour, such as self-sacrifice in battle ([1897] 1970: 222)
3 acute altruistic suicide, such as among members of a religious sect who believe that death will transfigure them into a truer form of existence.

## The regulative axis: anomie and fatalism

Broadly speaking, anomic suicide results from disturbances in the social order, such as dislocations resulting from industrial and commercial changes. This model of social crisis both draws on the sense of pathology with which nineteenth-century sociologists viewed European societies, and defines a theory of social dislocation that was subsequently to be highly influential. In these terms, anomie is seen as a social condition specific to contemporary societies in which the emphasis is not on integration but regulation. While Durkheim admits that anomic suicide has 'kindred ties' with egoistic, he believes that the two are fundamentally different, since with anomie, social regulation of human passions is lacking. His analysis of anomic suicide drew on comparative European material, on the basis of which he claimed that financial crisis produces an increased suicide rate – such as that in Vienna in 1873–4 when the suicide rate increased from 141 in 1872, to 153 in 1873 and 216 in 1874. Durkheim's explanation of such data was that a sudden deregulation of people's lives allowed suicidal motives to have greater influence than would otherwise have been the case. Thus it was not financial ruin in itself that produced a rise in suicides, but the moral effect of a sudden alteration in people's life situation ([1897] 1970: 242). During periods of prosperity a similar rise in the suicide rate occurs. Durkheim concluded that whenever an abrupt shift in social stability occurs, it alters the mechanism that places restraint on individual desires and social wants. Anomie then is a state in which the force of normative regulation is weakened.

In addition to these three main types, Durkheim outlined a fourth, fatalistic suicide, which he suggested was of largely historical significance. In the same way as altruism identifies suicide that results from an excess of social integration, fatalism indicates a form of suicide caused by an excess of social regulation. Whereas anomie refers to an absence of regulation, fatalistic suicide occurs where regulation is so oppressive that the certainty of death is preferable, such as slaves who seeing no alternative to enslavement under the master, take their own lives (p. 276). Although not greatly developed, this category completes the symmetry of Durkheim's typology.

*Suicide* is an attempt to explain differential data and establish central features of a sociological account, which in particular will be counterintuitive, since the results of scientific inquiry may challenge widely held beliefs, and will refer to society as a system of moral integration. However, *Suicide* has been subject to a wide range of criticisms. Some of the most important are the following:

- The reliability of official suicide statistics have been challenged and in particular it has been suggested that the way in which coroners categorize a problematic death is open to a wide range of social pressures, including sociological theories of suicide themselves (e.g. Douglas 1966; Atkinson 1968).[6]
- Durkheim identified apparent statistical correlations, then speculated as to the social meanings underlying them, and fails to seriously consider alternative explanations (Douglas 1966: 73ff).
- It is disputable whether self-sacrifice in battle (an example of 'altruistic' suicide) should be described as 'suicide' at all, and conflicts with a widespread social understanding that distinguishes between suicide and self-sacrifice.
- Despite Durkheim's claim to be using an objective observational method, he draws on intuition to frame his explanatory hypotheses. In constructing the contrast between Catholicism and Protestantism Durkheim implicitly asked what the experience of Protestant individualism was like, deploying a technique of empathetic understanding rather than positivistic observation (Outhwaite 1996).
- It is not always clear whether Durkheim was referring to types of suicide or types of social structure. Anomie for example is a general condition of disorganization in industrial societies (Lukes 1973: 31). In what sense is this a specific explanation of suicide as opposed to other forms of deviance?

## State, legitimation and individuality

One of the core issues addressed by classical sociology was that of secularization and its consequences for social integration. We have seen how, after the French Revolution, counter-Enlightenment theorists claimed that the sacred foundations of social order had been destroyed and in their place had been a doomed attempt to found society on rational principles. We have seen too how Saint-Simon and Comte attempted to reconcile the Enlightenment's progressive and rational outlook with the conservative problem of social order. These were solutions that involved developing a systematically organized secular religion within an authoritarian social order. With Durkheim we find a further solution to this problem, which avoids the need to construct a new religion while acknowledging the centrality of civil rights and individualism in modern societies. The annual journal that Durkheim established in 1896, *Année sociologique*, was (among other things) concerned both to explain morality and develop a system of secular ethics.

This question led Durkheim into analysis of the state and rights that attempted to reconcile individualism, republicanism with the need for sacred legitimation of the social order. Durkheim's general view of the state was that it was the 'organizing centre of a differentiated society', and in a *normal condition*, rooted in civil society, guaranteed rights and liberties (Durkheim 1969a). This view of the state was the basis of Durkheim's theory of moral individualism. An organic, differentiated society is no longer integrated by a common value system, but on the contrary by respect for human rights which is the only possible basis of legitimation in a democratic society. However, Durkheim does not have in mind here Weber's notion of disenchanted, soulless formal rationality, but on the contrary a 'cult of individualism' in which the rights of the individual acquire sacred significance (Bach 1990). Respect for individual rights is precisely the shared moral bond that offers institutional regulation of an organic society in which people have divergent interests and beliefs. Indeed, Durkheim's commitment to this view seems to have strengthened in his later work. In the *Division of Labour in Society*, he suggested that 'as all the other beliefs and all other practices take on a less and less religious character, the individual becomes the object of a sort of religion. We have a cult of personal dignity which, as with every strong cult, already has its superstitions' (Durkheim 1933: 140). However, here the cult of individuality only imperfectly replaces established religions in that while deriving its force from society, it binds people not to society but to themselves. Later, Durkheim's view of the cult of individuality is more positive, since it is 'neither anti-social nor egoistic', but involves 'sympathy for all that is human, pity for all sufferings, miseries and greater thirst for justice' (1969a).

An important intervening event here was the Dreyfus Affair, in which Durkheim became involved, and which rocked late nineteenth-century France. When in 1894, Alfred Dreyfus (1859–1935), a Jewish army captain, was falsely convicted of treason and given a life sentence of hard labour on Devil's Island, the simmering divisions in the Third Republic between the Catholic-Monarchist Right and anti-clerical, left-liberal republicanism erupted into open hostility and revealed high levels of previously latent antisemitism (Wilson 1973).[7] Many intellectuals, including Durkheim, were involved in the ensuing campaign for Dreyfus' release, which in turn brought severe criticism from the Right. Maurice Barrès (National Assembly Deputy, founder of nationalist and antisemitic movements) claimed that the 'great culprits' in this dispute 'are "intellectuals", the anarchists of the lecture room, the metaphysicians of sociology, a band of arrogant madmen [who] treat our social institutions as absurd and our traditions as unhealthy' (Lukes 1973: 335).[8]

Reflecting on this highly charged period, Durkheim (1969a) replied to such sentiments while attempting to provide a sociological account of individualism, as a religion in which the human person becomes a sacred object. Durkheim accepted the view of other organic theorists that ethics could not be derived from individual experience since society is an emergent property. However, by claiming that in modern societies it is precisely the *individual* who is a sacred object, Durkheim broke with the anti-individualism of these earlier theorists. Thus 'whoever makes an attempt on a man's life, on a man's liberty, on a man's honour, inspires us with a feeling of horror in every way analogous to that which the believer experiences when he sees his idol profaned' (Durkheim 1969a: 28). This is a religion of which 'man is, at the same time, both believer and God' (1969a: 28). The concept of human rights was embedded in a Lockean theory of natural law (see Chapter 2) but Durkheim offers perhaps the first *sociological* theory of human rights which regarded these as deriving not from the individual but from society and as such are evolving with the moral division of labour.

### Society, morality and religion

It has been seen already how Durkheim regarded the moral division of labour as exercising priority over economic institutions. The significance of religion increased in Durkheim's later work, culminating in *Elementary Forms of the Religious Life* (1912). This may represent a new phase in his work, in which the idea of a collective conscience, as the moral regulator of society, gave way to 'collective representations' which constitute the symbolic order of society, representing prevalent beliefs and ideas. Collective representations are found in religious doctrine, legal rules, legends, proverbs, customs and traditions, the ensemble of which is the symbolic constitution of society. They open up the analysis of society as a symbolic order, which, arguably, led through Marcel Mauss and Lévi-Strauss to Roland Barthes' semiotics and Foucault's discourse analysis (J. C. Alexander 1990: 8). In *Elementary Forms*, Durkheim set out to show that the social is indispensable to understanding the formation of all beliefs, institutions and conceptions, since in religion we find an 'essential and permanent aspect of humanity'. If we look beneath the symbolic level, to the reality which it represents and which gives it meaning, then religion is 'something eminently social'. Further, we saw above that, 'in the beginning everything is religious' and later epistemology has its origins in religious systems of classification. Thus to show that religious systems were representations of society would show too that categories of scientific knowledge were socially constructed.[9]

*Elementary Forms* was a work of 'radical sociologism' (Benoit-Smullyan 1969) which aimed to resolve sociologically the philosophical dispute between rationalists and empiricists. For rationalists, following Kant, categories of knowledge (e.g. space, time, causality) were presupposed in cognition and therefore *a priori*. For empiricists, following Locke and Hume, the mind received sense impressions from the outside world which was the only possible source of knowledge. Durkheim attempted to resolve this dispute by showing, with reference to mechanical societies, that categories of knowledge are socially constituted. Thus they are in part received from outside the individual subject, but in part too given in cognition, because they provide a fundamental way of establishing relationships in the world. Reason then goes beyond empirical knowledge, because individuals are both isolated beings and social beings, and we must agree on concepts of time, space, cause, number etc., if there is to be any contact of minds. We cannot abandon these categories and still feel really human. Society is represented within us and we feel its authority as an indispensable condition of all common action.

The idea of a 'class', which is fundamental to all cognitive systems, is an instrument of thought that has been socially constructed in the form of a hierarchy. In so doing, Durkheim argues, we must have employed a model, which we could have found only with reference to collective life. Thus systems of knowledge (and prior to them, religions) construct relations of subordination and coordination, which people would never have thought of organizing in this way if they had not known beforehand what a hierarchy was. 'Hierarchy', of course, 'is exclusively a social affair. It is only in society that there are superiors, inferiors and equals' (Durkheim [1912] 1976: 148). Similarly, an orientation to space comes initially from the spatial relations with which people are familiar, thus where the camp has circular form, space is conceived in the form of an immense circle and is subdivided in the same way as the camp (pp. 11–12). The concept of time is derived from the rhythmic activities which punctuate social experience, such as rituals, rites and cycles. The concept of cause as an arrangement of sequences is derived from the logical relations of social organization. Totemic forces (e.g. manna, wakan and orends) which represent the moral force of society impinging on our will, are prototypes of causal thinking. The mind then posits relationships of cause–effect in the world *a priori* derived from the model offered by society (p. 363ff).

*Elementary Forms* was primarily aimed at developing a theory of religion, in relation to which Durkheim advances four hypotheses: religion is socially determined; it is cognitive; ritual expresses and dramatizes social roles; religion is conducive to social solidarity. The essence of religion (as for de Bonald) lies in sacred rituals, which reaffirm social solidarity, and the division between the sacred and profane is an evolutionary universal, found in all societies. For Durkheim the sacred has six characteristics. It is always separated from other objects; rites set out how the sacred is to be approached; interdictions and taboos isolate the sacred; the sacred is superior to the profane; the sacred and profane form a unifying principle and basis for other oppositions in society; rites transform the profane into the sacred.

Support for these claims came, for Durkheim, from the study of 'simple' societies such as the totemic cultures of Australia and North America, which he believed would possess the 'elementary forms' of all religious practice. Here the totem is a symbol of collective life, standing for the true object of religious adoration. Totems are not products of pure imagination, but are derived from external reality, that is from society, and the object of worship is an anonymous and impersonal force independent of individuals. Aboriginal societies were divided into sub-groups whose distinctiveness was symbolized in their separate totem, while 'a foreign totem is never divine' (1969e: 85). Totemism is the emblem of the group, which represents the collective to itself through myths and legends. Totemic societies are organized around strictly enforced taboos or interdicts, which are the simplest form of veneration of the sacred. These may be either positive or negative. Positive taboos secure bonds between members of the group, such as the spilling of blood at a sacred rock, which reaffirms the common link between the collective and the object. Negative taboos create prohibitions on forms of contact and conduct as in the case of prohibited foods or sexual taboos. The incest taboo is both the first interdiction, defining relationships within the group and with others, and paradigmatic for all other taboos (1969e).

Collective solidarity moreover is periodically renewed through rituals that serve in different ways to reaffirm the power of the totem. In these assemblies a 'collective effervescence' is created which reaffirms social integration through four kinds of rites. Sacrificial rites symbolize the renewal of social bonds by reanimating the totem. In the Intichiuma of the Arunta (Australia) for example, young men mix their blood with the totem in order to reanimate the embryos of the new generation. Imitative rites symbolize the transmission of qualities of the totem, which are acquired through touch, suggesting ideas of both contagion and causality. Commemorative rites, such as ancestor worship, relive the mythical history of ancestors and sustain the vitality of beliefs by rendering them present. Finally, piacular (expiatory) rites involve mourning, fasting, weeping, with obligations to slash or tear clothing and flesh, thereby renewing the group to a state of unity preceding misfortune.

One of the most famous and controversial claims in *Elementary Forms* is that religion and piety are symbolic representations of the relationship between society and individuals. Society (we have seen) is experienced by individuals as superior and transcendent, a force demanding our acquiescence. It not only creates moral obligations that are external, but also is continuous while individuals die and are replaced. Thus, as a symbolic representation, the sacred too has features of immortality, transcendence and superior power. People have a dual existence, impersonal and personal, as a member of society yet as a particular person and body existing at a moment in time and space. In western societies, Durkheim argues, this dualism is represented in the religious idea of the soul, which is bound to the body, but only until death when it departs. The soul represents the immortality of society, which becomes part of us, enters our bodies, during our transitory physical membership of society. Religion thus appears as a moral power immanent in us but representing more than ourselves. This claim, for Durkheim applies as much to contemporary as to totemic societies. In mechanical societies religious symbols are totems that represent material forces such as animals, the elements, rivers, and deal with groups (clans, tribes, etc.) rather than individuals. With Christianity, ritual is less central than examination of one's conscience, and prayer becomes an internal meditation. As God withdraws, so to speak, into a transcendental realm, the world splits into matter and consciousness. This does not indicate a diminution of the power of the sacred, however, but symbolizes an increasingly complex social organization and division of labour, in which social control becomes individualized and society more abstract.

### Women and 'dark, mysterious sex'

It has been seen in earlier discussions that the 'woman question' became increasingly important in late nineteenth-century Europe. There is a view that Durkheim had little to say about women (e.g. Smith 1997: 550) but as Lehmann (1993) and others (Gane 1993; Shope 1994) have shown, Durkheim advanced fairly explicit views (not unlike Comte in some ways) that indicated objections to the prospect of women's emancipation, and more generally the ambiguous tension between society and nature in his work. By contrast with the involvement of women in the revolutionary public sphere, public life from the Napoleonic period onwards was an exclusively male, guarded realm of the modern, which was thought to reflect the natural order (Wagner 1994: 46). This belief in the naturalness of gender relations was widespread, and this was a view that Durkheim, though otherwise committed to the idea of society as a moral, not natural, reality, basically shared. Thus he used naturalistic arguments to develop a response to feminist writers. His views did pass through two phases though. In the first, primal equality evolved towards civilizational inequality, which then became fundamental to modern societies; in the second, primal inequality evolved towards functional separation which held out some prospect of equalization.

In his earlier work, Durkheim regarded the sexual division of labour as a source of conjugal solidarity. Following Morgan (as had Engels) Durkheim believed that in segmented societies women were equal to men, 'mingle in political life [and] accompany men to war'. Thus 'the further we look in the past, the smaller becomes [the] difference between man and woman. The woman of past days was not at all the weak creature that she has become with the progress of morality' (Durkheim 1933: 57). In complex societies, however, we find institutions of marriage, fidelity and division of labour – differences that are inscribed into physiology. In a curiously voluntaristic metaphor, woman 'retired' from warfare and public affairs and 'concentrated her entire life to her family', and as a result of this social separation, morphological differences of height, weight and average crania appeared (1933: 60).

This indicates an attempt to naturalize gender divisions on social-functional and physiological levels. Durkheim claimed that if the sexual division of labour were to recede below the level of conjugal solidarity institutionalized in marriage, 'an entire category of social life would be absent' (1933: 61). Conjugal solidarity is fundamental to social organization, it makes its action felt at each moment and is a model for differentiated sociality in general, of separation and mutual dependence. As in other aspects of his sociology, Durkheim's focus here is not on individual actors (men and women) but on the conjugal unit as a social bond, with its own pattern of functionally integrated differentiation. This is a differentiation not only of social functions, however, but also between the natural and social. Women are partly outside of society (therefore less subject to social forces such as suicidogenic ones) and are trapped in their biological constitution, just as men are enmeshed in the social. Patriarchy has emerged as a modern institution that reconciles women's and men's natural and social functions within the conjugal unit (Shope 1994). Indeed, conjugal society is a core unit of solidarity because it is the meeting place between men and women, the natural and social, mechanical and organic forms of solidarity (Lehmann 1994: 91). The argument for Durkheim is a scientific not moral or political one – defences or attacks on patriarchy are equally in vein since the system can be judged only against its social context (Lehmann 1994: 61).

While this indicates Durkheim's opposition to feminism, his later thesis revised some of these views, reflecting the wider shift in his sociology discussed above. In particular, he reversed his earlier view of primal gender equality. In 'The Prohibition of Incest and its Origins' (1898), which was a prelude to *Elementary Forms*, primitive society is no longer the site of archaic equality, but of extreme segregation and gender inequality. The taboos on endogamy, incest and blood symbolize male fear of women as 'dangerous magicians', and women's association with blood (through menstruation) reinforces men's fear of women as profane. Marriage and sexual rites are social institutions that aim to avert the consequences arising from the proximity of unequal subjects (Gane 1993), divisions that can be manifest even in the form of different languages for men and women (Durkheim 1969a: 77).

One consequence of this revised view is that rather than being a modern product, sexual divisions now appear archaic and evolve in complex societies in a different direction. That is, towards increasing respect for the individual, the body and the possibility of mutual reciprocity between private and public spheres (Shope 1994). Durkheim's later, cautious, acceptance of some of the demands of French feminism is tempered by warnings of too rapidly undoing the 'work of centuries', which would lead to anomie and increased violence against women. This, he predicted, would result from a situation where women would no longer be 'protected' by respect for the family and their place within it. Nonetheless, the moral and intellectual inferiority of women 'is no longer in keeping with our modern ideas' (Shope 1994) so demands for married women's rights to property, divorce, civic and legal equality are therefore justified. Durkheim remained committed to the family as the cornerstone of organic solidarity and to taboos on 'dark, mysterious sex' which violated the boundaries of the individual (Lukes 1973: 533; Gane 1993). Thus Durkheim condemned free love, advocated for example by Saint-Simonians such as Enfantin, as violating the principle of mutual respect between individuals, and expressed doubts about the moral consequences of explicit sex education. Describing himself as a 'feminist', Durkheim advocated equality of status for men and women but conditional on mutual recognition of their different capacities.

Perhaps it is the case, as Shope (1994) argues, that Durkheim's concept of women's emancipation reflected the thinking of contemporary French feminists campaigning for mutual respect for different functions ('separate but equal'). One may regard Durkheim's views as a product of his time. Even so, his treatment of the 'woman question' resisted any departure from the assumption that the combined effects of natural evolution had codified gender divisions in ways that were open to only limited social adjustment. According to Lehmann (1994) Durkheim's 'feminism' was a conservative defence of patriarchy which goes to the core of his sociology,[10] and he chose to reject more egalitarian pro-feminist writing available to him, such as Fourier, Wollstonecraft, Condorcet, J. S. Mill, Marianne Weber and Charlotte Perkins Gilmass (Lehmann 1994: 24). He cannot then be regarded simply as a product of his milieu but as a partisan participant in a passionate controversy, which he also hoped to neutralize by adopting a scientific stance. Durkheim could not view *gender* as socially constituted despite the radical social constructionism he applied to other institutions and practices.

## EVALUATION OF DURKHEIM AND EVOLUTIONARY SOCIOLOGY

Evolutionary thought was one of the most significant intellectual developments in the nineteenth century, which changed thinking in most of the human sciences. Its application to social life was and remains controversial not least because social evolutionary theory has a bias towards regarding existing social arrangements as natural and necessary. One problem evolutionary sociology confronts is that of drawing boundaries around the respective influence of nature and culture – at what point and how does the latter take over from natural development? One can identify a continuum between hard and soft approaches to this. At the hard end were biodeterminists like Hippolyte Taine (1828–93), frequently an object of Durkheim's critiques, since he reduced mind and morality to brain physiology. Then there were evolutionists like Spencer, for whom the social had a specific evolutionary trajectory (military to industrial organization) but was encompassed within a universal evolutionary process. In this context, Durkheim's approach is 'softer', in that he insisted on society as a symbolic, moral, cultural entity where natural evolution worked only in a highly modified way. The general issue here, of the limits of the natural and its possible effect on social organization, is one to which social science continually returns (see Runciman 1998).

The relationship between individual and society is a central theme in Durkheim's work. This is manifest in various ways: organic solidarity allows the expansion of individualism within an interdependent society; social facts are experienced by individuals as constraining and coercive; suicide rates are a function of four different configurations of individual and society; beliefs and concepts themselves symbolize the relationship between individual and society. The social is the source of the sacred, symbolizing the collective, while individual bodies with egoistic desires are the source of profanation. However, Durkheim's conception of individual, society and morality is problematic in several ways. Concepts of individual and society are used in various senses. 'Society' could mean cultural transmission, the association of individuals, socially prescribed obligations, system of rules, symbolic representations or just a national entity, as in 'French society'. 'Individual' could mean the presocial body, a collection of psychological elements (sensations, reflexes and instincts), an abstract property (the bearer of rights), the object on which social forces operate, or just people in general. It is not unusual to find sociologists using their core concepts in varying ways, but the individual–society dualism does so much work for Durkheim's theory that this ambiguity affects most of his other theoretical claims.

Further, he established a duality of 'self' versus 'society', which conflicts with his view of the primacy of the social. If the social was really the source of individuality (as he often claims) then our concept of the private self would be socially constituted too. Then the very antinomy of self–society would have to be seen as much a social category as he claimed was the case for space, time, causality, hierarchy and so forth. This is a step he did not take. Although the critique of utilitarianism is the rationale for much of Durkheim's sociology, he remained tied to a notion of the egoistic self in need of normative regulation. That such regulation is perceived as constraint, external to the individual, meant that despite himself, he resorted to an implicit concept of desiring and selfish individuals who stand outside of society.

Durkheim's duality of morality and the self did not separate social obligations from decisions to comply with them. We may feel an obligation to do something that we would prefer not to do, but whether or not we comply, we shall offer reasons justifying our action. So between obligation and action lie reasoned judgement as to the adequacy of possible reasons for complying or not. Durkheim himself implies that 'constraint' does not necessitate compliance based on coercion, which is a pathological condition. Rather, the 'normal' state of organic societies is based on consensual integration. Giving reasons, though, involves dialogue and the capacity to imagine how others will view our justifications, rather than simply acknowledging the external facticity of the social order. Durkheim did not differentiate *in his theory of morality* between those agreements that are based on the unquestioned, binding force of tradition (characteristic of mechanical solidarity) and those based on secular, post-traditional norms and consent (in organic solidarity). Had he done so, his view of **social action** might have become more linguistic, communicative and interactive, and he might have discovered a more indeterminate view of the social.

---

**Core concepts in moral-organic social theory**

- Nature, social evolution and naturalistic theories.
- Organic integration – the problem of complexity.
- The sociological dualism of individual and society.
- Moral integration has primacy over material accounts of the social.
- Social solidarity and the problem of order.
- The proper subject matter of sociology is society as a fact-like (external) entity.
- Human rights and the post-traditional social order.
- Religion, knowledge and society – sociological radicalism.

---

## FURTHER READING

Steven Lukes (1973) *Emile Durkheim: His Life and Work* (Penguin) provides a very comprehensive and detailed discussion of all Durkheim's writings. Jeffrey Alexander (1983) *Theoretical Logic in Sociology*, vol. 2 (University of California Press) offers a more theoretical discussion while Anthony Giddens (1978) *Emile Durkheim* (Fontana) provides a brief and lucid summary. Frank Pearce (1989) *The Radical Durkheim* (Unwin Hyman) and Mike Gane and Keith Tribe (eds) (1992) *The Radical Sociology of Durkheim and Mauss* (Routledge) challenge conventional views about Durkheim's conservatism. Jennifer Lehmann (1994) *Durkheim and Women* (University of Nebraska Press) gives a detailed account of Durkheim's attitudes towards feminism.

## NOTES

1 This methodological anti-individualism should not be confused with political anti-individualism. Viewing society as a binding moral order did not prevent Durkheim from endorsing human rights and increasing personal liberty, as his involvement in the Dreyfus Affair indicates (on which, see pp. 104–5).

2 This is not to say that all social constraint is normal or should be accepted. Constraint of 'one individual over another due to strength or wealth is abnormal and can only be maintained by violence' (Durkheim [1895] 1964: 123).

3 The increasing complexity of the division of labour itself is the consequence not the cause of the decline of segmented societies, since these could not themselves have stimulated a complex division of labour (Durkheim 1972: 152).

4 There is an echo here of Rousseau's claim that the transition from the state of nature to one of civilization involved increased unhappiness because in the latter people's desires multiplied, as did their sense of unfulfilment.

5 Durkheim could not accept the implication here that since marriage is an institution benefiting men rather than women, the latter, to preserve their moral health, should avoid marriage in favour of greater participation in the public sphere. See the discussion of Durkheim and women on pp. 108–10.

6 Durkheim was aware of this limitation. With reference to fluctuations in the rate in Paris 1870–1, he said 'the question has . . . been raised whether the cause of this momentary drop at a time of crisis might not be that the record of suicides was less exactly kept . . . however, the drop revealed by the statistics is too steady to be attributed to a brief inadvertence of administration' ([1897] 1970: 206).

7 By December 1898, 4,500 had signed the petition organized by the League for the Defence of the Rights of Man. Dreyfus was pardoned in 1899 and acquitted in 1906. But the affair had deep repercussions in France and beyond, foreshadowing the rise of European antisemitism in the twentieth century.

8 Maurice Barrès, writer, Boulangist deputy, was founder of 'integral nationalism' in France that depicted Jews as strangers, intruders, financiers and parasites (Wistrich 1992: 129).

9 Durkheim did, however, try to avoid the possibly relativistic implications of this view by insisting that truth, which requires long and specialist training, embodies the moral authority of the collective (Crook 1991: 47).

10 Lehmann admits that her definition of 'feminism' – the demand for 'equality of potential ability between men and women and advocacy of equality of actual treatment' – is 'arbitrary and anachronistic' in that it is a contemporary definition that was not shared by all nineteenth century 'feminists' (Lehmann 1994: 19).

# CHAPTER 6

# Critiques of positivism

Most of the writers we have considered thus far were committed in one way or another to the application of scientific methods to the study of society. Many (as we saw in Chapter 5) were further committed to an evolutionary approach, although the implications of natural evolution for sociology varied in the hands of different writers. I have suggested that although not following necessarily from Enlightenment thought, these two themes were developments of its rational and progressive ethos. Later in the nineteenth century though, the positivist evolutionary paradigm was challenged by the increasing popularity of anti-positivism, especially in the German-speaking intellectual world.[1] These critiques themselves drew in part on Enlightenment themes, especially philology and critical theology, Kantianism and Hegelianism, but also on the Romantic counter-Enlightenment's distaste for naturalistic methods.[2] The critique of positivism was generally linked to an insistence on essential differences between social and natural science, which were grounded in claims about the specific qualities of human culture. The ensuing debate, between naturalistic and anti-positivist approaches, become one of the most significant for the subsequent development of sociology and set the scene for classical theories such as those of Georg Simmel and Max Weber. This chapter examines the background to this debate in hermeneutic philosophies and their origins, in particular that of Wilhelm Dilthey (1833–1911), who laid the methodological foundations of hermeneutic sociology. 'The first condition of the possibility of historical science', Dilthey said, 'is that I myself am a historical being – he who studies history is the same as he who makes history' (1976b: 192). On this basis he outlined the foundations of an intuitive, historical methodology that was to offer an alternative to positivistic approaches for the following century.

## ■ WHAT IS HERMENEUTICS?

The word hermeneutics is derived from the Greek *herméneutikós*, associated with Hermes, the messenger, and connotes the process of understanding, interpretation and explanation. Hermeneutics is a philosophical approach to problems of understanding in general and the understanding of texts and actions in particular. It is concerned with interpretation where communication has become problematic as, for example, when encountering a foreign language, an unfamiliar culture, a distant epoch or pathological symptoms. Communication, in which we engage routinely in everyday life, is rarely transparent but poses problems of understanding, which we approach in various ways. Confronting a difficult text, for example, we may deploy a number of strategies to increase our understanding. We may take particular sentences and place them in the context of a whole passage, we may focus on individual words and discover their meaning from the way they are used in sentences, and we may consult other texts that offer clarification of the topics and language used. Then again, we may attempt to find out more about the author, the period and culture in which they lived, the debates in which they engaged and what their intentions were in writing the text. Each of these are hermeneutic devices that we can apply not only to texts, but also to other symbolic human products such as works of art, archaeological remains, political discourses, conversations, and so forth. Hermeneutics may begin with fragments of culture, complete works, or texts of historical events and reconstruct the world of meaning that makes them intelligible (see Figure 6.1).

These techniques have at least three important consequences for social theory. First, understanding is an activity fundamental to being human, since to communicate at all we need to be able to decode complex symbolic systems and orient our actions to other people's frames of meaning. This in turn may require **empathy**, that is the ability to place oneself in the context of another and reconstruct the world from their point of view, albeit imperfectly. Second, therefore, these activities

Figure 6.1  The hermeneutic circle

involve the elaboration of techniques of understanding that we use routinely in everyday life. This suggests that although hermeneutics may
involve elaborate techniques, its principles are already rooted in everyday life. Third, they suggest that the process of understanding is open-
ended and always incomplete, in that there is no final point at which one
could say that a text or work of art had been completely understood.
Thus not only is interpretation an issue of central concern for sociology, but also this approach suggests that the social world needs to be
approached in a very different way from the natural sciences. The development of hermeneutic approaches, then, has been central to debates
about the scientific status of the social sciences, the relationship between
subject and object, the meaning of 'objectivity', the formulation of
appropriate methods and the meaningful constitution of the object
(Bleicher 1982).

## HERMENEUTICS AND POSITIVISM

### Causal laws

Many of these debates are rather abstract and it may help to put them in
the context of broader questions about the nature of the social sciences.
These are bound up with disputes over positivism that took off during
the nineteenth century. There was (and to a large extent still is) a general
agreement that the aim of science is to produce generalizations, or laws,
stating the causal relations between phenomena. Natural science progressed by discovering invariant and necessary connections between
phenomena in an orderly universe. Newtonian physics for example could
predict events in the physical world with accuracy and symmetry because
(prior to the Einsteinian revolution) it seemed to be based on universal
laws that operated everywhere in the same way. Yet the exact nature of
'laws' was never subject to agreement among philosophers.

There were two disputes relevant here – the questions of what 'laws'
are, and whether they are useful to sociology (Outhwaite 1987)? Universal laws involved regularity and necessity: under the same conditions,
phenomena always behaved in a certain way and this regularity arose
from necessity. But what *was* necessity? This had been a problem with
Newton's theory of gravitation, an idea to which there had initially been
some resistance because it operated in an unseen way rather than through
a visible mechanism (Chalmers 1978). David Hume ([1748] 1975) had
argued that we observe regularities in 'constant conjunction', for example
that water at sea level boils at 100°C. But reason alone could not arrive
at the idea that heat *caused* water to boil. Any 'necessity' here is imposed
by the intellect. This argument was influential in positivist philosophy;
Comte regarded causal attributions as metaphysical (see Chapter 3) because they attempted to intuit the hidden nature of things. However,
J. S. Mill countered Hume with the theory of induction, that is, forming

general statements on the basis of accumulated observations. Mill argued that we infer from the uniformity of nature that what we know to be true in a particular case (e.g. water boiling) will be true in all cases which resemble it (J. A. Hughes 1990: 50). This was opposed to deduction (favoured by Comte) that sought to derive testable hypotheses from general, theoretical statements. But behind these disputes about the status of laws in science there were nonetheless some shared beliefs – that science was about reconciling the general with the particular; that the object of scientific inquiry was external to the investigation; that knowledge is based on observable regularities. It was these beliefs that were challenged by anti-positivists especially with regard to their application to understanding the social world and it is these arguments that we shall be examining in this chapter.

## Hermeneutic challenges

We saw in Chapter 3 that the Comtean positivist conception of sociology involved belief in the application of natural scientific methods to the social world, albeit with appropriate adjustments. For Comte, the human mind was progressing towards the development of a unified hierarchical science, organized in terms of universal laws which proceeded from the most abstract, mathematical to the most organic laws of sociology. In this unity of science, sociology would incorporate methods of observation, experiment and comparison. This involves the central assumption of naturalism – that the methods of the natural sciences were appropriate to understand social life – and organicism – that society was made up of functional parts, from which the individual institutions could be explained. On the basis of this knowledge sociologists would be able to intervene beneficently in the social body, just as medical knowledge facilitated interventions into the physical body. Most important perhaps, positivism assumed that society was an object independent of observers, with an inherent logic and structure that was knowable through the techniques of the natural sciences.

Hermeneutic approaches are often contrasted with positivism (e.g. Bauman 1978; Delanty 1997: 40ff); although there are good grounds for doing so, this should be done with caution, especially in relation to nineteenth century theorists. One issue here is that the German '*wissenschaft*', though often rendered into English as 'science' has a much broader connotation of systematically pursued knowledge than the more narrowly conceived English association with the *natural* sciences. So, philosophers such as Dilthey conceived of the *Geisteswissenschaften* as scientific in that they pursued a systematic and rigorous approach to mental life (Dilthey 1976b: 104). However, in distinguishing the natural and cultural sciences, hermeneutic theorists like Dilthey tended to accept a positivistic view of what natural sciences do, a view that many contemporary philosophers of science would challenge (for a classical statement of this argument, see Keat 1971). Dilthey further sympathized with, and was inspired by, Comte and Mill's desire to make human studies rigorous, empirical and scientific and shared their desire for concrete experience, rather than speculation, to be the basis for social theory (Palmer 1969: 93). However, Dilthey was opposed to their narrow concept of experience that equated scientific methods with those of physics or chemistry and insisted that the different subject matters of the natural and cultural worlds demanded different methods. He further held that a hermeneutic approach could out-do positivism in gaining access to social life, since humans could achieve a degree and depth of understanding of mental life that was impossible in the natural sciences.

Nevertheless, it is true that the implications of hermeneutics presented a challenge to the 'secular sobriety' of rationalist, French positivism (Bauman 1978: 11). Aside from the specific methodological claims made by different styles of hermeneutics (which will be considered shortly) they offered an alternative, humanistic vision of social life that eluded the precise, calculating spirit of positivism. Influenced by the Romantic Movement, nineteenth-century hermeneutics stressed subjectivity, description and consensus rather than instrumental objectivism. Empathy, Dilthey says, 'finds no analogy in the methods of the natural sciences but rests rather on reconstructing the relationship between expressions and the inner states [of mind] expressed in them' (Dilthey 1985: 163). Its objective is less to explain and consequently intervene in the world, so much as to understand and reconstruct meaning to regain the lost unity of the act of creation of a text, culture, artwork, institution or whatever. In this sense, as Delanty argues, hermeneutics had a more conservative orientation than positivism. Whereas the latter arose in the context of revolt against the authority of tradition and political absolutism, hermeneutics has tended to value community, be uncritical of social institutions and ignore power relations (Delanty 1997: 41–2). Positivism was informed by a reforming passion to improve the condition of humanity through the application of scientific rationality and the expulsion of metaphysics. But this contrast too should be treated with caution. The 'scientific' analysis of society was often associated with biological and evolutionary reductionism that emphasized difference among human (especially 'racial') groups. Meanwhile hermeneutic philosophers (in the nineteenth century) emphasized humanity's creative and meaningful commonality, which was revealed in the process of understanding. As Dilthey put it:

> Everything in which the mind has objectified itself contains something held in common between I and thou. Every square planted with trees, every room in which seats are arranged, is intelligible to us from our infancy because human planning, arranging and valuing – common to all of us – have assigned a place to every square and every object in the room.
>
> (Dilthey 1985: 155)

According to this separation of the sciences, the natural world follows causal patterns beyond consciousness or will; however, the social world was an arena of meanings, symbols and above all texts, that required interpretation and understanding. This meant not only that the methods of the two branches of knowledge were different, which they were, but also that the objectives were different too. The objective of the natural sciences was to *explain* phenomena, while that of the cultural or social sciences was to *understand*. Thus a division was established between two quite different conceptions of scientific activity, explanation and understanding, that was to underpin methodological disputes for the following hundred years or so. Bauman (1978: 28) says, understanding starts from establishing an affinity between its subject and object; or rather between two subjects, 'standing respectively at the beginning and the end of communication.' Similarly, for Habermas (1972) the natural sciences have an interest in control, while the hermeneutic sciences have an interest in mutual understanding. Rather than regard the social world as an object of explanation, the social world as a symbolic realm is read and understood like a text, or a dialogue. The possibility of understanding presupposes several conditions that suggest a different method from that of the natural sciences. In particular:

- Human action has purpose and intention, and is therefore ontologically different from nature.
- Social relations are meaningful and require interpretation rather than explanation. They are thus epistemologically different from natural science.
- An observer can rationally understand cultural products and shares an intersubjective consciousness with other subjects. The social sciences are thus methodologically different from natural science.

These and other key differences are summarized in Figure 6.2; to put it most simply, positivism aims to *explain* the social world, hermeneutics to *understand* it.

## THE HERMENEUTIC TURN

### Origins of sociological hermeneutics

Hermeneutics' origins are identified in diverse places but most commentators emphasize the importance of theology, brief mention of which should illustrate the distinctive nature of the approach. Hermeneutic problems arise particularly clearly in religions where texts are regarded as canonical, in that they are binding on the community of believers, yet where their true meaning has been distorted by generations of oral transmission, translations and changing cultural contexts. 'All we know of the texts we now call the Hebrew Bible', says Bruns, 'are rooted in centuries of scribal activity that originated, borrowed, compiled, despised,

**Figure 6.2** Differences between hermeneutics and positivism

|  | Positivism | Hermeneutics |
|---|---|---|
| Ontology | Society as organic system<br>Unintended consequences | Human action purposeful and<br>intentional, text-like<br>Objectified in culture and<br>institutions |
| Epistemology | Causal explanation<br>Interest in control | Understanding<br>Interest in mutuality |
| Methodology | Observer constructs hypotheses<br>Data external to subject<br>Induction/deduction | Subject interprets other subjects<br>Internal relation through<br>re-experiencing |
| Validity | Tested through observation | Reconstructs intentions and<br>meanings of actors |
| Procedure | Linear | Spiral |
| Subject-object | Objective – world of facts<br>independent | Intersubjective – knower and<br>known partners in dialogue |

amplified, and redacted various sorts of biblical material in ways no longer possible to describe' (Bruns 1992: 65). After the Jewish Diaspora (73 CE) the Torah (Pentateuch) was not only written and codified but also subject to a centuries long process of rabbinical disputation. This Midrash (Hebrew for 'interpretation') was to recover its true meanings and was a dialogic process of disputation, the aim of which was to think oneself into the text, rather than remain an analytic outsider. In Islam, Sufism developed a kind of Quranic hermeneutics that aimed to divine the meaning of a text that 'is a sea without a shore, a recitation of [another] text only God has seen, the *umm al-kitab* (the Mother of the Book). This was recited to Muhammad over twenty years, who recited it in turn to his Companions' (Bruns 1992: 126). Thus the meaning of the Quran cannot be fixed but is subject to interpretation and understanding. Again, the medieval Christian Bible was embedded in a history of interpretation and commentary that was added to the text in the form of annotations.

A more direct link with contemporary hermeneutics began with Reformation theologians who held that scripture could be understood without the mediation of ecclesiastical tradition (Müller-Vollmer 1986b: 3). To recover the true authority of the text, it was necessary to read the Bible structurally, placing a passage in context of the whole and within the time it was written. Thus through biblical hermeneutics seventeenth century, Protestant scholars developed a historical, critical method that sharpened the task of exegesis. It was to go deeply into the text to find moral truths hidden in historical events and thus to grasp the spirit (*Geist*) underlying the work. During the eighteenth century, however, these techniques became increasingly removed from theology and were applied to philology and the understanding of works of art. At the same time, its emphasis on grammatical and structural reading opened up critical biblical studies that treated the Bible as a text like any other, which contained historically specific meanings and myths that could be expunged (Palmer 1969).

## Post-Enlightenment hermeneutics

From the point of view of sociological theory, the most significant developments of hermeneutics took place in the aftermath of the Enlightenment, with the application of the method to classical art and literature. From the Enlightenment came empathy with an author's creative intention and belief in a rational order underlying history and culture. From the Romantic Movement came the ideas of the author creating a work which possessed inner stylistic unity that nonetheless allowed an infinite range of interpretations (Müller-Vollmer 1986b: 3). Wilhelm von Humboldt (1767–1835) for example argued that linguistic competence (*Sprachkraft*) involved the coproduction of meaning by listeners and speakers and interpretation required passing between part and whole of a text. These approaches drew on the Enlightenment concept of historical development, since classical antiquity was no longer seen as a place of timeless perfection, but as a historical society, posing challenges of understanding (Bauman 1978: 26). This required an intellectual journey back to the spirit of antiquity, which implied the possibility of a unity of understanding between cultures, since a total strangeness would be totally numb and speechless.[3] Two classical philologists, Friedrich Ast (1778–1841) and Friedrich Wolf (1759–1824), illustrate the way hermeneutic methods began to take shape early in the nineteenth century.

Friedrich Ast's (1808) studies of the classical world (*Grundriss der Philologie* and *Grundlinien der Grammatik, Hermeneutik und Kritik*, cited in Outhwaite 1975: 19–20) assumed an essential unity of human nature on the basis that anything humanly produced was understandable; an approach very different from that of French physiologists who were seeking to explain cultural difference in terms of biology. We could not understand either human dignity in general or individual documents and works of art, 'if our spirit were not essentially at one with the spirit of antiquity, so that it can absorb into itself this spirit which is only temporarily and *relatively* alien' (Outhwaite 1975: 19). Ast aimed to grasp the 'spirit' of antiquity through works that revealed a *Volkgeist* of life in general (Palmer 1969). Language was the means of transition between spirit and text and hermeneutics was the method of extracting spiritual meaning out of a text. Since we participate in spirit, which is the source of all development, it was possible to apprehend meanings from antiquity. The process of hermeneutic understanding proceeds in a circle with continual oscillation between the part and the whole. The part is understood from the whole in three aspects. historical, grammatical and its relation of the total view of the author and their period. These correspond in turn to three levels of explanation – hermeneutic of the letter (words); hermeneutics of sense (meaning in historical context); hermeneutics of spirit (view of life).

Friedrich Wolf aimed to grasp the intentions of writer and speaker, in order to understand their thoughts, as they would have wanted them understood. Note here that the emphasis is on reconstruction of the intentions of the writer/artist as key to meaning. Hermeneutics is a dialogue with the author that moves through the levels of grammar (the understanding of language), the historical life and times of the author, and the philosophical, which is proposed as a 'logical check' on the other two. The latter gestures towards a serious difficulty with hermeneutic methods in general – that of validity. How do we know whether our interpretations are valid, or indeed, given the subjective nature of understanding, that issues of validity arise in hermeneutics at all?

The theologian Friedrich Schleiermacher (1768–1834) is often regarded as the 'founder of modern hermeneutics' (Bauman 1978: 29). He followed the approach of Ast and Wolf but regarded interpretation as offering the possibility of understanding authors *better* than they understood themselves (Schleiermacher 1977). Whereas previous hermeneutics had been a 'pedagogical aid to recovering meaning by disciplined reconstruction' Schleiermacher went much further by treating *mis*understanding as a routine experience and therefore one that required universally shared techniques of interpretation (Gadamer 1976: 48). His concept of hermeneutics aimed to go beyond the subjective intentions of authors and artists to recreate the world of form and meaning within which they worked. This introduced the idea that a text could contain meanings of which the author was unconscious, which arose in the process of struggle between intention and the demands of form, so the end result was not a simple reflection of the author's intentions. In 1819 he called for a new conception of hermeneutics, involving an imaginative re-creation of the intellectual context within which texts are produced. Re-experiencing again proceeds through a circle – 'each part is understood only from the whole and vice versa. Within a given text, parts can only be understood in terms of the whole' (Schleiermacher 1977: 85). This conception of hermeneutics involves a continual dialectical play between subjective and objective moments, of comparison of part to whole, reference to sentence, text to author. There is no logical beginning where first principles lead to predicted conclusions, but a 'leap' into the circle. Hermeneutics uses intuition and (what would have been anathema to positivists) precognition – that is, prior knowledge of texts and cultural background, without which understanding would not be possible.

Further, following the philologists, Schleiermacher grounded hermeneutics in human language, which he saw as an autonomous living organ through which the author must think. Anticipating later, language centred theories of the social, Schleiermacher regarded the author of a text as an 'event in the life of language itself' (Bleicher 1982: 329). That is, the authors had to work through the medium of language, its system and rules, as a medium for expressing their intentions. Now hermeneutics was no longer occupied with decoding a given meaning but illuminating the conditions for the very possibility of understanding. In his *Handwritten Manuscripts*, Schleiermacher claimed that understanding is an 'unending task', analogous to speaking, since speech acts imply mutual understanding. Two phases in understanding can be distinguished – decoding language as a system of speech and understanding speech as part of the speaker's life process. This was to be an important distinction in Dilthey and Weber's sociology. Schleiermacher viewed understanding as an intersubjective process, since 'one can understand a word which one heard only because one could have spoken it oneself'. Meaning is coproduced by a listener and a speaker and requires creative imagination to produce a guiding vision of the whole (Müller-Vollmer 1986b: 14).

Speaking is the medium for shared thought since understanding speech always involves two processes – understanding what is said and understanding the thinking of the speaker. This 'art of understanding' is moreover embedded in social life and common to both scientific and everyday practices and draws on what would later be known as 'tacit knowledge' of social life (Schleiermacher 1977). 'Very often in private conversations', Schleiermacher said, 'I resort to hermeneutical operations, if I am not content with the usual level of understanding but wish to explore how . . . the transition is made from one thought to another' (*Hermeneutik*, 1838, in Bleicher 1982: 329). This is possible because each individual carries within their capacity for language the 'minimum of all others'.

In his later work, Schleiermacher separated language from psychology and argued that grammar constituted the objective rules of language while understanding required knowledge of the psychology of the individual author. The objective of Schleiermacher's hermeneutics was to transcend language to access inner processes of psychology and 'non-linguistic' individuality (Palmer 1969: 93). It is true that the idea that there is a private self, separate from and preceding language informs some nineteenth century hermeneutics, and that this would be challenged by later linguistic philosophies. But as hermeneutics developed from philological to wider social concerns the scope increased for applying its techniques in a broader social context.

## NEO-KANTIANS AND ANTI-POSITIVISTS

An important context for the development of sociological hermeneutics was neo-Kantianism, which influenced the methodology of the social sciences and set the scene for later debates in classical sociology. Kant's critical philosophy has been mentioned in earlier chapters and in many ways stands behind many of nineteenth century theoretical debates. In his *Critique of Pure Reason* (1781) Kant attempted to resolve one of the major philosophical disputes of the eighteenth century, between idealism and rationalism. In response to Hume's empiricism, Kant argued that there were indeed limits to what could be derived from the exercise of reason. We could not infer the existence of cause, nor of time and space, however, (*pace* Hume) empirical knowledge presupposed these categories *a priori*. That is, they are inherent in any act of cognition and are therefore (for Kant) subjective and prior to experience. Beyond the apprehended world of experience there is the unknowable world of 'things in themselves', the *noumena*. This is unknowable because we can never see beyond the categories that provide the form through which cognition occurs. Categories of space and time are real in that they are present in any object we perceive but they are also 'transcendentally ideal'. This means that considered with respect to the unknowable *noumena*, space and time are not real but subjective ideas (Körner 1977: 38–9). Kant's *Critique*, which was an exploration of the limits and conditions of knowledge became a model for hermeneutic attempts to understand the human sciences.

Kantianism had been in eclipse since Hegel's death in 1831 and after the 1848 revolutions was associated with dangerous ideas like liberalism. But it was revived by the neo-Kantian movement, associated with historical thought at the universities of Heidelberg and Marburg between 1860 and 1900, where the return to Kant was an expression of dissatisfaction with the dominance of positivist thinking and the failure of idealist philosophies. Leading members of the Heidelberg school were Wilhelm Windelband (1848–1915) and Heinrich Rickert (1863–1936) whose turn to Kant had the intention of drawing insights that would rebuild critical philosophy. The neo-Kantians did not slavishly follow Kant (who had had little to say about the social sciences) but radicalized his critique of pure reason to develop a critique of historical reason. This involved investigating the conditions of possible cultural knowledge and the separation between natural and social sciences (Delanty 1997: 45). A central issue here, as in the hermeneutic approaches, was the relationship between subject and object and indeed, how knowledge of the social is possible at all. This in turn raised a further question about the relationship between historical judgements and values – what were the bases for value judgements and what role did they play in historical and cultural analysis? I shall return to these in relation to Weber in Chapter 8.

A tendency among some neo-Kantians, including Dilthey, was to dispense with transcendental idealism. On the other hand Kantianism seemed to lay emphasis on the activity of the subject and escaped the passivity of the subject in positivism and materialism. We saw in the discussion of

Marxism (Chapter 4) that revisionists in the SPD, such as Bernstein, looked to Kantianism to give increased priority to the ethical dimension in Marxism. In the methodological debates of the 1880s, Kant was invoked to reinstate the subject as an active participant in the production of knowledge, which seemed particularly appropriate for the social sciences where the subjects and 'objects' were active, knowing beings.

## WILHELM DILTHEY (1833–1911)

Trees are not humanly made so we cannot understand them.

Sociological hermeneutics proper begins with Dilthey, whose work has been described as a 'declaration of independence on behalf of humanities' (Szacki 1979: 329).[4] Creating a methodological separation between social and natural sciences was central to his later philosophy, which attempted to justify the knowledge claims of human studies in terms of a philosophy of life.[5] Stuart Hughes comments that 'Dilthey was so old-fashioned that by the end of his life he had become a modern' (H. S. Hughes 1974: 192). His influence in philosophical and theoretical debates in Germany was greatest from the 1890s, shortly before he retired from the University of Berlin. Dilthey was absorbed in the philosophy of the late eighteenth and early nineteenth centuries – of Kant, the Enlightenment, the Romanticism of Schleiermacher, Fichte and Schelling. He also had respect for the aims of positivism, which is apparent in his desire that concrete experience rather than speculation be the basis for theoretical *Geisteswissenschaften*. Further, although influenced by the Romantics, and agreeing with them that intuition was possible in cultural life, the purpose of his theoretical hermeneutics was to preserve the general validity of interpretation against the inroads of (what he saw as) Romantic irrationalism and sceptical subjectivity. Thus his work embodies conflicts that run through nineteenth century thinking between the desire for immediacy and the need to validate theoretical claims with objective data, tensions that we shall see too in Weber. Dilthey's interests had come back into fashion partly because of methodological debates surrounding neo-Kantianism and the way he too applied Kantian reasoning to the problems of the cultural sciences.

### Life and textuality

Dilthey began with Schleiermacher, who was the subject of his major biography (1862). As with Schleiermacher, Dilthey's hermeneutics moved through the particular to recapture the general process of historical creation. Through understanding we comprehend living human experience partly through self-reflection and partly through re-experiencing (*Nacherleben*), one of Dilthey's central concepts. For Dilthey, Schleiermacher's architectonic method of oscillating between part and whole replaced the

dichotomy of induction-deduction, which as we have seen, was central
to the debate about the status of scientific laws. Positivistic conceptions
of science treated their object as external, to be approached through the
systematic formulation of concepts and hypotheses. However, hermeneutics offers a way of getting to the inner structure of the object, since as
Schleiermacher had shown, interpretation proceeds through engagement
with the organization and composition of a work. Irritated by the 'clatter'
of induction and deduction in J. S. Mill's work (Makkreel 1975: 73),
Dilthey regarded it as beside the point whether moral sciences first obtain
generalizations inductively from experience or deductively from theories.
Such discussions mistakenly presuppose that human studies are like the
natural sciences. On the contrary, hermeneutics involves understanding
(*verstehen*), an imaginative reconstruction of the worldviews, situation,
meanings and intentions of historical actors. Whereas positivist epistemology had substituted 'bloodless shadows' for living people who existed in
a world of experience (*Erlebnis*), Dilthey begins with the 'richly varied
experience of observers who are culturally and physically embodied'
(Rickman 1976: 14).

However, there is no timeless *Geist* at work here, since the meaning of
cultural products will change over time – the meaning of Shakespeare's
plays for example, will be different now than they were in the sixteenth
century. Dilthey turned Schleiermacher's approach in a more historical
and sociological direction, applying hermeneutics to the cultural sciences.
Sociological hermeneutics situates itself in the process of historical development. Understanding is not accomplished by isolated subjects removed
from time and place but is made possible (as for Hegel) by the process of
historical development itself. Dilthey says,

> [This is] a question of the utmost importance. Our actions always
> presuppose the understanding of other people; a large part of
> human happiness arises from sympathy with other frames of mind;
> the holding of philological and historical science is based on the
> supposition that this sympathy with the individual can be raised to
> the level of objectivity. The historical awareness built on this sup-
> position enables modern man to have humanity's entire past with
> him: he looks beyond the confines of his own age to past cultures;
> he absorbs the power of these cultures and then enjoys their magic:
> from this his happiness is greatly increased.
>
> (Dilthey 1976a: 104)

History is a process of self-objectification of mind, so from such cultural
fragments we can trace back to the spirit determining the age (*Zeitgeist*).

However, in reconstructing the original unity of the work, Schleiermacher had appealed to the *Keimensschluss* (from *Keim*, 'seed') in which
the whole was already prefigured at the outset. For Dilthey this failed to
take account of the important ways in which a historical perspective
contributes to our knowing the author better than 'he knew himself'.

Schleiermacher thus had a 'closed sense of the original unity of creative work' (Makkreel 1975: 269). Moreover, Dilthey replaced Schleiermacher's analogy of hermeneutics as a circle with the idea of a spiral – the circle never closes since understanding is never complete, and we enter it, provisionally, in the middle. The idea of a circle challenged the positivistic belief in a linear starting point. But Dilthey's concept is more flexible in that it invites the interpreter to shift their focal point in the course of engagement with a text. The artist creates a portrait from a focal point and to understand the work, a spectator needs to modify their normal apprehension and relocate the point at which other traits converge.

### Plan for Human Studies

In 1883 Dilthey drafted an *Introduction to the Human Studies* with the intention of combining historical with systematic approaches, in order to solve the problem of the philosophical foundation of the human sciences. What system of presuppositions justifies the judgements of historians, the conclusions of economists and the concepts of lawyers and provides criteria for establishing that they are true? The answers which Comte and the positivists gave to these questions seem 'to truncate historical reality in order to assimilate it to the concepts and methods of science'. On the other hand, he says, the reaction against them seems to sacrifice the independence of human disciplines and the fruitful power of their empirical methods to 'a sentimental mood which nostalgically seeks to recall, . . . a mental satisfaction which has gone forever' (Dilthey 1976b: 161). To avoid both of these, Dilthey sets out to base his programme in experience to reconstruct the categories of mind that make knowledge of the historical (and therefore social) world possible.

### *Categories of life: from experience to the social*

The argument here is fairly abstract, but it leads in an important direction. Dilthey argued that Kant's dichotomy between *a priori* categories and the noumena (see pp. 123–5) is valid for the natural but not for the social sciences. 'All historical understanding presupposes self-reflection to do justice to inner experience' and nothing *necessarily* transcends human understanding (Dilthey 1976b: 238). So there is no dualism between appearance and the thing-in-itself in the human sciences since these get access to inner knowledge of social life. This claim is based on Dilthey's central concept of experience (*Erlebnis*). It is an idea with clear *Romantik* overtones, however much Dilthey tried to distance himself from this position. 'It is the secret of life', he said, 'that a supreme purpose, to which all individual purposes are subordinated is realised in it' (1976b: 238). Thus life and history are meaningful narratives. We have access to the meaning of social life because our own life is invested with meaning, even though our understanding of this, as with history as a whole will always be partial. The meaning of our own life would become clear only when known as a totality (i.e. at the end) and similarly the meaning of history would be knowable only from its end. Hegel had envisaged an end of history, the point of absolute spirit (see pp. 59–61 for a brief account of this) but Dilthey had no such expectation. Thus the hermeneutic 'hovers' in this incomplete circle where the part (of life or history) is knowable only through the whole and vice versa (Dilthey 1976b: 236).

Understanding history is possible, though, because knowledge of the human world develops first in everyday life. Everyday experience contains within itself categories of understanding, which are basic principles of innate mental structure. Like Kant, he attempted to uncover what categories of thought make possible knowledge of the external, in this case social, world. But here Dilthey moved away from the abstract notion of the bloodless subject and introduced a social, intersubjective dimension. The important thing about experience is that when it becomes an object of our reflection, it is imbued with structure and time. Pure experience is trapped within immediacy – it exists for a moment and passes away. In fact, from the point of view of experience, there *is* no present, only a passage from past to future. It is through re-experiencing that experience is organized temporally. And what happens then, Dilthey asks, 'I lie awake at night worrying whether I shall be able, in old age, to complete works I have already begun' (1976b: 185). In other words, once we reflect on, and organize, experience it acquires a narrative structure, events are put in context, we move between past and present, whole and part and so forth. Now we see that the unity of life is something constructed in the mental activity of organizing experience. He proposed re-experiencing as part of a non-positivistic methodology for the social sciences that would go beyond the limitations of objective, observable phenomena and tap into a deeper more intuitive level.

This is possible because self-reflection is never, so to speak, something done alone. It is private but involves transcending the limits of our own experience and extending understanding over 'several people, mental creations and communities', which widens the horizon of the individual and opens up a path to the general (1976b: 186). Language is the medium of reflection and is of course held in common by communities, so re-experiencing rediscovers the 'I in thou'; it is always a dialogue between self and others, between particular and general. We understand ourselves as others might understand us, so the creation of objects of consciousness is a social process that is nonetheless grounded in our inner mental life.

Further, Dilthey claimed that reconstruction of the art of re-experiencing led to the identification of categories of historical knowledge, which are given in mental structure. These include (his list does not claim to be exhaustive) things like the ability to make typical connections between mental processes, so for example, perceptions give rise to memories, memories awake desires and desires prompt action. Our mental life is purposive and we are aware of affecting our environment and of being affected by it. Mental states are expressed physically, so we intuit inner states of mind from people's overt actions. We not only perceive the world around us but also evaluate it in terms of the feelings it arouses and the way it affects our purposes (Rickman 1976: 15).[6] Understanding is an interpretative activity that has developed from an everyday art into a discipline. This was possible because humans live within the culture that they study. It may sound a little odd to say 'we cannot understand trees because they were not a human creation but we can have a deeper understanding of the cultural world because it is a human creation'. But this expressed his concept of the distinctiveness of the social sciences. It further echoed the theme of hermeneutic approaches in general, that understanding of the cultural world is possible in a way that it is not in the natural world.

I did say that this argument is abstract. But it leads Dilthey to a concept of the social as both subjective and objective reality. Beginning with experience, Dilthey found his way to the social (all experience is intersubjective) and then to the process of objectification, that is, the way social life appears to take on an objective character independent of individuals, which is 'almost nature like' (1976b: 191). When experience is subject to reflection it becomes an external object, towards which we may adopt an attitude, attribute value, reinterpret and so forth. When we reflect we deploy language, values, ideas or other cultural material, that has been derived from the accumulated individuality of other people. Dilthey is trying here to grapple with the problem that has in one way or another been central to almost every sociological theory – the relationship between social action and social system. Let us turn to this now.

### Individual and society

Participating in understanding is a mutual relationship and the individual experiences a social power superior to the individual will. This relationship between 'I and things' (i.e. objects of consciousness) leads to differentiated states of the self, feelings of pleasure or exhilaration, desire for objects, fear or hope (Dilthey 1976b: 178). But there is no simple dichotomy here between individual and society since in a style of argument we shall find again in Simmel, the individual is the point where webs of relationships intersect. These webs possess an independent existence as they develop in differentiated systems of culture, art, philosophy and the economy. Two features basic to consciousness – awareness of inner mental states and the reconstruction of meaning based on empathy – enable human studies to grasp this process of sociation.

Dilthey suggested that this process of objectifying experience is inherent in the life process and gives rise to the objective spirit or mind (*Objektiver Geist*). This is a term derived from Hegel, although Dilthey uses it in a different way.[7] Objective mind contains differentiated systems – 'many lines . . . traverse the world of objective mind and cut across it' (Dilthey 1976b: 191). In particular there are two social systems with different consequences. A cultural system, based on free and voluntary association, is manifest in the arts, language, science, religion and economics. A social system of institutions, however, is coercive in that membership is not chosen but is based on social bonds bound by collective will and hierarchical relations. We are born into the family, tribe, state, etc. and these are 'independent of our will'. Even so, both are functional structures activated by individuals rather than autonomous entities (Makkreel 1975: 67).

The distinction here between voluntary and coercive is somewhat arbitrary in that participation in some activities, the economy being a prime example, may (as Marx said) be formally free but substantively coercive. One may be formally free to enter a labour contract but compelled to do so if the alternative is starvation. Freedom and coercion can be properly evaluated only in a context of power relations, which in the main are noticeably absent in Dilthey. Further, given that Dilthey acknowledges the existence of social institutions into which we are born and are therefore not the product of our consciousness, he may be open to a Durkheimian objection.[8] One could argue that precisely because individuals are born into precategorized social realities, which they find coercive, the source of these categories cannot be found in individual consciousness but in society as a reality *sui generis*. This point is worth pursuing briefly because it highlights one of the major divisions in most subsequent sociological theory, between individualistic (agent centred) and societal (system centred) approaches.

Dilthey could make at least four responses to the 'Durkheimian' critique. First, he could claim that his philosophical foundation of the social sciences did not refer to individuals *per se*, but to properties of mind that all individuals share. Second, (like Simmel) he argued that no human being is exhausted by any aspect of the cultural or social system, rather we partake in many different aspects at the same time. Individuals are always *more* than the roles or persona they manifest in various cultural systems, in which they are 'carrier and codeveloper'. Third, we live in a mind-constructed world and mind can understand only what it has created. We are surrounded by 'Roman ruins, cathedrals and summer castles', fragments of the history of mind that can be understood only by hermeneutic techniques grounded in the life process of individuals. We cannot therefore treat the social world as an organic system in the way that Durkheim and the positivists did. Fourth, Dilthey could point out that history takes place through the interaction of objective mind and individuals' understanding, which together 'determine the mind-constructed world' (Dilthey 1985: 158). He seems to be suggesting a view developed by many later sociologists, that society is the product of agents who are themselves socially produced. For example,

> It is important to keep in mind that the objectivity of the institutional world, however massive it may appear to the individual, is a humanly produced objectivity. Society is a human product. Society is an objective reality. Man is a social product.
>
> (Berger and Luckman 1967: 78)

Even so, while most sociologists have addressed this issue in one way or another, most have focused on one side of the dialectic of individual and society to the neglect of the other. Dilthey has far more to say about mental life and experience than he has about the social as an objective reality.

### Critique of Historical Reason

Among his later works, Dilthey began a *Critique of Historical Reason*, which was to widen Kant's *Critique of Pure Reason* to account for the historical dimension in the development of human thought. The *Critique* was unfinished and published only after his death in his *Collected Works* in 1926. Here again he argues that methods of interpretation in human sciences are derived from ordinary forms of understanding characteristic of human life and social interaction, in which concepts of historical knowledge are already present (Dilthey 1985). To appreciate Dilthey's importance for the subsequent development of social science – especially in Weber – we need to look briefly at the way he situates re-experiencing within a hierarchy of types of understanding. Dilthey identified various levels of understanding grouped into two broad categories of elementary and higher understanding. This is a kind of 'rules of method' although he was loath to set out formal rules for hermeneutics (1976b: 227).

### *Elementary forms of understanding*

1 The most formal level of understanding is based on signs, symbols, concepts and larger thought structures. These make a mental content intelligible but reveal nothing about the inner mental life of the subject.
2 **Direct understanding** – recognizing a symbol *as* something. This takes forms such as the communication of expressions, gestures and actions, the meaning of sentence or mathematical expression. The content may be symbolic but is understood directly, in terms of a regular relation between action and intention, state of mind and gestures or facial expressions. If we see someone hitting a nail with a hammer we infer from their action (and from our pre-knowledge of tools and their

uses) what their intention might be. Similarly, we recognize certain facial expressions as indicating grief or happiness.

3  Understanding objective mind. This (we have seen) refers to the various ways in which the things that individuals hold in common have objectified themselves in the world. Styles of life and social interactions relate to a system of purposes embedded in custom, law, the state, religion, art, science and philosophy. Individuals apprehend life-expressions against the background of knowledge about such common features. Civil law procedures, for example, are designed to secure the highest possible degree of perfection in the conduct of human affairs and we refer to them to understand particular judicial procedures and the legal machinery for carrying out decisions. Similarly, a sentence is intelligible only because a language (its words, inflections, and syntactical arrangements) is held in common by a community.

(Dilthey 1985: 156)

### 'Higher' forms of understanding

1  The greater the inner distance between a particular life expression and the person understanding it, the more often uncertainties will arise. For example there may be an intention to deceive. We make judgements about the character and capacities of individuals and the circumstances in which they are acting. But this is not to say that understanding is limited to the inference of direct communications with an agent. When we watch a play we direct our understanding towards the whole performance, the plot, the characters and interplay of events. We enter an objective world of form and only when we stand back from the performance and remember that what is being observed is an author's planned creation, does understanding pass back from the creation to the creator.

2  Empathy, recreating and reliving.[9] Empathy requires the ability to project oneself into a text or form of life and appropriate it on the basis of shared experience. To share the experience of poetic love, one must have loved, to imagine suffering one must have suffered and so on. Then on the basis of empathy arises the 'highest form of understanding in which the totality of mental life is active' – recreating or reliving the process of cultural production. There are two concepts here with different purposes. Empathy moves in *reverse order* to the sequence of events, from the completed product or event back to the context and intentions that inspired it. However, re-experiencing retraces the original line of events so that we progress with the history of the period or (say) a lyrical poem, through the pattern of lived experiences expressed in the final product. Re-experiencing does not involve literally recreating the mind of the author, but being able to relive experiences remote from contemporary life. For example, most

of us today are unlikely to undergo a religious experience in our own lives. However, Dilthey suggests, when reading the letters and writings of Luther, the reports of his contemporaries, the records of his religious disputes and councils, and those of his dealings with officials, we may experience a religious process, in which life and death are at stake. We can, he says, transpose ourselves into the circumstances and understand how they made for an extraordinary development of religious feelings. Limited by circumstances, we can 'yet glimpse alien beauty in the world and areas of life beyond our reach . . . Man, tied and limited by the reality of life is liberated not only by art – as has often been explained – but also by historical understanding' (Dilthey 1985: 161).

3 There is, finally, an objective, historical, context for the development of re-experiencing. These practices require an appropriate level of consciousness, which was articulated first in philology since 'the life of mind only finds its complete, exhaustive, and therefore objectively comprehensible expression in language'. But today it is hermeneutics, as a general science of social life that enters a context in which the human studies acquire the possibility of acquiring historical knowledge.

In conclusion Dilthey points out that 'we must acknowledge how little elementary forms of understanding achieve' compared with higher forms, which underscores the difference between naturalistic and hermeneutic approaches. Deeper understanding requires an intuitive leap into re-experiencing which has an irrational aspect (because 'life is irrational') and cannot follow a logical formula. Even so, understanding requires a form of induction – not where a general law is inferred from a series of cases – but coordinating cases into a structure or orderly system by treating them as parts of a whole.

## Validity and science

To summarize, the significance of hermeneutics for the development of sociological theory was to offer a challenge to positivistic and materialistic conceptions of the social. While the natural world was subject to causal processes, the social world was meaningful and therefore required interpretation and understanding rather than causal explanation. Language, culture, symbols and conversations all pose problems of understanding, but more than this, our capacity to perform as competent members of society rests on a number of presuppositions grounded in everyday life:

• Human action has purpose and intention.
• Therefore the social world is meaningful and systematically ordered.
• Whatever is humanly created can be humanly understood.

- The decoding of meaning involves a spiral of elucidation through 'dialogue'.
- Rather than an independent subject confronting an object world, the hermeneutic scholar shares an intersubjective world with what they study, of which we always have preunderstanding.
- The circle is never complete and can always uncover further layers of meaning.

As Bauman (1992: 125) puts it, 'hermeneutics is a dialogue rather than a soliloquy and interpretive reason is interested in continuation of dialogue even though it is unsure where to stop, treating each appropriation [of meaning] as an invitation to further exchange'. For both Dilthey and Schleiermacher there was no true starting point and no understanding without presuppositions, since we always understand within a historical and cultural horizon. But Dilthey still hoped to show how we can have 'universally valid knowledge of the historical world' (1976b: 191), which raises a crucial problem – how do we know whether our understandings are valid?

This is further complicated by Dilthey's view that objective understanding is in conflict with the 'practical tendencies of life', that is, particular interests arising from society and culture.

> Since historians, economists, political scientists and students of religion are immersed in life, they want to influence it . . . Even when they believe themselves to be operating free from presuppositions, they are determined by this horizon. Does not every analysis of the concepts of a previous generation show these concepts to contain components that originated in the presuppositions of the time? At the same time every science as such contains the demand for universal validity.
>
> (Dilthey 1976b: 183)

So, practical orientations posed a threat to objectivity while the more one is separated from the tendencies of life the greater the chances of being objective. Further, Dilthey suggested that the development of the objective mind was leading away from the practical tendencies of life. The chance of true understanding grows with time and distance, and social differentiation of occupations and the appearance of more specific specialisms with increased technical training may remove specialist knowledge from these practical tendencies (Habermas 1972: 177). As the cultural spheres of art, law and science separated, so they also become independent of their origins. Thus jurisprudence developed from Roman administration, politics from government of city states and art from religious ritual. In this process of cultural differentiation, discrete spheres become governed less by external interests and demands and more by internally defined criteria of relevance. Thus art pursues beauty, law and morality pursue justice and science pursues truth.

This approach to the problem of validity has drawn the criticism of 'covert positivism' in two senses. First, Dilthey is accused of accepting the positivists' account of science and using this as a basis for his contrasting account of social science. He does seem broadly to accept a 'Comtean' concept of natural science. For example, 'the natural sciences form a hierarchy of lowest stratum interdependent on the one for which it lays foundations', whereas in human studies everything is guided by understanding and is in a relation of codependence (1976b: 190). Gadamer regards Dilthey as too influenced by positivistic accounts of natural science when he might have challenged their status, suggesting that he 'succumbed completely to the modern concept of science' (Gadamer 1976: 48). Scientific work itself may involve hermeneutic procedures. When confronted by the results of an experiment, printed data, radio impulses from distant galaxies or whatever, scientists have to read these in particular ways and make judgements as to their significance. This will be a communicative process, which they will do with reference to dominant frames of meaning provided by scientific 'paradigms' (Kuhn 1970). Dilthey did, however, acknowledge the relevance of hermeneutics for the natural sciences although he also felt that its range of applicability to the social world was greater.

Second, there is the claim that although outlining a programme for the *Geisteswissenschaften*, Dilthey ends up with a naturalistic concept of uninvolved, objective description. Dilthey and Schleiermacher regarded the knower's embeddedness in a cultural tradition and historical location in a negative light – as prejudices that block understanding. Habermas claims that Dilthey reduced empathy to 'solitary re-experiencing', undertaken by an observer extricated from history and culture (Habermas 1972: 108ff) and Bleicher (1982: 321) argues similarly. On the other hand, Bauman (1978) sees Dilthey as a historical thinker for whom true understanding was the 'work of history' in that in the tradition of Hegel, Marx and Weber and the Enlightenment the historical process itself would create the conditions for valid knowledge. At any rate, both themes here – cultural differentiation and the problem of validity play an important role in Simmel and Weber's sociology.

## HERMENEUTICS AND THE SOCIAL SCIENCES

Hermeneutics has been influential in the social sciences and was one reference point, along with others to be discussed in Chapters 7 and 8, for the formulation of Weberian sociology. More recently, during the 1960s, there was a revival of interest in hermeneutics as again positivistic methods were subject to widespread critique. Rather than appearing as a conservative defence of community and tradition, however, hermeneutics then appeared to legitimize a radical attack on established sociology. In the meantime hermeneutics had been taken in various directions. In

*Being and Time* ([1927] 1996) Heidegger (1889–1976), impressed with Dilthey's theory of time, claimed to develop an ontology of understanding in which hermeneutics is an encounter with Being through language. Language centred hermeneutic approaches became influential following the philosophy of Wittgenstein and a variety of sociological approaches claiming some affinity to this, such as Peter Winch's *The Idea of a Social Science* (1958). Following more directly from nineteenth-century hermeneutics (filtered through Heidegger) Gadamer (1993) argued that the process of interpretation is infinite and our specialist understanding is in no way superior to those of everyday life, only different, 'if we understand at all'. Whereas Dilthey regarded the tendencies of life as an obstacle to understanding, for Gadamer our cultural context, or 'prejudice', is the starting point of all understanding. Understanding will always be context dependent, so our understanding of philosophy for example will differ according to our cultural and historical situation – the Plato of the Neoplatonists was different from that of the Renaissance and different again from that of nineteenth century German scholars. Understanding is a play of past and present, and is always a dialogue in which the question and answer will vary according to its purpose and audience. We can never escape the constraints of our tradition, although we might objectify them in the encounter with other cultures. Such later developments have made explicit the relativity of hermeneutic interpretations, and given up on what Emilio Betti lamented as the attempt to distinguish right from wrong interpretation (Palmer 1969: 56ff).

This is an issue of crucial importance for hermeneutics and the social sciences in general. I noted above that issues of material inequality, power and coercion do not get much treatment in Dilthey. It is not that he denies their existence but that it is not clear how these can be derived from categories of experience and consciousness, since they operate at levels that may escape the understandings of everyday life. The impact of global economic restructuring on local communities will of course be meaningful for those affected, but the ways in which they are interpreted will differ. Further, we may want to claim that some interpretations are more adequate than others. Marx provided a good example of this in his comments on thefts of wood in the Rhineland (see Chapter 4). The common right to collect dead wood had become criminalized with the enclosure of estates and the rising price of wood fuel. But to the Moselle peasants it appeared as if wood had taken on a fetishistic character. This is a pattern that has been repeated many times over in the industrialized and developing worlds. The rationale for political economy then was to explain these life events in ways that revealed the operation of powerful systems that otherwise occur, as Wellmer (1971: 14) put it 'behind the backs of actors'. More generally, hermeneutic decoding of meaning may have difficulty dealing with unintended consequences of actions, the effects of which were unanticipated and unwanted by actors. This became an issue of central importance in Weber.

---

**Core concepts in hermeneutic social theory**

- Understanding vs. explanation in methods of social science.
- Social and natural as objects of inquiry, defined by approach.
- Cultural development and history – self-understanding of Mind?
- Individual and society, agency and structure.
- Language as constitutive of meaning.
- Romanticism in sociology – the self as author.
- Experience as basis for cultural science.
- Cultural differentiation and progress towards objectivity.
- Neo-Kantianism and categories of social life.
- Problems of validity in interpretation.
- Universal human understanding.

---

## FURTHER READING

Zigmund Bauman (1978, reprinted 1992) *Hermeneutics and Social Science* (Macmillan) argues that each major sociological approach encounters hermeneutic problems – a good review, if demanding in places. Richard Palmer (1969) *Hermeneutic Interpretation Theory in Schleiermacher, Dilthey, Heidegger and Gadamer* (Northwestern University Press) is lucid and comprehensive. Kurt Müller-Vollmer (ed.) (1986) *The Hermeneutics Reader* (Basil Blackwell) is an excellent source with a very wide selection of readings.

## NOTES

1 Until unification in 1871, 'Germany' was a confederated collection of independent states. Debates about philosophy and the social sciences were always inflected by issues around the nature of Germany and its orientation – whether or not to follow a 'western' path.

2 The Romantic Movement (see Chapter 2) is hard to define since it included a wide range of philosophical and literary figures, such as Goethe (1749–1832), William Wordsworth (1770–1850), Friedrich Schlegel (1772–1829) and Novalis (1772–1801). Romantics tended to value ideas of individual uniqueness, free creative genius and to prefer community to other abstractions such as 'humanity'.

3 An illustration – the affinity between the Russian words *nemet'* (dumb) and *nemets* (German) suggests some initial hermeneutic difficulties in early encounters with Teutonic peoples!

4 Dilthey addressed a large range of philosophical and literary topics and his work on the philosophical foundation of the *Geisteswissenschaften* took shape later in his life. For a long time his interest in the cultural sciences was dominated by a psychological approach (Outhwaite 1975). This discussion will focus on works with particular relevance for sociological theory.

5 Nietzsche, Bergson and Dilthey developed the philosophy of life (*lebensphilo-sophie*) in different ways in the late nineteenth century. One theme of this was that life and organic reality consist in movement and a continual process of 'becoming'. Opposed to both materialism and idealism, it claimed that life is known by intuition rather than logical inference and consciousness is the ultimate level of experience. It was impossible 'to go beyond consciousness, to see as it were, without eyes or to direct a cognitive gaze behind the eye itself' (Dilthey 1976b: 161).

6 A further example of such categories would be our experience of time. In opposition to Kant, Dilthey argues that time is a category of experience and as such, is not a transcendent ideal, which is a 'meaningless doctrine in human studies' (1976b: 210). There never *is* a present – experience is always memory of what has just been present. So time is there for us through the synthesizing unity of consciousness creating simultaneity, sequence, internal duration and change.

7 For Hegel objective mind, in systems of law, morality and ethics, stands against the subjective will of institutions of family, civil society and the state. Both objective and subjective minds are stages towards the Absolute. For Dilthey this is a rational and idealist construct, while his own concept is based on historical realities and refers to all systematic products of human consciousness (1976b: 194).

8 So far as I know, Durkheim and Dilthey did not comment on one another's work.

9 Respectively: *Hineinversetzen* (to transpose oneself mentally into something); *Nachbilden* (to imitate and reconstruct something); *Nacherleben* (to relive something in inner experience).

# CHAPTER 7

# German critiques of capitalism

The dispute between hermeneutic and naturalistic methods in sociology was rarely just a matter of methodology, but frequently involved judgements about the fate and nature of western societies. Critics of positivism often regarded naturalism as part of the tendency in a scientific and technical culture to submerge meaningful life in the icy waters of calculation. Thus the debate was part of the wider process whereby sociology attempted to grasp and diagnose the disruption of the traditional order and the explosive development of a new commercial and industrial society. Sociological theory developed around contrasts between modern and pre-modern aspects of social order, which in some ways served as its rationale. We have seen how classical sociology addressed the disruption of the old traditional order and the explosive development of a new commercial and industrial society. This sense of a great transition was in many ways crystallized in Ferdinand Tönnies' famous distinction between *Gemeinschaft* and *Gesellschaft*, which can roughly be understood as 'community' and 'society'. His contemporary, Georg Simmel, similarly expressed (albeit more subtly) concern with the cultural effects of an urban and commercial society. Whereas most preceding sociologists of the great transformation were broadly, if not uncritically, progressive in their outlook, with Tönnies and Simmel, progressive optimism faded behind a more nostalgic and pessimistic motif. This was to some extent a reflection of a divergence between German as opposed to French and British intellectual traditions, but was to become a broader, recurrent theme in later sociology. A claim often to be repeated was that modernity's scientific and technical achievements had destroyed something authentic and meaningful that had preceded it. This complaint arose from the Romantic reaction to the Enlightenment and French Revolution (see Chapter 2), but grew in intensity amidst the growing *fin-de-siècle* pessimism of the 1880s and 1890s (H. S. Hughes 1974). This was not just a passing mood, though, but became a dominant theme with deeper resonance in European culture, where the biblical myth of the Fall associated knowledge with sin and expulsion from paradise. As Weber commented, the acquisition of wisdom from the Tree of Knowledge involved a transgression and disqualification from the paradise of naivety (B. S. Turner 1992: 133–5). Knowledge of nature that could be harnessed in an industrial-technological civilization meant that there could be no return to the enchanted cultures of the past. Some theories, notably Marxism, promised future redemption, but the later German sociologists saw little prospect of this.

## COGS IN THE WHEELS OF MODERNITY

Central to this motif is the idea of the loss of totality and 'wholeness'. This critique seemed particularly relevant in Germany where industrialization and urbanization had occurred later but more rapidly than in France and Britain.[1] Underlying the Romantic critique of capitalism and industrialism was the question, which one finds still in Weber's sociology, of whether German economic, cultural and political development should follow the 'western' materialist path of Britain and France or whether its destiny lay in a national, spiritual culture. These issues came to a head during Bismarck's modernization and secularization drives after unification, which included the 1870s *Kulturkampf* (cultural struggle) with the Catholic clergy. One example of the Romantic conservatism was Paul Lagarde (1827–91), whose work not only displayed but also heightened despair over cultural conditions in Germany after unification. Often regarded as an intellectual precursor of National Socialism, along with similar writers such as Langbehn and Möller, Lagarde was antisemitic, regarding Jews as cosmopolitan carriers of modernity bringing dissolution of the old order (Stern 1974).[2] Lagarde loathed liberalism, free-market economies, materialism and parliamentary government. Reacting against Bismarck's modernization, he hoped for a new faith (a national, Germanic religion) that would restore a lost, imaginary past. Although this nationalistic cultural pessimism was in some ways specific to the German context, it shared roots both with Rousseau's cultural criticism and hostility to what was seen as the mechanistic thought of the Enlightenment; ideas that resurfaced during this period in French anti-Drefusards such as Maurras and Barrès. They in turn drew on the conservatism of de Maistre and de Bonald. However, the close association between France and post-Enlightenment modernity lessened the influence of the latter writers, while Lagarde could appeal more directly to a German nationalism which had tended to regard liberalism and parliamentarianism as western, alien forms. In his *Deutsche Schriften* (1878) Lagarde argued that the core of 'man' was not reason but will, and these spiritual needs of the soul were the most important. In the secular Bismarckian state, he saw nothing but retreat from morality, levelling of the rising masses and frivolous cheapening of standards.

Lagarde was an extreme and highly reactionary example of this thinking and I am *not* suggesting that sociologists (like Tönnies) who shared some of his views were in any sense precursors of fascism.[3] However, later classical German sociology did share aspects of the Romantic diagnosis of the modern age, which was informed by a deep sense of loss: of tradition, customs, folk wisdom, social solidarity, morality and enchantment (Pappenheim 1959). In the emerging widespread critique, indictments of industrial capitalism included:

- mechanization of life engenders a calculating outlook towards nature and society and dissolves people's bonds with them
- the world of machines follows its own course and escapes human direction
- commercialization of culture and politics reduces public life to the lowest common denominator of monetary equivalence
- humans have become alienated from work, from themselves, society and nature
- there has been an increase in selfish instrumentalism and a decline in civic-mindedness.

These ideas were to appear under the broad heading of 'mass society' theories in the first half of the twentieth century often with a conservative agenda, highlighting the alleged mediocrity of the mass, degeneration of culture to the lowest common denominator, the instrumentalism of commercial society and the disintegration of communities (e.g. Ortega y Gasset 1961). Some of these ideas appeared too in the form of a Marxist critique of modernity in Adorno and Horkheimer (1973).

Generally, Marxists attempted to draw a distinction between industrialism *per se*, which they saw as both progressive and inevitable, and capitalism as an exploitative but historically specific and doomed form of social organization. Even so this distinction was not always clear. Despite Marx's admiration for capitalism sweeping away traditional society and the 'idiocy of rural life', he also conveyed a sense of an authentic moral community undermined by crass commercialism illustrated for example in his essays on the Jewish Question (1844). Marxism projected into the future a recovery of an organic community as a model for communist society (Arato 1974). However, German sociologists of the later nineteenth century tended, in different degrees, to articulate warnings not only about capitalism but the growth of scientific-industrial civilization in general. This is a critique that sometimes drew on Marx (as did Tönnies and Simmel in different ways) but differs from Marxism in at least two further respects. First, it emphasized cultural rather than economic processes. Thus both Tönnies and Simmel were primarily concerned with the cultural consequences of capitalism and Simmel's opus, *The Philosophy of Money* (1900), treated money primarily as a cultural and symbolic rather than economic entity. Second, these critiques have a nostalgic and tragic motif that derives in part from counter-Enlightenment Romanticism, in that the alienation caused by capitalism would not be overcome. No agent of historical emancipation would thunder to the rescue of humanity nor could there be any return to an organic, communal past. For Simmel this was part of the 'cultural tragedy' of lost wholeness and authenticity (and one sometimes finds a similar sense of resignation in Weber) while for Tönnies there was some, limited hope for a restoration of communal relationships through the social democratic and trade union movement. However, this style of critique was neither necessarily 'left' nor 'right' in orientation. The Marxist critique of alienation and commodification drew on Romantic as well as socialist themes and one finds both facets in the critical thought of the later nineteenth century and beyond. Thus Tönnies drew both on socialist sources of radicalism and on Largarde's radical conservatism.[4]

## FERDINAND TÖNNIES' CRITIQUE OF CAPITALISM

Ferdinand Tönnies (1855–1936) was a major contributor to sociological theory and is most closely associated with his distinction between two basic types of society, *Gemeinschaft* and *Gesellschaft*.[5] Like many other classical sociologists, these followed in evolutionary sequence, the former epitomized by small scale rural communities and the latter by industrial societies. The main factor differentiating the two though was not economic but moral. His system is summarized in Figure 7.1. The two types of society arose from two basic forms of human will: *Wesenwille and Kürwille* respectively. *Wesenwille* or **essential will** is an underlying, organic

**Figure 7.1** Tönnies' *Gemeinschaft* and *Gesellschaft*

|  | *Gemeinschaft* | *Gesellschaft* |
|---|---|---|
| **Action orientation** | Essential will (*Wesenwille*) | Arbitrary will (*Kürwille*) |
| **Primary social relations** | Intimate and private; familial; bound in 'weal and woe' | Public and anonymous; strangers |
| **Production** | Rural | Industrial |
| **System** | Living organism* | Mechanical artifact* |
| **Example** | Language; folkways | Business; travel; sciences and companies |
| **Temporality** | Solidarity and continuity | Coexistence and transitory |
| **Property** | Communal | Exclusive |
| **Ethos** | Instinctual and habitual | Intellectual |

\* Note that Tönnies gives these terms meanings that *reverse* Durkheim's use and instinctive driving force, while *Kürwille* or **arbitrary will** (from Old German *Küren*, choice) is deliberative, purposive and future (goal) orientated. That Tönnies grounded his social typology in concepts of will did not indicate a desire to found human behaviour in psychology. Rather, it indicated what would later be called an 'action orientation' in which social organization was regarded ultimately as the result of human actions and dispositions. Indeed Tönnies regarded as social only those interactions that contain a normative element, while individual and private actions would be the province of psychology (Heberle 1973). Thus for Tönnies, society was a moral-normative entity and different types of society must by definition involve different moral codes. He regarded society as a product of will expressed in interactions guided by moral codes. Indeed in his (often sympathetic) critique of Marx, Tönnies argued that Marx's materialism had overlooked the extent to which social relations are morally constituted (Cahnman 1973b).

*Gemeinschaft* (community) groups form around essential will, in which membership is integral and self-fulfilling, in the sense that it does not serve any external purpose. Craft production 'for the delight in creating and conserving' (Tönnies 1971: 146) and enjoying for its own sake the solidarity of cooperation with other people would be an example of *Gemeinschaftlich* activity. These relationships were (and where they remain, are) governed by solidaristic ties of belonging. Such interactions are diffuse in that they consume the whole of a person's being and relations of solidarity, such as familial and friendship bonds, demand participation of the whole of our sentiments. Your friend, after all, is supposedly interested in all aspects of your life – family, love affairs, money problems, work and so on – whereas your bank manager (for example) is interested only in the state of your finances. Friendship is characteristic of *Gemeinschaft* relations which demand that we enter into social relationships with the whole of our being, while *Gesellschaft* interactions are highly specific and therefore fragmented.

The family is an important example of Tönnies' concept and he regarded the relation between mother and child as a pure form of *Gemeinschaft*. Original, *Gemeinschaftlich* societies were patriarchal (he rather glosses over the evidence of earlier matriarchy) where authority was derived from the father and passed on to the first-born son. This familial principle was then extended to the authority exercised by the community over a shared habitat. At this point there appeared a '*Gemeinschaft* of the mind' which (for reasons Tönnies assumes rather than explains) is 'the only real form of life' based on the closeness and physical proximity of blood relationships extended to society. Thus we find here a commonality of will and spirit, shared language, proximity of living space and friendships based on intimate knowledge of each other (Tönnies 1971: 255). *Gemeinschaft* embodied the 'feminine' principle of creativity and solidarity (even though subordinated to male authority) which lives on, though under continual threat, in artistic and craft activities. Tönnies' social theory thus reflected the common construction of the feminine as primal and natural, a naturalness that is under threat from impersonal (male) systems within which, paradoxically, women are gaining increasing equality. Simmel takes up a similar theme in his account of **objective culture**.

On the other hand, a group in which membership is based on some instrumental goal or formal organization displays *Gesellschaft* characteristics. A central idea here is the contract as a defining aspect of modern societies, as it was for Spencer whose influence on Tönnies' is clear (Lukes 1973: 143–4). Whereas in *Gemeinschaft*, people in small-scale units of production are the 'original and dominating power' in that they 'determine their economic condition', once united into nations this control begins to diminish. With international trade and the rise of commercial societies, power shifts towards merchants who harness the labour force of the nation, a process that achieves its highest form in the 'planned capitalist production of large-scale industry'. Further, the nation itself loses power here in that 'this merchant class is by nature, and mostly also by origin, international as well as national and urban, i.e., it belongs to *Gesellschaft*, not *Gemeinschaft*'. Later all social groups and dignitaries and to a large extent, the whole people, acquire the characteristics of the *Gesellschaft*.

The emergence of *Gesellschaft* from *Gemeinschaft* occurred in the transition from communal-feudal to contractual social relationships. The village community developed into the town, which though complex, retained some characteristics of *Gemeinschaft* life, such as personal (face-to-face) interactions, strong kinship ties, craft production and local power over the economy. However, with the development of the city, communal characteristics were almost entirely lost. Individuals or families took on separate identities and their common locale, whether accidental or deliberately chosen, was no longer determined by traditional values and status. The city is typical of *Gesellschaft* in general, being essentially a commercial town and, in so far as commerce dominates its productive labour, a factory town. Capital thus became the means for the appropriation of products of labour or for the exploitation of workers. The city is also the centre of science and culture, which accompany commerce and industry. But while in *Gemeinschaft* art was expressive of religion, tradition and life, in *Gesellschaft* the arts must make a living and are exploited in a capitalistic way. Thoughts spread and change with astonishing rapidity. Speeches and books through mass distribution become stimuli of far-reaching importance. The 'mass' acquire increasing significance and 'strive for pleasure and entertainment' held in check only by limitations of money and state repression (Tönnies 1971: 150).

This led to a process of increasing global integration but above all, *sameness*. Cities grew into nations and yet entire countries and the world itself 'begins to resemble one large city'. Traditionally, the national capital, as residence of the court or centre of government, manifests some features of the city while retaining its national character. But increasingly, the city and capital are synthesized into the metropolis, which is the highest expression of *Gesellschaft*. Not only is it the essence of a national society, but also it contains representatives from a whole group of nations, i.e. of the world. In the metropolis, money and capital are unlimited and almighty. It is able to produce and supply goods and science for the entire earth as well as laws and public opinion for all nations. It represents the world market and world traffic; its newspapers are world papers, its people come from all corners of the earth, being curious and hungry for money and pleasure. We shall see in Simmel a similar, if more ambivalent, concern with social life in the metropolis as an epitome of modern conditions and the dominance of money.

By contrast with many social evolutionists, then, Tönnies did not regard the emergence of modern society as necessarily progressive. *Gesellschaft* is rather the cause of alienation and the fragmentation of life into discrete spheres of activity. Tönnies paints a picture of a mass of isolated people in the city: free persons who have contacts with each other, who exchange and cooperate, but without any solidarity. No community or common will develops among them except such as might occur sporadically or as a leftover from former conditions. In the main, these numerous external contacts, contracts, and contractual relations merely 'cover up . . . inner hostilities and antagonistic interests'. Whereas in *Gemeinschaft*, property was communal and based on traditional rights, in *Gesellschaft* it became individualistic and exclusive. As in Marx's critique of commodification, money is the key social relationship in modern society and reduces everything to the level of commodities, thereby equalizing the different social and cultural values and making them interchangeable. The yardstick of human relations is no longer intrinsic 'worth' but value measured by labour time and production costs.

Within *Gesellschaft* new cultural and economic inequalities arise. Only the upper strata, the rich and the cultured, are 'really active and alive' in the city and they dictate the standards to which the lower strata have to conform, which they do, in order to gain social power and independence. Yet the system is fraught with the threat of class conflict, for example between the rich and so-called 'cultured class' and the poor or servant class, as well as between capital and labour. This is interesting in part because it opens the possibility of a cultural-consumption, rather than purely economically, based definition of class. Tönnies was less concerned with the divergent material interests represented by these classes so much the way they exemplified different types of moral will. The 'two-fold' character of labour that Marx identified, as use and exchange value (see Chapter 4), was better understood as a contradiction between essential and arbitrary will, respectively (Cahnman 1973b).[6] The production of use values involved activities intrinsic to labour and presupposed cooperation and communal property relationships. Exchange value, on the other hand, involved treating objects and other people as means to an end (profit) and presupposed a society of competitive individuals.

Tönnies believed therefore that he had placed Marx's critique on a more sociological and less economic basis.

Unlike Marx, however, Tönnies did not expect an ultimate victory of the proletariat over all existing social conditions. Tönnies was warning that rational calculation and contractual relationships involved impoverishment, diminution and worsening living qualities especially through commodification. This demolished and despoiled personal qualities of life, of skill and enjoyment. Science itself, rather than a means of liberation, was a product of *Gesellschaft*, itself a 'leveller' which analytically reduced actualities to abstractions. Science produced a new associational world of specialization in which everyone pursued his or her own interests in a spirit of 'uncommitted rationality'. This threatened to result in the degeneration of moral choices through what might now be called the dominance of 'expert cultures' (e.g. Giddens 1990).

The transformation to *Gesellschaft* brings further changes in its wake. People change their temperaments in line with the pace and conditions of their daily life, which become hasty and changeable. Simultaneously, along with this revolution in the social order, there is a gradual change in the law. The contract as such becomes the basis of the entire system, and the rational will of *Gesellschaft*, formed by its interests, combines with the authority of the state to create, maintain and change the legal system. The state increasingly frees itself from traditions and customs of the past and the belief in their importance, thus the forms of law change from a product of the folkways and mores and the law of custom into 'purely legalistic law, a product of policy'. The 'numerous and manifold fellowships, communities, and commonwealths' of the past, which grew up organically, are replaced by bureaucratic public officials. Similarly, people's personalities undergo changes as they adapt to new and arbitrary legal constructions. So law based in folkways, mores and the conviction of their infallibility gives way to positive law based on convention and contract.

Finally, as a consequence of these changes and in turn encouraging them, there is a 'complete reversal of intellectual life'. While originally rooted entirely in the imagination, it now becomes dependent upon thinking. There is a Comtean sense here of belief in unseen forces ('invisible beings, spirits and gods') being replaced by observable nature. Religion, which was rooted in folk life or at least closely related to it, cedes its supremacy to science, which derives from and corresponds to *Gesellschaft* consciousness. Such consciousness is a product of learning and culture and, therefore, 'remote from the people'. Whereas religion made immediate contact with the people because its morality could be transmitted through generations, science receives its meaning only from observation of the laws of social life, from which it derives rules for a rational social order. So whereas Saint-Simon and Comte looked to science to provide the basis for a new morality, Tönnies sees science as the amoral epitome of an instrumental and rootless culture in which relationships can no longer be governed by social solidarity.

Thus Tönnies took an uncompromising stance against the new industrial order pointing out that unless elements of the old society were retained the prospect was for a Hobbesian war of all.[7] Not unlike Durkheim, he regarded the 'substance of the common spirit' in modern societies as 'so weak . . . that it has to be excluded from consideration'. In contrast to the family and cooperative relationships, there are only separate individuals without common understanding, lacking 'time-honored custom or belief' that might create a common bond (Tönnies 1971: 149). This unrestricted freedom allows all to destroy and subjugate one another, or, being aware of possible greater advantage, to conclude agreements and foster new ties. In the absence of social solidarity, 'only fear of clever retaliation restrains them from attacking one another, and, therefore, even peaceful and neighborly relations are in reality based upon a warlike situation'. The state protects this civilization through legislation and politics. In a swipe at those who regard such a dismal state of affairs as indicating human progress, he comments that science and public opinion, attempting to conceive it as necessary and eternal, glorify it as progress towards perfection.

*Gemeinschaft* and *Gesellschaft* was a turning point in the history of sociology in that it attempted to capture the experience of modernity in archetypes that can be recovered from all sociological data. The two types are ideal (simplified and extreme) not empirical concepts – one would never find a pure type of either and most social situations involve a combination of both. *Gemeinschaftlich* forms persist within *Gesellschaft* – for example in trade union organizations that offer the possibility of recreating new forms of social solidarity. However, there was for Tönnies, as for many German sociologists of this period, a widespread longing for *Gemeinschaft* that was romantically tinged, even when appearing in social democratic form. His account overlooked the question of whether the idea of communal society was a core myth of modernity itself (which I suggested in Chapter 2), as he did the negative aspects of *Gemeinschaft*, such as intolerance, uniformity and strict religious and moral constraints. The idea that community disappears from urban or modern life, leaving a soulless moral wasteland is a rhetorical rather than empirical claim. Actual communities not only survive (as urban villages) but also are recreated within modern societies, such as in industrially based communities. Talcott Parsons for example (following Durkheim) argued that professional communities recreate *Gemeinschaft* in systems of non-monetary regulation (e.g. Parsons 1973). Tönnies, as Durkheim argued, had an inadequate theory of the bases of social integration within *Gesellschaft*. The free play of interests among atomized individuals could not explain social solidarity within complex societies, which must be subject to underlying laws (Lukes 1973: 141–4). 'Contract', which for Tönnies (as for Spencer) was a key concept, needs to be seen as the product of social order not its foundation. Nevertheless, the contrast between community and society has been a point of reference for much sociology, especially that concerned to rediscover community within modern societies and the need to recreate community has been a recurrent theme in many political and social movements.

**SIMMEL – SOCIOLOGICAL FLÂNEUR**[8]

There were important differences between the sociology of Tönnies and Georg Simmel (1856–1917). Simmel saw social fragmentation and alienation as general features of modern society rather than a class project of the bourgeoisie. Both writers stressed the interactive nature of social relations, but Simmel gave far more attention to the nuances, the apparently unimportant aspects of everyday life than any previous sociologist. Simmel was thus more sensitive than Tönnies to new forms of integration and sociability in modern society. Like Tönnies, Simmel rejected the positivist view of society as an objective system dominating its members and in neo-Kantian style saw human agents as actively constructing the categories of the social. Both were significant in promoting the idea of 'society' and social relationships, rather than the state or other formal structures, as the main object of investigation. Simmel regarded society as an intricate web of multiple interruptions and relations between individuals, which together embodied the principle of association. Both, again, rejected the organic holistic concept of society and sought to differentiate sociology from other disciplines especially biology and psychology (Swingewood 1985: 134–5).

With Simmel the emphasis of sociology shifted away from exclusive concern with macroscopic, public sphere issues, towards individuals and interactions, and often, the apparently mundane. Simmel was interested in, among other things, social types, such as the miser, pauper, spendthrift, stranger and the adventurer. In his sociology apparently unimportant nuances of everyday life – courtesy, coyness, fashion, even sociology of the glance – are brought into the foreground. For a long time he was neglected, but has recently been rediscovered, especially in cultural studies, as a writer who appreciated the fragmentary and fleeting character of social life. For this reason he is sometimes described as a **postmodernist** *avant la lettre*, who deconstructed the Romantic notion of the subject (Weinstein and Weinstein 1993: 203).

Ambivalence is the keynote of Simmel's sociology. It is often noted (e.g. Coser 1991a) that Simmel was a 'stranger in the academy', not gaining a full-time professorship until 1914, three years before his death. Perhaps as a consequence, he rejected conventional academic style and wrote as an essayist, aiming to capture the fragmentary moments of social interaction. He rarely cited references and often digressed from the main argument. He was reluctant to define terms unambiguously and often developed an argument in one direction, only to pull up short and turn it around. For example, having elaborated his central concept of the meaning of 'form' as opposed to 'content' in sociology, he said 'of course, what is form in one respect is content in another' (Simmel 1971: 25). He was a controversial figure and more orthodox sociologists were often critical of the style and content of his work, although it had an important role in intellectual circles in Berlin and Heidelberg, where his lectures were popular. According to David Frisby (1981):

> No sociologist before him had sought to capture the modes of experiencing modern life nor the fleeting moments of interaction. Simmel's sociological texts are richly populated with fortuitous fragments of reality, with seemingly superficial phenomena, with a myriad of social vignettes.
>
> (Frisby 1981: 103)

The background to Simmel's work was diverse. It included Spencer's evolutionary theory, and his emphasis on conflict and competition and social atomism, in which individuals were the unit of study. It further embodied hermeneutics,[9] the idea of intuitive understanding and the neo-Kantian revival, which as we have seen, informed a widespread reaction against positivism and evolutionary theory. Neo-Kantianism influenced his methodology, which applied to the social sciences questions such as 'How can the human mind arrive at knowledge?' and 'What is society?' Like the neo-Kantians, Simmel rejected the idea of the mind as a passive object of either natural stimuli or social forces, conceiving of it rather as active, constituting its object and imposing order on nature. Simmel's critique of sociological reason focused on the activity of subjects who internalized, but nonetheless constructed and manipulated social types, which were the categorical basis of social life. The major influences and impact of Simmel's work are summarized in Figure 7.2, which is elaborated at the end of this chapter.

Simmel shared with Durkheim an early and in some ways formative interest in Spencer. Thus Simmel understood social evolution in terms of increasing social differentiation in the transition from tradition to modernity, although he was ambivalent as to its consequences. His sociology develops themes of differentiation, individualism and competitiveness, although these are taken in directions that Spencer would not have anticipated. Further, Simmel had no sympathy with functional approaches to the social and emphasized the ubiquity and centrality of conflict, albeit understood largely in terms of individual and group competitiveness. Competition, moreover, was not necessarily destructive but was rather a form of association in its own right. Like Spencer (and unlike Durkheim) Simmel rejected the idea of 'society' as an organic unity, arguing instead that 'society' was a metaphor, a collective noun for **forms of association** that were abstractions from everyday life. Simmel attempted to view society simultaneously from the standpoint of the individual and social, since for him individuals were both 'in and outside' society. We reveal parts of ourselves in social interaction but hold parts of ourselves

**Figure 7.2** Mapping Simmel's impact on sociology

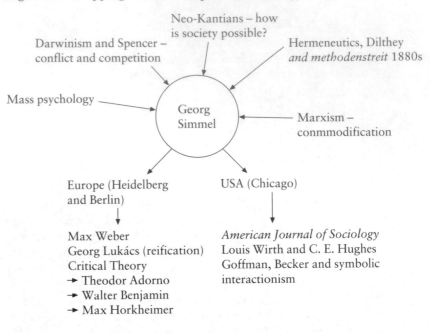

Neo-Kantians – how
is society possible?

Darwinism and Spencer –
conflict and competition

Hermeneutics, Dilthey
*and methodenstreit* 1880s

Mass psychology

Georg
Simmel

Marxism –
conmmodification

Europe (Heidelberg
and Berlin)

USA (Chicago)

Max Weber
Georg Lukács (reification)
Critical Theory
→ Theodor Adorno
→ Walter Benjamin
→ Max Horkheimer

*American Journal of Sociology*
Louis Wirth and C. E. Hughes
Goffman, Becker and symbolic
interactionism

back. We present different aspects of the self in different interactions. 'We see the other person as generalized in some measure . . . We think of him in terms not only of his singularity but also in terms of a general sociological category' (Simmel 1971: 24).

The elliptical and unstructured nature of Simmel's style has been the subject of considerable attention. His sociology was not generally written in a way that appealed to data for support (one will find very few statistics in Simmel) but rather he invoked a kind of shared intuition, inviting us to recognize the ways of the social in his vignettes and descriptions. For example, when Simmel said 'there is more than a little satisfaction in the misfortune of a friend' (1971: 93) he attempted to capture the pervasiveness of competition in everyday life and the ambivalence of intimate relationships. Neither friendship nor competition are quite what they first appear, but are interwoven in complex sociality. But he suggests this by appeal to shared social experience rather than to a body of objective evidence. Simmel's style is that of an essayist, a street café voyeur, a *flâneur* rather than a scientific sociologist.[10]

### Form, content and types

This is not to say that Simmel's sociology was entirely intuitive and unsystematic. Indeed, he was sometimes criticized for writing in an overly formalistic and descriptive way; Sorokin for example saw formal sociology as a 'purely scholastic and dead science, a kind of almost useless catalogue of "human relations"'(Tenbruck 1959: 64). Simmel's 'formal sociology' was to study the forms of association that made generalized and routinized social interactions possible. Experience is inescapably organized in forms. Try for example to imagine colour: one cannot imagine 'pure' colour, but only colours appearing in particular shapes, or forms (Weingartner 1959). There are then two components to experience, a formal, organizing aspect and content, what is perceived. Another way of understanding this is through Simmel's analogy with geometry. He described sociology as the 'geometry of social life' (Simmel 1971: 28ff) in that just as geometry was concerned with the abstract relational properties of the material objects, irrespective of their particular content or nature, so sociology would describe the forms through which the content of social life took place.[11] 'Contents' are the materials of sociation – everything that is present in individuals, such as drives, interests, purposes, inclinations and psychic states (Simmel 1971: 24).

To the question, 'How is society possible?' Simmel answered that it is an ongoing creation of its subjects, and hence unlike nature (in Kantian terms) society needs no observer, since it is directly realized by its own elements. This occurs through **typification**, the process whereby we construct social categories. In order to interact socially, we must continuously add to and subtract from another's individuality, as Simmel put it. We never encounter anyone as unique (this would be 'formless' experience) but always as 'more and less than they are'. More, because we typify someone as a parent, sister, student, teacher, or whatever – attributing characteristics that extend beyond the individual. Less, because we thereby subtract from someone's individuality by relating to them as a bearer of a general category. Society is possible only because of these abstractions that are the basis of formal associations. Forms are relatively stable features of social life – such as superordination and subordination, exchange and competition, inclusion and exclusion – that have regular features irrespective of the particular contexts in which they appear. So conflict and competition, for example, will have a recognizable structure and dynamic whether they appear in the family, in a royal court, or between nations. But Simmel's emphasis was not on formal *structures* so much as on social *relations*, that is, interactions that always contain the capacity for innovation and change. Thus *unlike* geometric relations, their particular nature and intensity will vary with the circumstances in which they appear.

Even so, Simmel believed that it was possible to separate form and content analytically in (relative) abstraction, if one follows rules for their identification (see Figure 7.3). First, one must identify the same form in different contexts, then show that a particular 'content' is realized in dissimilar forms. Thus to describe the form 'competition' one would find it in different settings, such as families, between political parties and states. At the same time familial, political or national interests would be

Figure 7.3 Simmel and the 'geometry of social life'

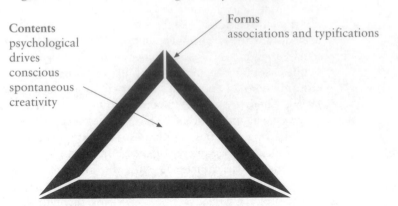

**Contents**
psychological
drives
conscious
spontaneous
creativity

**Forms**
associations and typifications

BUT what is form in one context can be content in another . . .

manifest in various forms, such as conflict, super-subordination, cooperation and so forth.

Further, there is a balance of individuality and abstraction in different
social forms – some are more abstract and impersonal than others. Money
exchanges represent a high degree of impersonality and abstraction,
whereas love relationships have low typification and higher degrees of
individuality. Thus the affective structure of intimacy is based on what
each of the two participants gives or shows only to the one other person
and to nobody else. Intimacy, then, is based on the exclusive content of
a relationship between members, regardless of its specific nature. However, when intimate relations become formalized, as in marriage, their
character changes. Marriage is no longer simply an intimate exchange
between two people, but is socially regulated and historically transmitted,
requiring the official recognition by external authorities of law or religion.
Nonetheless, modern marriage, Simmel says, seems to have a weaker
objective character than unions of the past, allowing a greater degree of
individuality, creativity and differentiation (Simmel 1971: 227ff).

This approach is thus more nuanced than later formulations of the
'social role' (e.g. in Parsons) since Simmel aims to capture tension between
contents and forms in dynamic interaction. The increasing social differentiation and multiplication of forms has ambiguous consequences. On
the one hand, it results in a blurring of boundaries between our public
and private selves. While relationships of intimacy are becoming less
formalized, some public interactions are more relaxed – for example
exchanges between superiors and subordinates become more courteous
and apparently egalitarian. This (as Tönnies also noted) reflects the way
that social encounters are unlikely to consume our whole being and can
therefore be approached with a degree of distance. On the other hand,
social interaction is increasingly stylized in that (precisely because of the
process of social fragmentation) it is pursued playfully as an end in itself,

detached from specific contents. Conversation, for example, becomes an 'art' to be pursued with tact following unspoken rules, that for example, you should exclude references to your personal character, mood and fate. Similarly, eroticism as the pursuit of sexual interests is subordinated to coquetry, the play of 'hinted consent and hinted denial' where all participants understand that this is a game not meant to lead to actual seduction (Simmel 1971: 134). Thus sociability as a playform becomes an end in itself which mirrors and parodies the serious business of social life.

Yet the analysis of social forms may reveal a whole world of social relations in apparently unimportant facets of social life. This is illustrated by his concept of the 'senses as forms' (e.g. Simmel [1916] 1997: 109–19). A social world may be encapsulated in a glance, revealing mutuality, self-disclosure, concealment, and subordination or superordination. The erotic glance contains an 'absorbing moment of playful delight' when two people's eyes meet and both are drawn transiently into an absorbing moment of experience, of 'mutual conspiracy beyond convention'. The glance among lovers constitutes communion and conspiracy beyond social norms. Thus the eye has a 'uniquely sociological function' of establishing reciprocity and intimacy, a gift to the other, which assumes equality. However, inequality inhibits the glance (it was considered subversive for a Black in the southern USA to look a White in the eyes) and where no reciprocity is possible the eyes are hidden. Thus we close the eyes of the dead and place a hood over the face of the executed or executioner.

## Modernity, money and alienation

The formation of an objective culture, in which social forms become autonomous and self-sufficient, is the outcome of a long developmental process of the human spirit, which passed through several stages in which the influence of Hegel and hermeneutic theorists is apparent:

⇒ The desire for gratification and self-consciousness, pure experience.
⇒ Preliminary forms in which skills are developed and objects have use value.
⇒ Protoforms in which specialized skills and crafts develop.
⇒ Objective forms in which action is pursued for its own sake and liberated from the requirements of practical activity.
⇒ World forms – language, morals, art, legal systems, technologies.

This is not a simple evolutionary scheme, however, in that there is a dialectical tension between the appearance of cultural forms in which activities are pursued increasingly as ends in themselves and the increasing instrumentality and greyness of everyday life. While social forms become increasingly self-sufficient and detached from mundane purpose, life in the modern city, governed by the cash nexus, generates increasing uniformity that belies the appearance of diversity. Fashion for example reveals the desires for both individuality (to stand apart) and for conformity, since its *raison d'être* is to be a *follower*. Modernity establishes atomized 'cool reserve and anonymous objectivity' (Simmel [1900] 1990: 457). This diagnosis is reiterated in Weber, for whom the tendency of complex organizations was towards increasing formal rationality, bureaucratization and loss of meaning (*Sinnverlust*).

The instrumentality and calculability of modern life is analysed in Simmel's longest work, *The Philosophy of Money* ([1900] 1990) as well as essays such as 'The metropolis and mental life' (1971b). In these works he juxtaposes freedom and impersonality with the sense of a lost or threatened culture typical of *fin-de-siècle* German sociology. The development of money, he argues, is an element in a profound cultural trend. Like Tönnies' (one might call) 'culturalized Marxism' Simmel analysed money, the quintessential symbol of materialism, precisely *as a symbol*, and stressed its cultural meanings. Indifferent to all specific purposes, the elevation of money stands for the dominance of means over ends in society. The money economy creates a paradoxical kind of freedom in that impersonal relations facilitate individuality (the wageworker is more free than the serf) yet the decline of what Simmel called 'the old social obligations' promoted the atomization of society and the 'colourlessness of modern life' ([1900] 1990: 177).

This is further illustrated in what Simmel depicts as the 'blasé attitude'. After warning about the dangers of an immoderately sensuous way of life, Simmel suggests that cities cultivate a blasé attitude because an overload of sensations leads to indifference between things – the meaning and value of distinctions are lost. This psychic mood is the subjective reflection of a complete money economy – money takes the place of all qualitative relations between things – reduced to the distinction 'how much?' This is a partial echo of Marx, except that for Simmel money is a cultural trend, rather than the expression of property relations. Money is a leveller that flattens everything to a single dimension, such that anything can be bought and sold. Only self-interest appears logical while selfless motives appear not to be natural, flowing from irrational forces of feeling and volition (Simmel [1900] 1990: 439). Cool reserve and anonymous objectivity dominate modern exchanges, such that the 'slot machine is the ultimate example of the mechanical character of the modern economy' in which the human relationship is completely eliminated (p. 461). Cultural consequences of this include increasing cynicism, along with a loss of integrating beliefs,[12] and depersonalization as essential human qualities become interchangeable. There is antipathy towards money which, being impersonal, may be regarded as an inappropriate gift, not corresponding to the moral economy of friendship. Prostitution is degrading because the most intimate relations are reduced to their generic content, sex, while money itself resembles the quantities of prostitution – indifference, infidelity, lack of ties and complete objectification.

Simmel saw no possibility of return to pre-capitalist harmony; even if socialism were to replace capitalism it would simply intensify bureaucratic impersonality and the complete calculability of life. This theme of the cultural tragedy of lost wholeness became more explicit in Simmel's last works, such as the 'The crisis of culture' ([1916] 1997), in which he develops Dilthey's notion of the World Spirit while drawing on Marx, Hegel and Romantic dissatisfaction with modernity. The tragedy of modern culture arises from the increasing objectivity of life in which world forms (like language, morals, technical and legal systems) lose links with the subject and take on a life of their own. We are left in a world of cultural fragments devoid of meaning. This is a tragedy in the classical sense, in that like the character whose otherwise noble qualities are fatally flawed, the destruction of the unified subject is the necessary result of the very nature of social life. To be social is to engage in interaction creatively, generating types and forms of association that are ultimately destined to take on an alienated character (Nedelmann 1991). The human being becomes the 'bearer of the compulsion with which this logic rules developments' (Simmel [1916] 1997: 72) opening a new phase in the age-old struggle between life and form. The dominance of money does not give rise to cultural alienation though, rather it is itself an expression of the prevalence of means over ends and the cultural trend towards increasing objectivity (Simmel [1900] 1990: 56).

The development of money as a social form further reflects a modern pattern of differentiation between symbolic and material relations. Symbolism was as much a part of 'primitive' as of highly developed cultures. But the latter frees us from symbols in cognition (which becomes more empirical) while making us more dependent on them in practical matters of everyday life, as in the case of money, which is essential to condense what would otherwise be impossibly complex transactions. Similarly, Simmel suggests, conflicts will be played out not only directly, in strikes, wars etc., but also (and more often) symbolically through negotiation in which contending parties imagine the relative strength of the other and the consequences of action ([1900] 1990: 148–9). Written prior to the world wars of the twentieth century, this view now appears hopelessly over optimistic. Yet in a sense the Cold War was a war in the imagination, perhaps the epitome of symbolic conflict – with computer simulated wargames and exercises, ritual confrontations, not to mention continuous cinematic and televisual scenarios.

Money is interwoven with the reordering of spatial relations, creating new dimensions of proximity and distance. Money stands in between people and products as an intermediary preventing immediacy (Davis 1973). Inequalities are relations of space both in the literal sense that classes are divided by residential areas, and in the sense that inequality creates social distance – hierarchy is a spatial concept of 'higher' and 'lower'. The stranger moves through space – a synthesis of wandering and detachment, presence and absence in ways facilitated by money. The stranger is interested in money because it provides chances that are open to fully entitled persons or indigenous people through personal relations. The trader is a stranger but the stranger is also disposed to become a trader, especially once settled within the group (Simmel [1900] 1990: 224–5). From this, Simmel argues, we can understand the popular association between Jews and money – Jews are permanent strangers generally prohibited from owning land but exempt from laws against usury. Moreover, popular resentment against finance houses (wrongly associated with Jews) is resentment against an indifferent, characterless force whose essence seems to be personified by strangers (p. 227).

Money not only is evidence of increasing abstraction, but also itself becomes more abstract. Once tied to an apparent guarantee of value (gold) it now floats freely and expands into more abstract forms like credit, spending money you have not got, trading on future prices etc. – imaginary and symbolic worlds that Simmel did not directly anticipate but his analysis suggested. Money, then, is iconic for the modern age, bringing freedom and depersonalization, proximity and distance. Money and the urban economy reduce spatial distance between people while separating 'nature' from modern life, for which it becomes an object of contemplation. The stylization of nature means it is constructed as something internally unattainable, a promise that is never fully kept and an entity that responds to our most passionate devotion. Money has allowed urban people to take flight into nature yet stands between them and nature ([1900] 1990: 476–8). Where new territories are opened up for mass exploration (such as the Alps) this appears as a standardized, 'framed' and already 'pictured' landscape (Frisby and Featherstone 1997). Although, like Tönnies and Weber, Simmel mourned a wholeness of meaning, he also hints that this was probably always an illusion constructed by modernist sensibilities.

### Women and objective culture

Like other 'founding fathers' Simmel was aware that the transformation of gender relationships is one of the core elements of modernization. He went further than most others (although Tönnies had hinted at this too) in regarding the very process of the formation of objective culture as gendered. The separation between subjective and objective culture is also a divide between feminine and masculine culture, in that objective culture was founded on a 'male way of seeing' (Vucht Tijssen 1991). The features of a male culture were the pursuit of grand ideals in a goal-orientated way; increased specialization of the division of labour; separation between professional activities and subjective rationality; repression of emotions and subjective experience. Capitalism intensifies the dominance of male culture as money creates a division of labour between domestic (female) work and the (paid) work of men, with the consequence that a woman's economic value loses substance and she appears to be supported by her husband, a liability which gives rise to dowry (Simmel [1900] 1990: 375). He draws attention (not unlike Engels) to the paradox that proletarian women had been chased from the home while bourgeois women were confined within it. Therefore economic autonomy would be a curse for one but a blessing for the other.

This male culture appears universal because of the naïve identification of 'human' with 'man', an association made explicit in languages where the generic term is masculine. Indeed, Simmel noted, in many cultures feminine adjectives are applied to men to denote inadequate performance. Men have recognized neither the male bias in objective culture, nor the autonomy of the female principle, because the master does not need to think about the fact that he *is* master (Vromen 1987).

Thus far, Simmel's analysis resonates with some contemporary feminist theory, but gets more problematic when he goes on to discuss 'female culture'. This reflects the view, which we find too in Comte, Durkheim and Tönnies, that women are closer than men to 'nature' – thus forgetting his own argument that the 'natural' is itself a social construction. Women, he argues, transcend the division of objective and subjective labour, and have a wholeness of being, such that while men involve only part of themselves in sexual relationship, women commit the 'whole of their being'. In short, men are more inclined to be rational while women do not need rationality 'to get to the realm of absolute'. Indeed, 'women are more embedded in the species type than are men' so women are 'closer to the dark, primitive forces of nature' (Simmel 1971: 122). As more 'whole' beings, women are less fragmented and are therefore more sensitive to criticism and more faithful. A female objective culture then would value activities such as medicine, theatre, art and performance, home and socialization, which best suit women's natures.

Simmel's remedy for the dominance of masculine culture is a reappraisal of the female form of life and the reinforcement of the position of women in society. This could lead towards an independent female culture or to a culture common to men and women that had more female nuances. Marianne Weber (1998), who had also taken issue with Durkheim's critique of feminism, argued that Simmel confuses facts with values by confronting femininity as an autonomous phenomenon with roots in nature. He had not addressed what women themselves might want and had limited the sphere of female creativity to those spheres that would avoid a duality of life and form. In the process he had projected an unacceptable idealization of home and service. Like earlier social theorists, Simmel projected on to women a set of 'natural' attributes that men find it hard to fulfil themselves (Marianne Weber 1998). This further illustrates how classical sociology theorized the transformation of gender relations in terms of the nature/society dualism – which was to become a centrally contested division in subsequent sociological theory.

I leave no spiritual heirs . . .[13]

Despite his reluctance to leave a school of followers, Simmel's work exercised diverse influence over the formation of subsequent theories (see Figure 7.2). A true 'follower' of Simmel would not attempt to apply his ideas so much as absorb them and move on to enrich a variegated vision of social life. Indeed, his influence does seem to have become manifest in the works of theorists whose indebtedness was rarely acknowledged. Two areas are mentioned here – western Marxism and symbolic interactionism.

### Western Marxism

Several young students, who attended Simmel's lectures and his informal Sunday gatherings, subsequently became theorists of 'western Marxism'. This was a broad theoretical tendency that included Critical Theory (e.g. Adorno and Benjamin) and Georg Lukács (1885–1971), which avoided the doctrinal rigidity of Soviet Marxism and was generally philosophical and cultural in orientation. One can see echoes of Simmel's attention to the minutiae of social life in Theodor Adorno's concept of 'unintentional truth' where the apparent trivia of popular culture encapsulates a whole world of social relationships (Buck-Morss 1977: 77–81). Simmel's critique of modernity was generally significant for western Marxism, even where his influence was vehemently denied. Lukács at one point regarded formal sociology as part of the intellectual context for fascism, as 'subjectivism, complacent cynicism, frivolous dilettantism elevated into methodology destroying objective scientific spirit' (Lukács 1980: 452). But later he claimed that 'he had seen Marx tinged by Simmel and Weber and . . . the properly scholarly use of knowledge of Marx was greatly influenced by the philosophy and sociology of Simmel' (Tokei 1972).

During the 1910s Lukács adhered to a generalized Romantic anti-capitalism, which manifested a more tragic dimension of resignation in the intellectual milieu of the *fin de siècle* (Löwy 1979: 48ff). The dominant theme, which we see in Tönnies and Simmel, was the opposition of culture and civilization, in which *Kultur* referred to the universe of religious values, spiritual and aesthetic traditions. On the other hand, *Zivilization* referred to material, industrial and technical modernity with its ambivalent and often destructive consequences. This kind of philosophy lent itself to both 'left' and 'right' critiques of modernity, the combination of which was portrayed in the character of de Naphta, the Jesuit Communist in Thomas Mann's *The Magic Mountain* ([1928] 1960), another product of this milieu. Lukács' early (and probably most influential) work *History and Class Consciousness* (1923) was a classic of western Marxism and combined a cultural critique of capitalism with a theory of class consciousness and proletarian revolution. Not unlike Simmel, Lukács interpreted Marx's critique of commodity fetishism as a cultural critique of reified consciousness in which social relationships, the objective products of human subjectivity, took on the appearance of things – natural, independent and unalterable. This Simmelian view was given a Leninist twist in that for Lukács, proletarian consciousness could escape reification precisely because it was the 'unified subject-object of history' – its interests coincided with those of universal humanity. Thus the revolution would be a grand moment of transcendence and authenticity in which subjectivity and objectivity were reunited. However, Lukács shared the Romantic (and Leninist) distrust of the masses, in that the 'empirical consciousness' of the proletariat may be 'false' (distorted by a reified culture) so the repository of true consciousness lay with those who adopted the 'standpoint of the proletariat', that is, the Party.

### Simmel, symbolic interaction and the self

On the other side of the Atlantic, Simmel (and Tönnies') works were used in quite different ways than in central Europe. The earliest English translations of Simmel appeared in the Chicago based *American Journal of Sociology*, where he was interpreted as a sociologist of urban space and interpersonal interaction. However, there is some affinity between Simmel's idea of the self as continually presented in social interaction, from which we stand back and observe reflexively, and symbolic interactionism developed by theorists such as George Herbert Mead (1863–1931), Charles Cooley (1864–1929) and Herbert Blumer (1900–87). Simmel was not a direct precursor of symbolic interactionism, which owed more to pragmatism (Ritzer 1983: 299ff), but both approaches differ from structural theories by placing the actor at the centre of analysis. Charles Cooley's *Human Nature and the Social Order* (1902) argues that the imaginations that people have of one another are the solid facts of society, thus what he called the 'looking glass self' has the capacity to see ourselves as we see any social object. This means that we can imagine how we appear to others; imagine judgements likely to be made about that appearance; develop a sense of self based on these. This also opens capacities to see oneself as possessing dispositions or general features of a role and to reflect on the construction of our identity. We can extend this self concept to external objects such as clothes, a football team, a car, or indeed, any external object.

Mead's *Mind, Self and Society* (1933) argued that consciousness was reflexive and interpretative because it was possible only through language that allows us to reflect on the meaning of symbols and offer a variety of interpretations of them. Language is unique in this respect as a symbolic system. We might understand that a red star is a symbol of communism, or gesture (such as shaking a fist) is a symbol of anger and so forth, but the star symbol cannot explain other symbols, the gesture cannot explain other gestures. Language, however, has the capacity for infinite layers of interpretation since we must use words to explain the meaning of other words. Now, if the self is constructed through language then the

dynamics of the self and others are open to complex layers of interpretation and reflexive distancing. It is this property that symbolic
interactionism has attempted to elaborate.

For Mead the self was constructed through stages of development
through which we learn to adopt more complex relationships between
self and others. These briefly are as follows:

- Play: where a child learns to take roles, develop a sense of reality
  through adopting roles the child is familiar with, such as those of a
  parent, sibling or teacher.
- Game: where a child takes the role of all others and learns to know
  relations between them. The game analogy is important and has a
  resonance with Simmel's social theory – through understanding the
  rules of a game and how players are related in the team to the rules,
  we understand how social roles are integrated. But this is still a stage
  largely external to self, learned from significant others especially parents.
- Standpoint of the **generalized other**, where we internalize expectations
  of others as standards for the self. This is the self-reflexive level, because
  we know that there are rules, we know that other people judge us
  according to these rules, but we form a concept of self formed by these
  rules.

Adopting the standpoint of generalized other involves a split between 'I'
and 'Me', that is between my reflecting self ('I'), and the self on which I
reflect ('Me'). If we think for example, 'I am not a very nice person' or
'I think I did that rather well', we are applying the standards of the
generalized other to Me. This dialogue between aspects of self makes
social interaction open to complex levels of interpretation, a theme
developed by Bulmer, a student of Simmel's and subsequently by Erving
Goffman (1920–1980), who drew on both Mead and Simmel (e.g.
Goffman 1959: 75).

Like Simmel, Goffman pointed to the sociology of hidden sociality –
such as the dynamics of embarrassment, uneasiness, self-consciousness
and mental illness – to gain a better understanding of how social integration is possible. Again like Simmel, Goffman viewed social interaction as
performative and dramaturgical – in presenting ourselves in interaction
people sustain a stable self-image through a dynamic interaction between
themselves and an audience. This requires impression management – a
technique that actors use to maintain certain impressions. Impression
management conceals errors and presents the finished product in a way
that does not reveal the preparation but the accomplishment, conceals
dirty work, anticipates the criticisms, hides the effects of insults etc. This
involves distance from both audience and role – treating the role not as
something one is constrained to do but as an object. This for example
creates the potential for self-parody, to indicate that you really should be
doing better than this, self-deprecation (to indicate sincerity perhaps) – all
with differing degrees of cynicism or authenticity. The upshot of this style

**Figure 7.4** Simmel's core concepts

| Core concepts | Meaning | Example |
|---|---|---|
| Form | Innumerable contents given meaning in forms of association | Social types; always abstract from and add to individuality |
| Reciprocity | Meanings not fixed or intrinsic All meaning relational | Dynamic of exchange creates new social forms |
| Distance | Properties of form and meanings function relative to distances between individuals | Money; impersonality is social distance |
| Dualism | Conflicts and contrasts between individually opposite categories | Fashion – conformity and individuality |

of sociology is a nuanced concept of the self and society in which the maintenance of social relations becomes a practical accomplishment of actors.

With Simmel the idea of the social comes into its own in a way that is less apparent in earlier classical sociology. The social becomes a relational realm of interactions and mutual typification. Simmel's core concepts of form, reciprocity, distance and dualism (see Figure 7.4) foreground the social to the extent that the state and political society almost disappears from view, while economic processes are treated as symbolic cultural trends. There are limitations to this approach, though. Formal sociology risked becoming an entirely descriptive collection of 'interesting cases' with no integrating theory and unable actually to explain anything. Despite Simmel's tragic conception of the fragmented subject, there perhaps remained a residual concept of a virtuoso subject, a kind of universal *flâneur*, standing outside of the social looking in. This in turn seems to draw on a rather unsociological and romantic concept of the soul or spirit of the authentic individual which was characteristic of German anti-modernism.

---

**Core concepts in formal sociology**

- Critique of modernity as instrumentalism and destruction of community.
- Cultural tragedy as the fate of modernity.
- Interactive view of individual and society and break with deterministic theories.
- Form vs. content
- Conflict and competition as integrative forms of sociality.
- Sociology of nuances and everyday life.
- Sociology of spatial relations and the metropolis.
- Sociology of the senses, especially vision.
- Links to diverse schools, including Marxism and interactionism.

## FURTHER READING

David Frisby (1981) *Sociological Impressionism* (Heinemann) presents a lively and accessible account that discusses Simmel's sociology in the context of his milieu. Deena Weinstein and Michael Weinstein (1993) *Postmodern(ized) Simmel* (Routledge) provide a fresh examination of Simmel, deconstructing the subject and the social. Georg Simmel (1971) *On Individuality and Social Forms* (University of Chicago Press), edited and introduced by Donald Levine, is an excellent collection of Simmel's work, and David Frisby and Mike Featherstone (eds) (1997) *Simmel on Culture* (Sage) bring together his main cultural writings.

## NOTES

1 During the 1890s German rural population declined from 57 to 45 per cent of the total, and between 1880 and 1899, steel production grew from 0.6 to 6.3 million tons. In the wake of this rapid industrialization several anti-capitalist movements were formed, such as the antisemitic peasant Bund (Barkin 1970: 109–11).

2 This association of Jews with modernity, arising partly from the stereotype of 'Jewish finance', was widespread in Germany and the rest of central and eastern Europe in the later nineteenth century (Bauman 1988; Horkheimer 1982–3).

3 Tönnies himself, it should be said, remained an anti-fascist activist into his old age and campaigned for the Social Democrats in the July 1932 general election (Cahnman 1973a: 284–90).

4 Tönnies' central concepts of *Gemeinschaft* and *Gesellschaft* are similar to Lagarde's dualism of nation (as an organic unity of the people) and state (as a formal and mechanistic institution).

5 Tönnies' major work, *Gemeinschaft und Gesellschaft* (first published in 1887), is available in English translation (Tönnies 1973). Tönnies' ten other books, of which the major work dealing with sociology is his 1931 *Einfuhrung in die Soziologie* ('An Introduction to Sociology'), plus most of his essays, still await English translations. A full bibliography of Tönnies' work can be found in *American Journal of Sociology* 42 (1937): 100–1.

6 Like Marx's critique of the Jews which Tönnies invokes, social atomization and the rule of the commodity has brought us to see ourselves as buyers and sellers. It is hard not to see an echo of Marx's essay on the Jewish question in Tönnies' claim that the merchant class is by nature and origin 'international', suggesting (has had Marx) that capitalism and its agents were from an alien, non-German culture.

7 In 1889 Tönnies produced an annotated new edition of Hobbes' *Human Nature* (1650). But whereas Hobbes had regarded the state of war as original, Tönnies regarded individualistic, asocial competitiveness as a feature of *Gesellschaft*-like society.

8 *Flâneur*, literally a 'lounger' or 'loafer', is also a literary allusion to the stylized spectator and detached salon intellectual, following Walter Benjamin's analysis of Baudelaire. This is said to apply to Simmel too, as 'the stroller

through the city . . . who wanders through a variety of social situations [yet] remains detached from them, because he is merely an observer' (Frisby 1981: 78).

9 Levine (1997) points out that Dilthey and Simmel shared mutual antagonism, from which he concludes that the former exerted little influence on the latter. However, Simmel did participate in the broader climate of interest in intuitive, self-reflective and anti-positivist methods, which included hermeneutic approaches.

10 In a review of Simmel's *Philosophy of Money*, Durkheim (1979) said, 'Imagination, personal feelings are . . . given free reign . . . and rigorous demonstrations have no relevance . . . I confess to not attaching a very high price to this illegitimate speculation (*spéculation bâtard*) where reality is expressed in subjective terms'.

11 Simmel did stress that geometry, in contrast to sociology, isolates absolutely pure forms whereas in sociology abstraction is merely an analytical device. But the analogy is interesting in that it emphasized visual and spatial social relations.

12 Each previous period had a unifying philosophy of life. In Greek classicism, this was Being; the Christian Middle Ages, God as the source of reality; from the Renaissance, supremacy was accorded to Nature as the embodiment of truth; but in the modern age people's specialist occupation, rather than belief, is most likely to govern their lives (Simmel [1916] 1997: 79–80).

13 'I know I shall die without spiritual heirs (and that is good). The estate I leave is like cash distributed among many heirs, each of whom puts their share to use in some trade that is compatible with *their* nature but which can no longer be recognized as coming from that estate' (Bottomore and Frisby 1990: xxv).

# CHAPTER 8

# Max Weber: the triumph of reason?

The debate with the Enlightenment was in part about the extent and value of reason in human society and with the sociology of Max Weber (1864–1920) rationality becomes an unfolding theme in human history. In the process he synthesizes many of the themes raised so far in this volume. These include naturalistic versus hermeneutic approaches, problems of historical understanding, agency versus structure, materialist as against ideational and cultural approaches and more generally, the fate and implications of modernity. Weber's approach to these questions was influenced by his participation in the intellectual and political milieu described in Chapters 6 and 7. In common with many German social scientists, he was concerned with issues of rationality, the relationship between social, cultural and economic development and the costs of modernization. Above all, perhaps, Weber situated these issues within a comparative and historical perspective in which human behaviour tended to become increasingly rational and further removed from a world of enchantment. Echoing Tönnies and Simmel's depiction of modernity as fragmented experience, Weber identified a loss of meaning in modern societies with the decline of integrated worldviews that in the past had been provided by religious and philosophical systems. In this respect he shared some of the nostalgic pessimism of Tönnies and Simmel, yet I shall suggest that he was as much an advocate of modernization as he was its critic.

## ACTION, METHODS AND VALUES

Weber's methodological contribution to the formation of the sociology has been immense. It has also been appropriated piecemeal according to the preoccupations of the day. So there is Weber the 'patron saint of value-freedom' (Gouldner 1963); the pioneer of interpretive sociology;

the action theorist; methodological individualist and so forth.[1] He attempted to resolve major philosophical disputes pragmatically (especially those associated with the *Methodenstreit* in the 1880s) and this pragmatism has left his work open to varied interpretations, depending on where the emphasis is placed.

### Weber and the *Methodenstreit*

Prior to the emergence of clear and policed disciplinary boundaries in the twentieth century, the lines between sociology, history, psychology, political economy and jurisprudence were unclear and frequently crossed. Classical sociologists tended to regard economic action and institutions as a part of the social realm rather than as narrowly self-contained and subject to specific laws. Thus Comte thought that economics was too abstract; Durkheim wrote of the non-contractual bases of contract; Marx regarded the apparent autonomy of the market as a fetishistic illusion; Simmel regarded money as an expression of the stylization of culture. Weber shared this broad and historical view of the integration of economic and social analysis, reflecting the influential German Historical School. However, this view was challenged in the *Methodenstreit* ('dispute about method') conducted among German social scientists in the 1880s.[2] One consequence of the *Methodenstreit* was the separation of sociology, concerned with broad social and historical questions, and economics, dealing in abstract concepts of market behaviour. Weber regarded this separation as a disaster and continued to situate economic processes in a broader sociohistorical context, although the fundamental methodological problems the dispute raised were central to Weber's methodology.

The *Methodenstreit* was a dispute about the relationship between natural and social scientific methods and addressed two issues in particular: subject matter and theory of knowledge (Morrison 1995: 265–70). On the question of subject matter, Carl Menger (1840–1921) argued that economics was hindered by its failure to follow the exact sciences. Since all human action is reducible to simple economic exchange founded on utility and self interest, economics could and should discover the regularities of social life and propose general laws of behaviour like those in the natural sciences. The leading representative of the Historical School, Gustav Schmoller (1838–1917), disputed Menger's positivism, arguing that since societies develop historically and at any period in time are at different stages, a generalizing methodology would not take into account the individual character of societies. Schmoller further disputed Menger's concept of human motivation, arguing that no rational motive underlies action since it is bound up with various (non-rational) political, religious and social beliefs. Economics then was a historical and ideographic discipline, concerned with specific and non-generalizable forms of social organization.[3]

In terms of the theory of knowledge, Rickert (see pp. 124–5) offered an alternative view of method, which emphasized the process of concept formation. Modifying Dilthey's dichotomy between the natural and social sciences (see Chapter 6), Rickert argued that differences between sciences were based on logic rather than subject matter. As a neo-Kantian, Rickert argued that human beings had no way of knowing the world independently of the frames provided by their concepts. He regarded facts as constituted out of experience and given form by mental activity, which always involved selection and judgement. Methods are developed with reference to these 'interests' that guide our knowledge – so if our interest is in nomothetic, generalizable knowledge the appropriate methods are those of the natural sciences. If, on the other hand, the interest is in ideographic, specific historical knowledge, then the appropriate methods are those of the cultural sciences deploying techniques of understanding and empathy (J. A. Hughes 1990: 91). In the cultural sciences judgements of relevance will be developed with reference to values, which are embedded in the cultural context of the enquirer. Two implications of Rickert's view were first, that judgement and selectivity were prior to knowing; second, that the dispute between the positivists and anti-positivists could be resolved into questions of perspective and appropriate approach. However, this was a solution with relativistic implications (much as Rickert tried to avoid this) that did not satisfy the positivists (Abel 1929).

However, for Weber this seemed to open up a way of resolving the dispute over methods. Weber rejected both the positivist view that the aims of the natural and the social sciences were basically the same, and the German historicist doctrine that it is impossible to make generalizations in history. Against the historicists, Weber argued that the method of science always proceeds by abstraction and generalization, and against the positivists, he argued that social relationships could not be understood solely with reference to objective characteristics but also to their underlying meanings. For Weber, as for Rickert, the difference between natural and social sciences did not derive from their respective subject matter but from the intentions and interests of the scientist. Both forms of knowledge face a similar problem – how to derive order from chaos, that is, how to abstract sufficiently clear conceptualizations from the complexity of real life. Natural science is primarily interested in those aspects of natural events that can be formulated in terms of abstract laws, and while social science may search for such lawful abstract generalizations in human behaviour, it is also interested in the meanings which human actors ascribe to their actions. Any scientific method must make a selection from the infinite variety of empirical reality. When social science adopts a generalizing method, it abstracts from unique aspects social reality which are conceived as 'cases' or 'instances', to be subsumed under theoretical generalizations. The individualizing approach, by contrast, neglects generic elements and concentrates attention on particular features of phenomena or concrete historical actors. Both methods are defensible, provided neither is held to grasp phenomena in their totality nor regarded as superior to the other.

Similarly, Weber developed Rickert's theory of judgement into a methodological principle of **value relevance**. Particular research problems and levels of explanation depend on the values and interests of the investigator; thus there is no absolutely 'objective' scientific analysis of culture or of 'social phenomena' independent of special and 'one-sided' viewpoints. Rather, these are expressly or tacitly, consciously or unconsciously, the principles according to which facts are selected, analysed and organized, so what is considered worthy to be known depends upon the perspective of the inquiring scholar. Hence there is no insurmountable chasm between the procedures of the natural and the social scientist, but they differ in their cognitive intentions and explanatory projects.

Further, like Dilthey, Weber argued that while our knowledge of nature must always be from the outside (observation of the external courses and uniformities of events) we can gain more intimate knowledge of the social worlds of which we are a part. Thus we can understand (*verstehen*) human action by penetrating to the subjective meanings that actors attach to their own behaviour and to the behaviour of others. Only meaning and our mutual capacity to understand it confer intelligibility on social action. Indeed, Weber regarded the method of *verstehen* as essential to arriving at a 'causal explanation of . . . cause and effect' (1964: 88). Like Dilthey, Weber distinguished two levels of understanding, direct (*aktualle*) and explanatory. Direct or current understanding involves understanding the meaning of symbolic expressions, such as the Pythagorean Theorem, the expression '$2 \times 2 = 4$', or that certain facial expressions indicate anger, pleasure and so forth. It is on the basis of this kind of understanding that everyday social interaction can take place at all. **Explanatory understanding** involves appreciating the meaningful connection between events and expressions along with the motives, intentions and emotions underlying them.[4] This is explanatory since it shows how actions follow from actors' systems of meaning. For example, if you observe someone writing down an equation you could explain why they were doing it at that time and in that particular way if you knew, perhaps, that they were balancing a ledger or making a scientific demonstration (Weber 1978b: 8). Weber (initially) followed Dilthey in proposing to reconstruct the actual motive guiding the actor whose action we wish to understand, although he departed from Dilthey's view that objective social institutions are the observable traces of *Geist*. As a consequence, Weber regarded the outcome of his approach as necessarily more hypothetical and fragmentary than Dilthey's (Weber 1964: 104).

Several issues follow from this. If 'adequacy at the level of meaning' is essential to any thorough account of the social, then clearly there are differences between the natural and social sciences that arise from their different subject matters and are not attributable only to differences of interest or value relevance. Even so, Weber wanted to demonstrate that the differences between the two forms of knowledge were not fundamental, but that explanation was possible in sociology through using *verstehen*. Indeed, *verstehen* generates only causal *hypotheses* and does not constitute knowledge in itself, however plausible an interpretation seems (Outhwaite 1975: 49). The validity of the explanation needs to be established empirically. As Bauman (1978: 86) points out, sociologists who see Weber as the champion of interpretive and subjective sociology miss the central point in his famous claim in *The Methodology of the Social Sciences*. Namely, 'granted that meanings are subjective; granted that historical categories, to make sense, must be relevant to these meanings; *we can still have objective social science*' (emphasis added). This is not a celebration of the diversity of knowledge but a plea for objective rigour in social science, an aspiration that became increasingly dominant in Weber's later work. His contribution to the *Methodenstreit* then was in part to effect a compromise between positivism and hermeneutics but in the process to move decisively away from the latter, through empirical validation of interpretations.

### Social action and ideal types

One of the principal differences between the natural and social sciences for Weber then was that the latter dealt with meaningful action that could not be understood simply through observation. He defined social action as 'behaviour to which subjective meaning is attached. It takes account of others and is thereby oriented in its course. Action is social when directed to the behaviour of others *meaningfully*' (Weber [1913] 1978b: 4). For example, a collision of cyclists previously unaware of each other is a behavioural event not involving shared meanings. But the attempts to avoid collision, or the insults which follow a collision are social actions because each participant is orientating their action to that of the other. Sociology is confined to the study of social action, thus non-social influences (e.g. biologically inherited traits) are outside sociologically relevant behaviour. He identified four types of social action that may each be found in contemporary society although they are distinguished by their respective degree of rationality and represent a developmental trend towards increasingly rationalized and formalized conduct.

1  **Traditional action** is rooted in a fixed body of traditional beliefs. Customary habits of thought and an automatic reaction to habitual stimuli which guide behaviour in a course which is repeatedly followed, as for example, with the clergy following church doctrine. A great deal of everyday action approaches this type which is really on a borderline between the social (meaningful) and pre-social (unreflective).

2  **Affective (or emotional) action** is anchored in the emotional state of the actor and is not primarily goal directed. This is expressive action

that is motivated directly by an emotional response, such as anger, revenge, sexual desire etc., and is not directed towards the attainment of a goal. An example might be the ecstasy expressed at evangelical religious services.

3 **Value-rational action** (*wertrational*) is striving for a substantive goal (e.g. salvation) by rational, that is, calculated means (e.g. self-denial in pursuit of holiness). This type of action is rational in that the means are judged logically necessary to achieve the goal.

4 **Goal-rational action** (*zweckrational*) weighs up the ends, means, secondary consequences and alternative courses of action so that the goals themselves have been rationally chosen. This form of action really includes at least two subtypes. First, instrumental action pursued in order to achieve a reward such as profit and loss calculations. Second, formal-rational action in which the objective is procedural, where following the rules (as in a judicial or democratic political system) becomes an end in itself.[5]

The implicit dichotomy here between the first two (non-rational) and the latter two (rational) types follows the distinction made by Tönnies and others between intrinsic and calculated forms of behaviour. These in turn correspond to action predominant in pre-modern and modern forms of society, respectively, since in modern societies the extent of rational types of action extends and the scope of the former two diminishes. However, this is an abstract typology and actual behaviour is likely to involve all four in different degrees. It might be difficult (as Weber showed in his *Protestant Ethic* study) to find purely rational action that does not on some level seek to realize a substantive goal, while even traditional action may be rule-following and involve choices. If *all* action, at least implicitly, involves some purpose and goal, then the distinctions appear to overlap considerably.

For this reason, Bauman (1978: 81–2) regards the 'notorious typology' as untenable and out of keeping with the rest of Weber's work. It is true that Weber did not develop the typology further than his presentation in the first volume of *Economy and Society* (1913). However, his typology surely depicts the 'way in which action gets uprooted from its random flow and transformed into meaning based regularities', which constitutes one of the central themes of Weber's sociology (Kalberg 1997: 217). We are never so free, Weber said, as when we are behaving rationally, in self-awareness of goals and the most adequate means of attaining them. Thus if the history of human societies involves the gradual expansion of reason then it also entails increasing freedom. Weber's view was rather more complex than this (like Simmel, his understanding of freedom was ambivalent) but his typology suggested that the more rational social behaviour is, the more transparent it becomes, precisely because it then appears as codifiable and logical. Yet his separation of rational and non-rational action reveals a deeper purpose – to show how intentions and reality do not always coincide and people must follow non-rational demands (Schluchter 1987).

His typology is an example of his use of **ideal types** to clarify an otherwise impossibly complex reality of 'infinite and multifarious historical life' (Kalberg 1997: 219). Further following Rickert's principle of judgement and selection, Weber developed the heuristic device of the ideal type as a way of conceptualizing patterned orientations of social action. Ideal types allowed the generalization of patterns of action without claiming either to provide an exhaustive description of social reality or to formulate laws. The ideal type is a conceptual pattern which brings together certain relationships and events of historical life into a complex which is conceived of as an internally consistent system. It does not attempt to portray an average nor an 'ideal' state to be achieved, but the central tendency of action that delimits it as a type. 'Modern society' for example contains a vast array of economic, social, political and cultural forms (as well as pre-modern survivals) which can be conceptualized from different points of view – such as urbanization, organizational action, values and beliefs, economic life and family relationships. Further, within any of these systems of action one may wish to emphasize particular action orientations, such as the expectations that characterize the modern, as opposed to pre-modern bureaucrat. Ideal types may in addition be rooted in historical particularities such as 'the western city' or emergent forms that occur at various times such as 'bureaucratic administration'.

As well as abstracting core orientations within patterns of activity, ideal types aim to proceed from 'the most rational forms reality *can* assume' to attempt to find out how far certain rational conclusions, which have been established theoretically, have been drawn in reality (Weber 1964: 92). For example, we may develop a model of how a stock exchange would operate if actors behaved in a rational and predictable way and compare this to what actually happens when panic breaks out, that is, when actors behave irrationally. We should note that *causal* explanation was introduced where actual outcomes deviate from rationally based expectations and that affective action (e.g. panic) along with misinformation, logical fallacies, errors etc. were assumed to be non-rational. Thus causal explanation is relevant only where action does not conform to the logical model of a means–end relationship. This has two further implications. First, the development of rational systems of action involves an escape from causality towards increased conscious choice, albeit choice that is highly constrained by the requirement to select the most efficient means. Second, the place of hermeneutics in this conception is considerably weaker than in Dilthey. This is partly because hermeneutics is deployed largely in relation to non-rational behaviour, where the meaning of people's action lacks transparency, but it also becomes linear rather than circular. The idea of proceeding back and forth through successive layers of understanding largely disappears in Weber.

In summary, then, Weber used ideal types in three ways: to facilitate the conceptualization of diffuse empirical reality; to construct a particular empirical research problem; to enable identification of significant causal relationships. The technique does pose some difficulties though. In the course of empirical research, how much deviation from the ideal type is acceptable before we must conclude that it bears too little resemblance to reality to be useful? How do we know anyway that we have abstracted central tendencies of a particular form? The rational reconstruction of actions involves 'thought experiments' (which Weber regarded as legitimate) where we pose the question 'What would have happened if . . .' actors had behaved differently, rationally rather than irrationally. This clearly poses problems of validation, which Weber attempted to resolve with a combination of empirical evidence and judgements of plausibility (Weber 1978c: 111–31).

## Values, science and validity

Should social science overtly hold political commitments or are these a diversion from the pursuit of knowledge? This proved to be one of the most vexed methodological questions in sociology. It was raised in part in the *Wertertielstreit* (dispute over values) which ran on from the *Methodenstreit*. Two of Weber's teachers, Roscher and Knies, had argued that economics embraced the whole field of social science and was committed to value judgements. Thus moral indifference could not be justified by a claim to scientific objectivity, a position reflecting that of the *Verein für Sozialpolitik* (Society for Social Policy), the main forum for German social science.[6] Weber challenged this view, arguing within the Society for value free research and the separation of the 'vocations' of science and politics. Two contexts were important here. German universities were highly politicized, with professors using the unquestionable authority of the chair to make political pronouncements that were often xenophobic and nationalistic. Weber regarded this as unacceptable and further regarded the commitment of the Society to social and political values a hindrance on sociology's professional autonomy. Unable to persuade the Society of the need for value freedom, he broke with it and founded the German Sociological Association in 1909.

'Value freedom' should be distinguished from value relevance mentioned above. Ethical neutrality implies that once the field of research has been selected, sociologists must suspend moral judgement *as sociologists* in relation to their data. We are compelled to pursue our line of inquiry whether or not the results fit with our cherished commitments. In this sense value freedom is a normative injunction that requires science to be committed to the ethos of neutrality, although as *citizens* we are entitled (as Weber did) to engage in political debate. The basis for this separation between the vocations of politics and science is the philosophical disjunction between the world of facts and the world of values, and the impossibility

of deriving moral positions ('ought statements') from facts ('is statements') and vice versa. An empirical science, Weber argued, could never
advise anyone what they should do, although it may help them clarify
what they *want* to do. The scientific assessment of values can make
logical judgements as to the internal consistency of the desired end, clarify
and make explicit ultimate standards, and can estimate the likely consequences of any form of action. However, this placed Weber at odds with
those who argued for morally based science, and distinguished him not
only from the older generation of the Society for Social Policy, but also
from the positivistic tradition of Comte and Durkheim. The latter, following the Enlightenment idea of rationally founded morality, had looked
to science to provide guidance for what constituted the 'good life'. Science, for Weber should not lend its authority to political values – and
cannot 'partake of the contemplation of sages and philosophers about
the meaning of the universe'. To do so would 'create only fanatical
sects'. This meant that the realm of moral values lay ultimately beyond
reason, as 'a realm of warring gods demanding allegiance to contradictory ethical notions' (Weber [1913] 1978b: 82).

One challenge to Weber's position is the argument that since social
science operates within a moral universe, it cannot avoid moral evaluation
of its data – indeed 'impartiality' may be an abdication of responsibility.
For example, one neither could nor should research the relationship
between poverty and health without finding poverty and its effects morally and politically objectionable. The question for Weber though is
whether one voices these values as a sociologist or as a politically active
citizen. A more fundamental challenge questions the very fact–value distinction itself. Max Horkheimer (a leading figure in the Frankfurt Institute
for Social Research) for example argued that positivism (which in this
context included Weber) relegates ethical judgements to matters of irrational decision, while reason is limited to the evaluation of facts. Once
morality is placed beyond reason it becomes a matter of personal pre-
ference, so 'if irrational power politics [i.e. fascism] should replace
enlightened self-interest' in people's minds no moralist could object because no moral choice could be condemned as irrational. The result was
that 'reason had committed suicide' (Horkheimer 1982–3). In this sense
Critical Theorists like Horkheimer regarded the debilitation of reason as
one of the intellectual preconditions for German fascism. More recently,
Jürgen Habermas has attempted to show through the reconstruction of
rules governing speech, that any attempt to reach mutual understanding
implies certain shared values. For a consensus to be reached guided only
by the force of better argument, he claims, *whether we recognize it or
not* we routinely assume certain conditions. Namely, that each participant has an equal chance to deploy, initiate and perpetuate speech acts
and that reasons for propositions will be evaluated in terms of whether
they are comprehensible, true, legitimate, appropriate and sincere. If this
is so, then not only has Habermas found a core of necessarily shared

values, but also the ways we evaluate judgements of fact and value do not essentially differ, since both involve giving and evaluating reasons for statements and conduct.

## MARX AND WEBER

There is a long-running debate over the extent to which Weber was engaged in a 'debate with Marx's ghost'.[7] Weber shared the Marxists' belief in the importance of economic forces, and Weber's analysis of the economic preconditions for capitalism identified many of the same factors as had Marx. These included the existence of a mass of wage-labourers, breaking the power of medieval guilds, technological development, and separation between the household and workplace. Weber's accounts of religious social movements were to some extent compatible with Marxism and echo the latter's concept of ideology. For example, for privileged strata, salvation religions can function as legitimation of the social order, expressing the divine origin of their good fortune, while for the underprivileged, they emphasize the messianic, future attainment of social justice (Weber [1913] 1978b: 490–2). While some commentators, such as Karl Löwith (1982), see an underlying compatibility between Weberian and Marxist approaches, others, like Wolfgang Mommsen (1991), regard them as essentially antagonistic. Mommsen claims that Weber was resolutely opposed to materialism and regarded Marxism as justifiable only in two ways. First, as a revolutionary political theory founded not on scientific truths but on ethical convictions, albeit ones that Weber did not share; second, as a system of ideal-typical hypotheses that enables us to investigate society.

There were, indeed, many differences between Marx and Weber. First, Weber's analysis of class emphasized market position, rather than property, as the main criterion, which enabled Weber to regard differentiated segments of the labour market as separate classes. Classes in this sense may (but may not) become 'conscious' of their interests, although the conflicts resulting from this will not polarize society in the way Marx had expected. Rather, there is a tendency towards increasing complexity of social structure, the multiplication of hierarchies rather than the polarization of society into two hostile camps.

Second, class position was for Weber only one dimension of stratification, the others being status (high or low esteem) and power, or position in organizational hierarchies. Status groups are normally communities held together by shared consumption patterns, lifestyles and social esteem, rather than market position or property, and they will generally restrict social interaction with those outside the circle. It is true that in capitalist society the economically dominant class will also acquire high status, yet in principle, propertied and propertyless people may belong to the same status group. At times, an economically weak group, such as the East Elbian Junkers, may exercise influence because of its exalted status. Moreover, status reward and the fear of its loss may operate as motives for political action as strong as class based modes. Power is a further dimension of stratification that cannot be reduced to class. Power for Weber was people's ability to realize their own will in communal action, even against the resistance of others. He did not dispute the Marxist claim that power is often rooted in economic relations, but argued that the emergence of economic power may be the consequence of power existing on other grounds. High officials in bureaucratic organizations, for example, may wield considerable economic power even though they are only salaried employees. Moreover, power may be valued 'for its own sake' rather than as a means to enrichment.

Third, Weber had a multidimensional view of historical development as occurring through **elective affinity**, a term he took from chemistry, which understood events as possessing a kind of mutual attractiveness such that they affect one another in unpredictable ways. A famous example of this is the alleged affinity between Calvinism and capitalism that while decisive for human development was the accidental confluence of two quite different processes – the emergence of commercialism and the Reformation.

Fourth, in contrast to Marxist claims to objective understanding of history, Weber regarded historical understanding as always interpretative and dependent on the principle of value relevance described above. There is no single meaning of history or one way of understanding capitalism, but multiple interpretations relevant to our interests. An account of capitalism in terms of the emergence of 'rational' features such as accounting, labour regulation and market discipline will look quite different from one written in terms of the disposition of peasants or the accumulation of capital through the slave trade. This is elaborated below with reference to the *Protestant Ethic* thesis.

Two further points follow from these. First, apparently incidental factors (e.g. battles) might be of great importance to historical outcomes – thus the defeat of the Persians by Athens in the Battle of Marathon (490 BC) was decisive for the subsequent development of western civilization. Second, history flows along several paths and follows a logic of unintended consequences, which is at odds with the Marxist notion of development through stages determined by the mode of production. Despite all this though, Marx may not have been Weber's main target and Marshall (1982: 33) claims that 'Weber is debating, not with the ghost of Marx, but – via German historical economics – with that of Adam Smith'. This is one reading of the *Protestant Ethic* essays.

## RELIGION, ECONOMY AND THE 'BUTTERFLY EFFECT'

If this essay makes any contribution at all, may it bring out the complexity of the only superficially simple concept of the rational.
(Weber 1974: 193)

Weber's *Protestant Ethic* essays provide one of the richest explorations of the interplay of economy and culture in his sociology. The thesis has implications far beyond a narrow debate about the relationship between Calvinism and the development of capitalism, though this is one of the issues it raises. The essays reflect a number of Weber's concerns. These include his insistence that economic action is culturally embedded and that capital accumulation was no more or less 'rational' than any other cultural goal. This is in contrast to the view of neo-liberal economists arising from the Austrian School, that entrepreneurial and self-maximizing behaviour arises naturally so long as it is not artificially constrained.[8] The essays further illustrate Weber's aversion to closed accounts of historical development and the irony of the logic of unintended consequences. That an obscure dispute over predestination among Reformation sects could have such cataclysmic consequences as to trigger the growth of capitalism, indicates the importance Weber attached to unintended consequences and an unpredictability slightly akin to what is now described as the 'butterfly effect'.[9]

### The Protestant Ethic thesis

Weber's *Protestant Ethic* thesis, which began as a series of lectures in 1904–5, gave rise to one of the central and longest running disputes in sociology, partly because it brings together many theoretical issues, crossing a wide disciplinary spectrum (Ray 1986). The thesis should further be seen in the context of the dispute over the fate of German culture and society (discussed in Chapter 7) which generated extensive work on the origins and nature of capitalism (e.g. Swingewood 1985: 159–64). In order to understand the thesis in the context of Weber's work one should see it as only one part of his account of the development of capitalism, which was complex and multidimensional (see Figure 8.1). His account of the origin of *capitalism* referred to a complex interaction of social, economic and cultural factors, while the *Protestant Ethic* essays had the more limited objective of explaining the origin, not of capitalism *per se*, but the *spirit* of rational accumulation.

Weber began with the observation that capitalism seemed to be associated with the Protestant countries and that many entrepreneurs were Protestant. Yet the conditions for capitalism – a money economy, banking, the separation between home and work, mercantile trade, technology, small scale factory production – had existed elsewhere in the world. Searching for the specific catalyst for capitalism in western society, Weber argued that what had taken place was the transposition of the religious goal of salvation into the secular goal of success, including the pursuit of profit. Important to Weber's argument is his claim that capitalism, as opposed to the desire for money, was not universal but historically specific:

**Figure 8.1** Weberian causal chain (Adapted from Collins 1980)

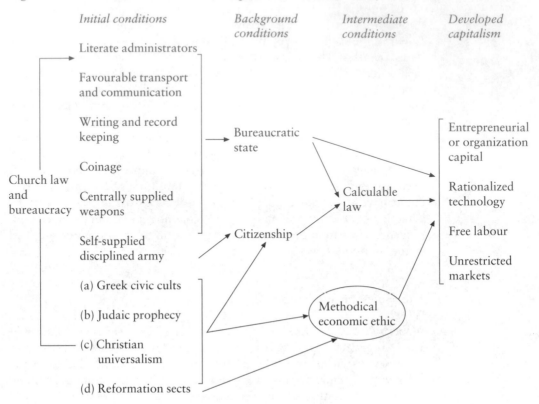

The impulse to acquisition, pursuit of gain, of money, of the greatest possible amount of money, has in itself nothing to do with capitalism. This impulse exists and has existed among waiters, physicians, coachmen, artists, prostitutes, dishonest officials, soldiers, nobles, crusades, gamblers and beggars.

(Weber 1974: 17)

What then, is capitalism? In ideal-typical terms, capitalistic activity is the pursuit of profits through exchange and more specifically (cf. Marx) 'the pursuit of profit and forever renewed profits', that is, accumulation as an end in itself. This, Weber believes was peculiar to seventeenth century northwestern Europe, where capitalists reinvested earnings rather than enjoy them in conspicuous consumption. Capitalism was linked with disciplined, rule following, methodical conduct, a view Weber derived from writers like Benjamin Franklin:

Be prudent, diligent, and ever about your lawful business; do not idle, for time is money; cultivate your credit-worthiness and put it to good use, for credit is money; be punctual and just in the repayment of loans and debts, for to become a person of known credit-worthiness is to be master of other people's purses; be vigilant in keeping accounts; be frugal in consumption and do not waste money on inessentials; and finally, do not let money lie idle, for the smallest sum soundly invested can earn a profit, and the profits reinvested soon multiply in ever increasing amounts.

(Weber 1974: 48–50)

By contrast with the Austrian School, Weber claimed that there is nothing spontaneous or natural about the pursuit of accumulation. For classical economists entrepreneurial energies would emerge once people were freed from the shackles of the state. But Weber argued that since accumulation for its own sake is irrational when compared with the traditional moral economy of self-sufficiency, its origin required explanation.

Weber claimed that an ascetic (austere or rigorous) religious concept of calling (Beruf) was transposed into the ascetic secular concept of disciplined work and accumulation. With the Protestant Reformation, the calling to an ascetic lifestyle broke free from the confines of the monasteries and entered the everyday life of devout followers of early Protestant sects. Medieval monastic orders such as the Cistercians had developed refined techniques of production, such as new techniques of labour organization and economically effective technologies – mills, water technology and wool production. These remained locked up, so to speak, until social disruption (in this case the decline of feudalism) and rapid social change released innovations from the monasteries into social development (Collins 1986: 52–4). What for the monk had been a *cause* of salvation, for the Puritan was *evidence* (Weber 1978a).

Once ascetically methodical behaviour became the way of life of whole groups of people, salvation no longer necessarily required other-worldly retreat, but rather the pursuit of this-worldly activity. Indeed, Calvinist theology demanded activity in the world, rather than monastic withdrawal, and evolved in such a way as to sanctify capitalistic activity. Central here was the Calvinist belief in predestination.[10] Since God was omnipotent and omniscient, He must have determined the whole pattern of Creation for eternity. To suggest otherwise was in effect to impose a limit to God's knowledge and power and to imply that the Universe might in part be unknown to Him. The belief in predestination applied to personal salvation – only a part of humanity was saved, and this had been ordained for eternity. To suppose that as a mere mortal one could affect the predetermined plan of the universe was in itself sinful arrogance. One might think that this was not a very promising ethic from which worldly activity could commence, but the meaning this belief was to have for Calvinists became crucial for the development of a capitalist spirit.

Weber's analysis involves reconstruction of the meaningful context of

Calvinism and interpretation of its consequences for action. A major consequence of the belief in predestination was an 'unprecedented inner loneliness' among believers. '"The question – am I one of the elect?" must sooner or later have arisen for every believer and have forced all other interests into the background' (Weber 1974: 110). One had a duty to consider oneself chosen yet faith had to be proved by its objective results – by increasing the glory of God through a life of systematic self-control. In particular, Weber argues, the Calvinist, knowing that there was no hope of salvation through good works or through sacraments, sought evidence of salvation in worldly success. Calvinists were alone in the world and were forced to rely on individual conscience for knowledge of grace. This provided a major incentive for worldly activity orientated towards proof of election, for one thing was certain: that the pursuit of any pleasure was contrary to God's law, and thus a dissolute, hedonistic or idle life was prima facie evidence of damnation. This was a novel resolution of the tension between the ethical demands of religion and the necessities of the marketplace – which had previously been resolved by other-worldly withdrawal, the pursuit of mystical knowledge, or contemplation. Calvinism, in Weber's account, sanctified the profane and thus fused the religious quest for salvation (or certainty of it) with the secular goal of success. Thus, 'Calvinism not only had a quite unique consistency, but . . . its psychological effect was extraordinarily powerful' (Weber 1974: 128). Further, once successful, Calvinists were prohibited from the relaxed enjoyment of life, conspicuous consumption, and so work became an end in itself. Thus the elective affinity between economic conditions and the ascetic capitalist spirit was established through a series of transpositions between religious and economic goal-orientations.

The pursuit of salvation as an end in itself carried over into capital accumulation also then pursued as an end in itself. The once sacred goal became a secular goal, although both were pursued through disciplined methodical ascetic conduct. As the pursuit of worldly success acquired a sacred significance and became an end sufficient to itself – accumulation became the goal of economic activity. These action dispositions then gel with the wider economic preconditions for capitalist development, including the emergence of a money economy; wage-labour; removal of state monopolies; technology; separation between household and workplace.

In the course of debate over the thesis Weber emphasized certain aspects more than others. The 'predestination paradox' gets less emphasis in later accounts although his 'anti-critical last word' does insist on the importance of the compatibility of personalities of Puritans and capitalists (Weber 1978a). On the other hand his *General Economic History* (1927), which is the basis for Figure 8.1, gives considerably more attention to the structural preconditions for capitalism than to the Calvinist motivational complex. Moreover, idealistic and materialistic accounts of the process are possible. 'It is not my aim' Weber says at the end of the essays, 'to substitute for a one-sided materialistic an equally one-sided spiritualistic causal interpretation of culture and of history. *Each is equally possible*' (1974: 183, emphasis added).[11] Further, the *Protestant Ethic* thesis illustrates Weber's methodological eclecticism and his multicausal approach to historical explanation. No underlying structure determines historical development; rather social spheres such as religion and the economy follow their distinctive patterns of development. Their elective affinity though, such as occurred in seventeenth-century Europe, can have crucial consequences for subsequent social development. That the resolution of a theological dispute can turn the tide of history suggests that social systems display chaotic levels of complexity. This in turn emphasizes the importance of the ironic logic of unintended consequences. 'The cultural consequences of the Reformation were to a great extent unforeseen and even unwished-for results of the labours of the reformers' (Weber 1974: 172). This was unintended in that a theological dispute among relatively small Protestant sects acted on wider socio-economic developments to stimulate the development of the capitalist ethos. It was ironic (and in Simmel's sense tragic) because the fully developed system of capitalist materialism would have appalled them.

### Main criticisms of Weber's thesis

Almost every aspect of Weber's thesis has been subject to criticism and debate. While historians have often been hostile, theoretically informed disciplines have tended to give the thesis a sympathetic if critical reception. It has further been influential in other debates, such as that over the origins of the scientific revolution in the seventeenth century (e.g. Hill 1965; Merton 1990). Figure 8.2 summarizes some main critical themes, with some possible responses and comments.

**Figure 8.2** Critique and defence of the Weber thesis

| Criticism | Response |
| --- | --- |
| Weber illegitimately replaced a materialistic thesis (Marxism) with an idealistic one (Fischoff 1944; Seé 1959; Rachfahl 1968). | Weber frequently denied this. But he *did* suggest capitalism could not have developed without the Protestant Ethic. |
| Capitalism predated Calvinism, so the influence was the reverse of that claimed by Weber (Tawney 1975; Pellicani 1988) or both arose from an independent source such as urbanization (Samuelssen 1961). | Evidence for the pre-existence of capitalism is itself subject to dispute. Cities existed in the ancient world and in Asia without the existence of capitalism. The priority argument is difficult to resolve. |

**Figure 8.2** (cont'd)

| Criticism | Response |
| --- | --- |
| Sometimes Weber referred to Calvinists (who believed in predestination) other times to Protestant sects in general, for whom the predestination paradox did not apply (Marshall 1982). | The force of this criticism depends on how much the paradox is emphasised, as opposed to a methodical and this-worldly orientation. |
| Weber misunderstands Calvinists, who did not have the personality structure he claims, and anyway would have been certain of their salvation (Trevor-Roper 1963; Pellicani 1988). Calvinism actually made provision for confirmation of salvation by 'good works' (MacKinnon 1994). | Some at least do seem to have had anxieties and faced a crisis. Again this depends on the importance of this aspect of the thesis. |
| Many Calvinists (especially early on) were anti-capitalist. The Anabaptists were in some ways precursors of socialism, with property held in common in egalitarian communities (Habermas 1984). | Weber does not deny this. The thesis is about unintended consequences of action. |
| Calvinism was more conservative than Catholicism, which was not hostile to capitalism. Italian cities had complex banking systems (Razzell 1977). | May be true, but again, Weber's thesis is about the consequences of Calvinism, not its essential beliefs. |
| Marginal and migrant status (Puritans, Quakers, Jews) was a more important stimulus to capitalistic activity than content of belief (Trevor-Roper 1972). | If true, one still has to explain why Puritan sects preached this-worldly asceticism at that time and with these consequences. |
| Weber defined the Protestant 'calling' in terms compatible with the spirit of capitalism. His selection of texts was unrepresentative (Fischoff 1944; Kitch 1967; Marshall 1982). | Maybe there is some truth in this. It is a problem with the construction of ideal-types. |
| The correlation between elements of 'economic' and 'religious' action is too simple because the terms are too broad. Over 300 years or more the meaning of both will have changed (Samuelssen 1961). | Given his commitment to reconstructing actors' meaning, one might have expected Weber to address this. Even so, economy and religion were differentiated by their respective goal orientations. |

## LEGITIMATE DOMINATION AND BUREAUCRACY

Weber's typology of legitimate domination (*herrschaft*) has exercised a lasting influence over the sociology of political rule. In keeping with Weber's emphasis on meaningful social action, the basis for his analysis was that power (the probability that a command will be obeyed) is in itself an insufficient basis for social order. Weber claimed that every form of rule attempts to establish and cultivate the belief in its legitimacy, although there are several modes of exercising authority. Ruling a considerable number of people requires a staff, that is a special group trusted to execute general policy and specific commands. Members of administrative staff may be bound to obedience in several ways – by custom, affective ties, material interests or values – from which arise different modes of legitimacy. It is important to note that Weber's discussion of legitimate authority is linked to his concept of bureaucracy, since for a regime to be legitimate it is only necessary that the ruler's commands should be regarded as valid among those who have to execute them. Weber did not regard it as necessary that the mass of people accorded the system legitimacy, and authority in the modern state does not require their consent, but is experienced 'externally' in a 'quasi-traditional' way (Weber [1913] 1978b: 1117).

Weber constructed three 'pure' types of legitimate authority – traditional, charismatic and rational-legal. **Traditional** legitimacy refers to the sanction of immemorial traditions and belief in the legitimacy of those exercising authority under them having 'always existed'. This does not mean that the authority of the ruler is unquestioned but that resistance will be founded on the claim that rulers have failed to observe the traditional limits or requirements of power.[12] The traditional (patrimonial) bureaucracy will be heavily based on personal loyalty and obligations to the ruler, indicating a continuation of the principle of personal rulership. Thus the exercise of power is highly discretionary and personalized, rather than rule-following, and judgements are likely to be made by viewing each case individually. There will be no clear separation between private and official spheres of action and a benefice such as land or wealth, rather than an income will reward loyalty to the ruler. The benefice is further likely to become the disposable property of the office holder and hence transferable through sale or inheritance (Weber [1913] 1978b: 235–6).

**Charisma** refers to the belief in the exceptional sanctity, heroism and exemplary character of an individual person, whose rule will typically be theocratic. The ancient world offers many examples of this but so too does modern society – the authority of leader of the 1979 Iranian Revolution, the Ayatollah Khomani, was based on belief in his spiritual qualities and his ability to identify himself with the holy Shi'ia martyr, Hussein. This illustrates, however, how charismatic leaders will often draw upon traditional imagery, such as a prophetic tradition. Unlike tradition though, charisma is a powerful revolutionary force, which disrupts 'rational rule as well as tradition altogether', 'overturning all notions of sanctity. Instead of reverence for customs that are ancient and hence sacred, it reinforces the inner subjection to the unprecedented and absolutely unique and therefore Divine. In this . . . sense charisma is indeed the specifically creative revolutionary force of history' (Weber [1913] 1978b: 1117). Charismatic authority is by its nature not bureaucratic and administrative functions are carried out by disciples selected for their belief in the leader's powers. Again an example would be the Iranian *pasdaran* (Revolutionary Guards) selected for their Islamic zeal, publicly self-flagellating and affirming their readiness to die for Ayatollah Khomani. However, charisma is subject to a process of routinization in that it must eventually face the problem of succession, which requires some principle of selection. At this point charisma is no longer focused on the qualities of the leader but the legitimacy of the selection procedures, whether these are resemblance to the original leader, revelation, election or personal endorsement of the leader. Since it must always be replaced by some form of procedures, charisma will tend to develop into either traditional or rational-legal authority (Weber [1913] 1978b: 246–8).

**Rational-legal legitimation** refers to belief in the legality of enacted rules and the right of those elevated to authority to enact them (e.g. in democratic republics). Formal-rational legitimation is impersonal and procedural in that authority does not rest with individuals as such but is founded on a belief that commands should be obeyed because they are legal. Although both democratic political systems and rational bureaucracies embody rational-legal principles there is a tendency for bureaucracies to encroach on the parliamentary system because their decision-making procedures are faster and more efficient. Similarly there is a tendency for collegial peer group regulation, typified by professional associations and universities, to be displaced by bureaucratic organizations because 'Collegiality . . . obstructs the promptness of decision, consistency of policy, the clear responsibility of the individual and ruthlessness to outsiders (Weber [1913] 1978b: 280). By contrast with the personalized rule in patrimonial bureaucracy, the modern formal-rational organization tends towards the following features:

- Hierarchical authority in which lower offices are supervised by higher ones. Once fully developed, hierarchy is monocratically organized, with a single command centre, from which orders emanate and are acted upon.
- Impersonality and separation of office from the office holder. The workplace will be separate from the official's home and will not be the holder's personal property. Officials receive a salary, are graded according to hierarchy, and unlike patrimonial bureaucracy, cannot use the office for personal benefit.
- Written rules of conduct. The modern office is based on written documents, which are preserved in original form, which requires a 'staff of subaltern officials and scribes of all sorts'.

**Figure 8.3** Typlology of action and legitimation

| Action | Legitimation | Example |
|---|---|---|
| Habitual | Traditional | Monarchy (e.g. Divine Right of Kings) |
| Affective | Charismatic | Theocracy (e.g. Iran after 1979) |
| Value-rational | Substantive | Welfare state |
| Formal-rational | Rational-legal | Democratic republic |

- Each office holder has a clearly defined sphere of competence to which the person is appointed not elected, and promotion through a career structure is based on merit not patronage or favour.
- The modern bureaucracy is based on a specialized division of labour and expert spheres of competence and training.

Weber did further hint at a fourth type of legitimation, in his introductory discussion of legitimation and his account of **substantive rationality**, which involves 'the provisioning of given groups with goods under a criterion of ultimate values such as social justice'. This idea (which Weber regarded as 'full of ambiguities') referred both to values and resource allocation in which given groups are provided with goods under a criterion of social justice, a system also known as 'social eudaemonic' or performance legitimation (Holmes 1992: 11). Weber associated this form with 'social dictatorships', such as revolutionary states that distribute welfare in order to secure the loyalty of cadres, a notion that has been developed in relation to Soviet societies (Rigby and Fehér 1982; Ray 1996). This mode of legitimation can combine aspects of charisma (e.g. cadre recruitment) with rational legality. The development of labour protection legislation and social welfare exemplify a move towards substantive rationality within a formal-legal state.

If the three pure types of legitimation plus the undeveloped notion of substantive legitimation are placed alongside the four types of rational action outlined above then we can see some symmetry in Weber's thinking about action and justification. This is shown in Figure 8.3, which illustrates his tendency to understand the development of modern social organization in terms of a tendency towards increasing rationality, both in interpersonal interaction and state systems.

This typology has been subject to considerable debate and extension. David Beetham argues that Weber's schema was inadequate since he was not able to give a clear account of the structural interrelationships between economy, social structure and government (Beetham 1985: 256) and exaggerated the importance of legitimizing *beliefs* (Beetham 1991: 9). Further, legitimation problems of the later twentieth century capitalist state became considerably more complex than Weber envisaged. Writers such as Habermas (1976) and Offe (1984) have argued that through postwar systems of social welfare and redistribution, the state engaged in a series of complex exchanges with society which restructured public and private domains, while generating new sources of legitimation crisis (Ray 1978; 1993: 50–3).

Many of Weber's core assumptions have been challenged. Three of these we could describe as centralization, convergence and colonization. First, Weber assumed that the model of centralized hierarchical, command-action organization was most efficient for dealing with complex societies. Yet high degrees of centralization can create unwieldy structures with poor information flows, along with excessive rigidity, which are not well suited to deal with fluid and increasingly complex societies. Thus decentralization, increased initiative, less specialized divisions of labour and more collegial structures may be more successful organizational designs (Reed 1992: 39–44). Second, Weber assumed that the pursuit of efficient and rational decision making would generate convergence around a core organizational design. Yet research since the 1950s has found that organizational structure is likely to vary considerably with contingencies such as technology, size and market types, as well as the strategic choices made by dominant coalitions in the organization (Child 1970). Third, Weber assumed that bureaucracies would colonize many areas of socio-cultural life, such that 'The future belongs to bureaucratization [and] is distinguished from other historical agencies of the modern order of life in that it is far more persistent and "escape proof"' ([1913] 1978b: 1401). Some argue that this expectation now appears exaggerated because the diversification of organizational forms points towards increasingly flexible systems of management (DiMaggio and Powell 1983) and virtual organizations, as 'organization becomes the art of deconstructing organizations that can re-organize themselves' (Stark 1991: 57). All of which brings us to consider Weber's concept of rationalization.

## RATIONALIZATION AND THE 'IRON CAGE'

Although Weber did not have a deterministic theory of history (e.g. Hennis 1987), he suggested that there was a long run cultural tendency towards increasing 'rationalization'. This is a complex and often misunderstood concept that actually appears late in Weber's work, in his *Sociology of Religion* (1965), and is then frequently 'read back' into earlier texts.[13] Rationalization is essentially a feature of worldviews and developed 'with full force' in Occidental civilization but is evident elsewhere. Although 'empirical knowledge, reflection on problems of the cosmos and of life, philosophical and theological wisdom' are universal, 'only in the West does science exist at a stage of development which we recognize as valid'. Thus 'in architecture, pointed arches have been used elsewhere as a means of decoration in antiquity and Asia . . . But the rational use of the Gothic

**Figure 8.4** Charisma and rationalization

| Charisma | Rationalization |
| --- | --- |
| Personality forces its way into history | Intellect and impersonality |
| Non-bureaucratic | Bureaucratic |
| Creative | Adaptation to values or material goals |
| Revolutionary | Routinized |
| De-differentiating | Differentiating |
| Often religious | Disenchanted |
| Ephemeral (becomes routinized) | Persistent |
| e.g. Puritan asceticism | e.g. spirit of rational accounting |

vault as a means of distributing pressure . . . does not occur elsewhere' (Weber 1974: 15). Rationalization involves the following features:

- The shaping of all scientific practice according to the model of the natural sciences and the extension of scientific rationality to 'the conduct of life itself'.
- Secularization or 'disenchantment' of the modern world, where systematic worldviews decline causing a loss of integrating meaning. This is closely linked to the growth of impersonal institutions of the market and bureaucracy.
- Secularization leads to the growth of means–end rationality – social action governed by goal of efficient calculation of means to achieve a goal. This is apparent in the impersonal organizational form of the modern bureaucracy.
- Growth of rational calculation in ethics and privatization of belief. Public life is dominated by procedural formality and substantive belief becomes a private matter – you do 'whatever your god or demon tells you to do'.

It is important to appreciate that rationalization is a tendency located within worldviews and is neither law-like nor unilinear. For example, Christianity was less rationalized than Judaism or Islam and charismatic movements can break through bureaucratization. In his later work Weber counterposed charisma to rationalization and it is through charisma that personality forces its way into history, which is exemplified by Puritan asceticism (see Figure 8.4). By contrast, the tendency towards routinization and impersonality was exemplified by the routinization of Puritanism into the capitalist spirit (Mommsen 1987: 35–51).

As an underlying process of *longue durée*, rationalization originated in the decline of magic and taboo, which give way to norms according to which certain actions were construed as religious abominations. These were such things as dietary restrictions, unlucky days, regulation of marriages and impurity of those outside the caste. Any breach of norms carries sanctions, and to this extent as the will of the gods becomes an ethical system, the world becomes predictable and transgression results in evil and punishment; piety results in salvation. This is a cognitive as well as ethical development since the emergent system of rules is a knowable rather than a gnostic or mystical experience, and gives rise to a unified view of the world in which everything has a systematic and coherent meaning.

On one level, rationalization occurs in all worldviews and is not limited to the Occident. In all world religions, the cosmos is understood as a system, knowable at least by the priesthood, rather than subject to capricious forces, and knowledge of ethics is the basis of action affecting outcomes in this world and another. World religions subsumed the world under categories and adopted attitudes towards it – as a profane and indigent world was set against the community of believers. Examples of these 'world attitudes' are adjustment to the world (Confucianism), overcoming the world (monasticism), world flight (Hinduism), world mastery (Protestantism) and submitting to the world as fate (Islam). In this context, salvation is an important concept because it viewed the self and life as based on rule following conduct rather than magic or the intercession of spirits. It was the prototype of goal-setting behaviour.

On another level though, rationalization developed furthest in the west. Weber regarded 'inner-worldly asceticism' as highly significant and tried to accord it a universal significance (Schluchter 1987). Protestantism furthered this tendency by conceiving of life as a path orientated towards an ultimate goal, which had to be achieved through methodical and disciplined conduct. Calvinism was a hyper-rationalized worldview in which the whole cosmos was preordained. Early modern Protestant sects addressed the tension between the ethics of Christian communities and the unscrupulous cut-throat ethics of business. With the development of merchant capitalism though, the tension between world affirmation and retreat became more sharply defined since the market tended to push instrumental action into the interior of communities, eroding the possibility of other-worldly withdrawal. The religious ethic of 'brotherliness' came into sharper conflict with market impersonality. The crucial role of the *Protestant Ethic* was to resolve this tension in a historically novel way, if only temporarily, by renouncing universal love in favour of a personal relation with God and a practical attitude towards the world.

In the *Protestant Ethic* essays, Weber comments that for Baxter, the care for external goods should lie on the shoulders of the 'saint like a light cloak (*ein duenner Mantel*) which can be thrown aside at any moment'. However, 'fate decreed that the cloak should become an iron cage (*ein stahlhartes Gehäuse*)' since the spirit of asceticism has escaped into everyday life in victorious capitalism. The 'iron cage' has been one of the most influential metaphors in Weber's sociology, influential both in analyses of bureaucratization and more global critiques of modernity (e.g. Adorno and Horkheimer 1973). This draws on the romantic critique of modernity that also informed Tönnies and Simmel. Thus in the rationalized nightmare,

> The performance of each individual worker is mathematically measured, each man becomes a little cog in the machine and aware of this, his one preoccupation is whether he can become a bigger cog . . . it is horrible to think that the world could one day be filled with these little cogs, little men clinging to little jobs, and striving towards bigger ones . . . this passion for bureaucracy is enough to drive one to despair.
>
> (Weber [1913] 1978b, vol. 2: 1401)

The possibility of a socialist future offered little comfort since this would create even larger bureaucracies in a single hierarchy, and 'would be similar to the situation in ancient Egypt, but it would occur in a much more rational – and hence unbreakable – form (Weber [1913] 1978b: 1402).

The 'iron cage' metaphor is now very familiar and is often treated as synonymous with Weber's assessment of modernity and the evils of bureaucratization. However, two qualifications should be noted. First, Weber's *stahlhartes Gehäuse* (steel-hard shell) can be interpreted as a metaphor of the inescapable fate of modernity – the *Gehäuse* into which individuals are born – rather than a prison (Chalcraft 1994). Weber did after all regard the expansion of rationality as an extension of freedom. Second, the broader process of rationalization was for Weber not a single unitary process but took place unevenly in differentiated value spheres. Modernity was a process of differentiation into categories of experience such as Kant had described between science, morality and aesthetics. Weber in addition referred to religion, economy, erotic and political life. In these terms, rationalization could be seen as a multidimensional process, which led to fragmentation but not to the total constraint of thought. If, as Simmel and Dilthey also argued, modern culture separates into self-contained spheres of activity, then total control becomes less rather than more likely, because institutional sites of rationalization are as likely to pull each other apart as combine together (Roth 1987). One conclusion from Weber's analysis then is that the sheer complexity of differentiated social orders renders bureaucratic management inefficient. At the same time a formal-rational order relegates matters of ultimate moral value to private conscience which has the consequence of establishing a multiplicity and relativity of beliefs rather than rigid common beliefs. So it is possible to read Weber in a way that suggests a more open and nuanced conception of modernity than simply an iron cage, though I should stress that these are *possible readings* of Weber and not those made most overtly in his work.

## WEBER AND MODERN SOCIOLOGY

Weber's work represents one of the most systematic and comprehensive attempts to develop a comparative methodology through which he hoped to illuminate the specific and peculiar rationalism of western culture. But there are many readings of Weber. Merton (1990) took what he understood to be Weber's idealist explanation of the rise of capitalism as a model for his account of the effect of Puritanism on the rise of science. For Bendix (1966), Weber was a political theorist and idealist historian, while for Gerth and Mills (1948) he was a kind of multidimensional Marxist. Parsons' (1949) Weber was the cornerstone of functionalism, although J. C. Alexander (1983) has construed him as a multidimensional Parsonian. Eisenstadt (1968) read Weber as the evolutionist of world-historical rationalization. Again, there is Weber the methodological individualist, the relativist (Sprinzak 1972), phenomenologist (Schutz 1972) and even Foucauldian (Lash 1987). There are 'left' and 'right' Weberians, and so on. Randall Collins (1986) comments (in a somewhat mixed metaphor) that 'the ghost of Max Weber, torn limb from limb, has spread over the landscape and now is almost coextensive with the warring states of current sociology'.

Weber is often hailed as the sociologist of meaningful action, although we have seen that his aim was to combine hermeneutic and objective approaches. Subsequent theories of action and meaning have developed but also called into question Weber's methodology. For example, do reasons exist prior to actions (thus explaining them) or does performing a certain action logically entail certain reasons? The bookkeeper mentioned above is following *rules* when writing down figures in particular columns, so perhaps the key to understanding behaviour is to know these, rather than actors' meanings or intentions. If actions follow logically from the acquisition of social rules, then 'meanings' and 'actions' are not independent of one another. Perhaps we act as competent members of society in the same way we speak a language, by following rules, as Winch (1958) was to argue.[14] More recent linguistically based social theories have tended to displace the problem of meaning and its juxtaposition of subject and action through the concept of discourse. According to such theories (Foucault's is a prime example) meaning is generated not by actors but discourses that constitute a field of objects and language embedded in power relations (May 1996: 180–96).

Weber is often regarded as a nostalgic but fatalistic critic of modern society who regarded history as the negation of ethical activity (B. S. Turner 1987; 1992). He was a 'tragic liberal individualist' who defended democracy and the market against socialist bureaucratization but knew that capitalism was heading towards the iron cage anyway (Craib 1997: 233). These pessimistic dilemmas perhaps arise from intellectual uncertainties over the process of German modernization discussed in Chapter 7. Yet other recent work has minimized this account

(Schluchter 1987; Scaff 1988) to retrieve the 'other Weber', that is less pessimistic and regards the future as offering multiple possibilities. It is this Weber whom Seidman (1983) invokes when he says:

> Whatever despair Weber may have felt about the prospects for meaning and freedom in modernity, his sustained analysis of modernity – rather than occasional rhetorical flourishes – represents a much more nuanced and complex view of modernity than is usually presented.
>
> (Seidman 1983: 276)

Even so, Weber, like much classical sociology, was not entirely comfortable in the modern world.

The most interesting issue here perhaps is that nearly eighty years after his death we are still in search of the authentic Weber. This somewhat reverential or canonical attitude suggests something quite important about sociology. We could after all treat classical theory eclectically, simply as a source of hypotheses, in which case Weber's pessimism, nostalgia etc., would not be very important except perhaps for the sociological biographer. It clearly still does matter, at least to a considerable number of sociologists, because sociology is still engaging with the classics as a living tradition.

---

**Core concepts in Weberian sociology**

- Problems of historical explanation – economy vs. culture; systematic vs. elective affinity.
- Multiple social structures – especially class, status and party.
- Comparative methods and the fate of the west.
- Economy and society as integrated through embedded institutions.
- Types of action orientation and modes of legitimation.
- Rationalization and disenchantment as key processes within worldviews.
- Bureaucracy and modernity.
- Religion and society, history.
- Social differentiation and cultural value spheres.
- Critique of modernity as loss of meaning.

---

## FURTHER READING

Every sociologist should read Max Weber's (1974) *Protestant Ethic and the Spirit of Capitalism* (Allen and Unwin). It is clearly written and concentrates many crucial sociological debates into a single study. Gordon Marshall (1982) *In Search of the Spirit of Capitalism* (Hutchinson) provides a good and lively review of the debate and for an account of recent debates see Hartmut Lehmann and Günter Roth (eds) (1993)

*Weber's 'Protestant Ethic': Origins, Evidence, Context* (Cambridge University Press). Bryan Turner's (1992) collection of his essays *Max Weber: From History to Modernity* (Routledge) contains discussion of wide range of Weberian themes including Weber and postmodernism, Islam, rationalization and the body, Simmel and Nietzsche. Scott Lash and Sam Whimster (eds) (1987) *Max Weber, Rationality and Modernity* (Allen and Unwin) bring together some of the foremost Weber scholars who frequently question accepted interpretations.

## NOTES

1  Methodological individualism claims that only individuals are real – in contrast with holism which regards collective entities such as classes, states and societies as real *sui generis*. Marx and Durkheim exemplify holistic theorizing. There is some basis for regarding Weber as a methodological individualist – his stress on social action for example – but much of his work treated collective forms (religions, states, economic structures etc.) as real in their own right.

2  The *Methodenstreit* really began with Dilthey's challenge to the idea of the methodological superiority of the natural sciences (see Chapter 6).

3  The details of this debate, which referred specifically to nineteenth-century German political economy, are now of less interest than the way it posed the general problem of the relationship between natural and social sciences, an issue that became a central methodological issue in the twentieth century.

4  'Motives' he describes rather ambiguously as a 'complex of subjective meaning which seems to the actor himself *or to the observer*, as adequate ground for the conduct in question' (Weber 1964: 98–9, emphasis added). Weber acknowledged that there were considerable difficulties in attributing motives for actions.

5  This action is likely to be highly formal and therefore predictable, such as the case of traffic circulation systems, which (when functioning properly) require calculated behaviour, orientated to other drivers' actual and expected behaviour and in pursuit of goals of efficiency and survival.

6  Founded by Schmoller in 1872, academics of the society are often described as 'socialists of the chair'. They regarded social science as having a responsibility to address the 'social question' of welfare and workers' rights, in order to consolidate the stability of the state. Thus science should not (even if it could) be detached and objective.

7  There is of course the question of how familiar Weber was with Marx's own works as opposed to the deterministic and evolutionary versions around in German Social Democracy. Mommsen (1991) suggests that until 1906 Weber referred only to vulgar-Marxist interpretations.

8  The Austrian School of economists, whose most famous twentieth century representative was Freidrich Hayek (1899–1992), was stimulated by Menger's *Principles of Economics*. In this sense Weber's *Protestant Ethic* thesis could be seen as a further contribution to the *Methodenstreit*.

9  This is the idea that complex systems are sensitive to minute, unmeasurable variations in their initial conditions such that the mere flap of a butterfly's wing can make the difference between a hurricane occurring or not.

10  While Calvinists (arguably) believed in predestination, Protestant sects such as the Pietists, Methodists and Baptists did not, although they shared an ascetic this-worldliness (Weber 1974: 128–54).

11  If taken at face value, this often quoted passage has dramatic methodological implications. If both are really possible are they also of equal value? If so, Weber could be viewed as an extreme pluralist or even relativist as Sprinzak (1972) suggests.

12  In these terms a great deal of protosocialist protest was 'traditionalistic' in that it resisted capitalism by invoking ancient rights and obligations (e.g. Eldridge 1994).

13  Parsons is often held responsible for this – appending Weber's Introduction to the *Sociology of Religion* to his translation of the *Protestant Ethic* essays thereby creating the impression that the latter was an example of 'rationalization' (Marshall 1982).

14  This is a view Weber had rejected in his critique of Rudolf Stammler, who argued that the central element of social life was regulation by external rules, which constitute society (Morrison 1995: 278; see also Weber 1978c: 99 110).

# In conclusion: retrospect and prospect

Sociology was a debate with the Enlightenment. While absorbing and furthering some themes, such as the possibility of secular ethics and the idea of radical social transformation, sociology was critical of Enlightenment individualism and rationalism. Sociology further defined the space of the social, separate from yet encompassing the spheres of the private and the state. The emergence of the social drew on a long process of intellectual development stretching back to classical antiquity. The social was to be the terrain on which contrasting theoretical positions took shape and through which sociology would distance itself from Enlightenment individualism and rationalism. For Saint-Simon, Comte and Durkheim, eighteenth-century social theory had been excessively negative and critical while giving inadequate attention to the sources of social solidarity. An important early theme was that of regulating social change in an orderly yet progressive direction that gave due regard to the non-rational, quasi-sacred foundations of sociality. In addressing the (primarily moral) crisis of industrial society, sociology sought the sources of communal solidarity and belonging that the Enlightenment had dismissed or ignored. To this extent, the search for community and a critique of the alienating and atomizing tendencies of industrial society was a guiding theme. Classical sociology tended either to look for sources of community to be reclaimed in the future, or lamenting their irretrievable loss as the tragedy of modernity. One should not imagine though that this is a concern only of the past, for it is a powerful theme today in the theory and politics of communitarianism, whose exponents often (possibly unknowingly) echo the critique of the Romantic counter-Enlightenment.

Although this tendency was particularly marked in moral-organic approaches, it was present too in Marxist materialism, which had begun by denouncing capitalist society as an alienating phase in the long struggle of humanity for self-realization. But Marxism elaborated the revolutionary ethos of the Enlightenment, revolutionary in the sense that unjust conditions need not be endured and that social order is subject to radical transformation. Marxism remained largely silent on questions of morality, attributing justice to the agency of the proletariat, whose historical role was derived from a philosophy of history. The limitations of a purely materialist conception of theory and practice were thrown into relief by Marxism's encounter with feminism and the appearance of multiple social movements in the early twentieth century. While Marxism could and did address these, the fractures in a theory centred round a single subject-agent became increasingly apparent in the course of the century.

The scientific-industrial civilization that was celebrated in different ways by both Marxism and Positivism lent support to the idea of social science as a naturalistic activity. The claim to scientificity was not only methodological but also connoted and valued the historical evolution of a scientific modernity. Hermeneutic approaches took issue with the principle of naturalism in social theory and justified the separation between natural and cultural sciences in terms of a different understanding of the social. This gave primacy to neither the moral nor material but to symbolic and cultural relations. The crucial facets of the social were the linguistically mediated background meanings whose acceptance was essential to sociality and retrievable through methods specific to the cultural sciences. The blending of hermeneutic approaches with the cultural critique of capitalism was to become a major strand of social theorizing and enabled some western Marxists to rethink the theory in more culturally inflected ways. Simmel was a central figure in this process whose work took sociology (and the inquiry into the constitution of the social) into previously neglected domains of everyday life.

The emergence of the social as a terrain of rational action was a central theme in Weber's synthesis of naturalistic and hermeneutic, material and cultural dimensions. Rational action made social life more transparent yet the accompanying disenchantment and loss of meaning threatened to create bureaucratic greyness and instrumentality. History was the unfolding of reason, but this was less enthusiastically endorsed than it had been by Condorcet or in Hegelian philosophy. Even though rationalization was a tendency inherent in worldviews and social organization, this was not an underlying law of historical development. History was rather an alteration between phases of rationalization and charismatic innovation although the former was the underlying tendency. Although Weber's synthesis was incomplete, it left a rich legacy of theoretical and methodological issues for subsequent sociology. Of particular importance was the theory of complex causality in which major events are the unintended outcome of an affinity of cultural and material factors. Similarly the method of ideal-typical construction, as well as the particular concepts Weber developed, have been influential in almost every area of sociological inquiry. Whatever Weber's intention in using the iron cage metaphor, it has crucially affected sociological perceptions of modernity.

This raises a further question of how the classical tradition should best be appropriated? I noted in Chapter 1 that the classics are not a fixed corpus and will be reinterpreted and reappropriated according to our current concerns. Thus there is a 'postmodernized' Simmel (Weinstein and Weinstein 1993), Marx the theorist of modernist fluidity (Lash and Urry 1994), Weber the precursor of almost every contemporary position, and so on. Of course, the classics are sources to be mined for whatever purposes we choose, but to discover, for example, 'Simmel the post-modernist' may not be the most interesting thing to say about a classical theory and may obscure more than it clarifies. It may be more revealing and cautionary, to see how the problems and dilemmas of our attempts to theorize the social have been anticipated and addressed by classical theory. This is valuable not only to avoid reinventing the wheel but also to see how the concepts and antinomies of our theorizing still play with those defined by earlier sociologists.

It is true though that classical sociology dealt with a very different social world from that of the early twenty-first century. They addressed industrial capitalist societies with polarized class systems, in which socialism was a future vista, where 'society' was organized in bounded nation states, where European colonial empires dominated the world, and patriarchal relations were largely taken for granted. Social theory understands the present age extensively by contrast with much of this – hence the popularity of the prefix 'post'. The present is post-industrial, post-socialist, post-colonial and global in ways that question conventional understanding of the boundaries of 'society'. It is further a period in which fluidity, uncertainty and flexibility have replaced what is seen as the solidity and certainties of the world of classical sociology. These concerns are central to contemporary social theory and do separate us in important ways from the classics.

This does not mean that the classical tradition is no longer significant. Not only do we still think to large extent in the categories of classical sociology, but also we deal with a legacy of its conceptual dilemmas. In the formation of a multipolar concept of the social, several themes have recurred and been addressed by all major classical and contemporary theoretical schools. In current dilemmas we find underlying classical polarities. Take for example the contrast that goes to the heart of our understanding of political and social organization, between the politics of redistribution (class and economic justice) as opposed to recognition (identity and cultural politics) (e.g. Fraser 1995). Not only does 'recognition' have a Hegelian theme, but also the opposition deploys a range of contrasts between the symbolic, material and moral. Again, the debate over the 'culturalization' of the social and the emergence of 'post-material' values and politics (e.g. Ray and Sayer 1999) reaches back to classical oppositions between the moral, cultural and economic and the various ways these may be articulated.

Three further issues are worth mentioning. We experience ourselves as agents, initiating actions that have effects, yet society appears as an objective symbolic and institutional order. The agency-structure polarity is a central sociological issue that all theories have attempted to resolve. Some (e.g. Marx, Comte, Durkheim) proposed holistic-organic theories that derive individual subjects from the social; others begin with experience or interaction and attempt to derive from this society and an objective reality (e.g. Dilthey, Tönnies, Simmel and to an extent Weber). Some, such as Talcott Parsons (e.g. 1949) and Anthony Giddens (e.g. 1979: 93–129) have attempted to reconcile the polarity in new conceptual formulations. Such 'resolutions' though have been unable to resolve the debate and have eventually come down on one side or the other. Parsons for example set out to develop an action theory but ended in highly abstract systems thinking. Giddens, however, resolved the duality largely by understanding structure as an aspect of agency. This could tell us something about the nature of such contrasts – they cannot be resolved because they are antinomies fundamental to theorizing the social.

Second, the social was defined in opposition to nature and so created a continual play of social against natural. This book has shown that most classical theorists acknowledged how modern societies were reordering gender relations, although they mostly viewed these through the lens of nature vs. society. The social is a naturalized place in that the natural is 'authentic', serves as a legitimation of existing institutions and established parameters of what cannot be changed. But nature is a socialized place in that it is subject to interventions of society through labour and (as Simmel recognized) is a symbolic and cultural construct. This play of nature and society runs through classical sociology, which theorizes it in various ways, but by and large, does not seek to challenge it. Subsequent Freudian theories of the primal tension between instinct and civilization took their place comfortably, despite the controversy they caused, within this polarity which organized social thinking for much of the twentieth century. But in contemporary theory the social and the natural are being subject to wide ranging deconstruction. Feminist theory has shown how the natural/social duality is a gendered division that encodes as 'natural' cultural and politically defined concepts of masculinity and femininity. The rapidly growing field of the sociology of the body (e.g. Shilling 1993) has challenged traditional divisions between biology and the social, drawing in part not only on Foucault's concepts of power and discourse but also on Weber's rationalization (B. S. Turner 1992: 115–38). This debate could become one of the most significant and challenging for sociological theory in the following decades in view of the already apparent resurgence of genetic accounts of human behaviour.

Finally, where do we now stand in relation to the Enlightenment? The promise of sociology was that it would contribute to human freedom and social progress by revealing the laws of society to enable people to control their destiny. Institutions, laws and social customs would be redesigned to conform to truths about human nature and social order. This view no longer commands such confidence. Bauman (1992: 166) has argued that the Enlightenment dream of a rationally planned society ended in the nightmare of the concentration camps and that the failure of communism demonstrated the impossibility of modernist visions of social reconstruction. This in turn reflects the controversy surrounding postmodernism that rejects ideas of historical narrative, objective meaning and rationally grounded critique. By contrast with postmodernism, a persistent theme in sociological theory has been to offer a critical diagnosis of society that points towards a good society. Sociology has generally located the range of possibilities for social development in a historical awareness of emergent forms. Each of the classical sociologists (whatever their claims to scientificity or objectivity) critically engaged with modernity (as disorganized, alienating, anomic, instrumental bureaucratic or whatever) and implicitly therefore had a view of what would be a good society. This is still apparent when the postmodern scepticism is countered by arguments derived from post-Enlightenment concepts of rationality and justice (e.g. Habermas 1987). The debate with the Enlightenment continues.

# Glossary of terms

The following provides a brief account of some of the main concepts used here. Where a word in the definition is in bold, this indicates that it is listed as a separate entry.

**Affective action** (Weber): action that expresses the emotional state of the actor and is not directed towards the attainment of a goal.

**Alienation** (Marx): the separation of workers from the products of labour, other people and from their true natures, as creative beings.

**Anomie** (Durkheim): a state of social disorganization caused by lack of normative regulation.

**Arbitrary will** (Tönnies): instrumental and purposive action underlying **Gesellschaft**. Contrasts with **essential will**.

**Charisma** (Weber): social movements based on belief in the expceptional (often religious) qualities of an individual. Charisma is a major source of social change but usually dissipated as it is subject to **rationalization**.

**Civil society**: associated with eighteenth century political theorists, describing a sphere of contract, the market and voluntary association separate from the state (political society).

**Commodity fetishism** (Marx): the process whereby capitalism creates the appearance that social relations between people are relations between things (thus natural and inevitable) rather than the product of a historically specific configuration of class relations.

**Dialectic** (Hegel, Marx): though originally used by Plato, modern usage comes from Hegel where it refers to the movement of history through transcendence of internal contradictions that in turn produce new contradictions, themselves requiring resolution. Dialectical thinking claims to go beyond conventional logic by permitting the existence of logical contradictions. Marx and Engels claimed to develop a 'materialist dialectics' in which, through the struggle of social classes, historical contradictions were resolved.

**Direct understanding** (Dilthey, Weber): understanding the meaning of an expression e.g. that $2 \times 2 = 4$. Contrasts with **explanatory understanding**.

**Egoism** (Durkheim): a state of the moral division of labour based on individual responsibility, rather than collective control.

**Elective affinity** (Weber): a principle of explanation in which otherwise independent processes (e.g. religion and the economy) have mutual attraction and combine in interaction.

**Empathy** (Dilthey): re-experiencing the life situation of actors to recreate the process of creation through which events and cultural objects were formed.

**Enlightenment:** an eighteenth century European social and intellectual movement, which challenged authoritarian and metaphysical practices and beliefs through scepticism and reason. See also **Postmodernism.**

**Essential will** (Tönnies): the organic force of social solidarity underlying **Gemeinschaft,** which creates strong personal bonds. Contrasts with **arbitrary will.**

**Exchange value** (Marx): the price at which commodities (including labour) trade on the market. Contrasts with **use value.**

**Explanatory understanding** (Dilthey, Weber): understanding the meaningful connection between events and expressions with reference to actor's motives and intentions. Contrasts with **direct understanding.**

**Forces of production** (Marx): the human capacities, instruments and techniques that are required to produce goods. See also **mode of production** and **relations of production.**

**Forms of association** (Simmel): patterns of social relationships that recur in many different contexts (e.g. conflict, competition, domination/subordination) and express contents, such as interests and emotions.

**Gemeinschaft** (Tönnies): often translated as 'community' and refers to close social bonds, generally found in pre-industrial societies, in which actions are performed for their intrinsic worth. Contrasts with **Gesellschaft.**

**Generalized Other** (Mead): the organized community or group whom the individual takes as a reference point for their sense of a unified self.

**Gesellschaft** (Tönnies): often translated as 'society' or 'association' and refers to impersonal and instrumental social relations, generally found in **industrial societies,** dominated by monetary considerations. Contrasts with **Gemeinschaft.**

**Goal-rational action** (Weber): action in which the objectives, consequences and means of attainment of a course of action have been rationally calculated.

**Hermeneutics:** method for understanding cultural and symbolic systems such as language, texts, art and beliefs that move in circle (or spiral) progressively uncovering deeper layers of meaning. See also **naturalism.**

**Ideal types** (Weber): abstract, rational constructs of action or processes that can be compared to complexity and irrationality in the real world.

**Ideology** (Marx): this has various uses but refers in particular to (a) perceptions of reality distorted by class interests; (b) the ideas, legal forms and culture that arise from class relations.

**Industrial societies** (Spencer): these have a complex division of labour, functional differentiation and integration, governed by relationships of contract. Contrasts with **military societies.**

**Jacobins:** revolutionary faction of radical egalitarians, including Louis Saint-Just (1768–94) and Maximillien Robespierre (1758–94) that ruled France 1793–4 during the 'Republic of Virtue'. This coincided with the height of the Terror – the mass executions of alleged enemies of the revolution. Though short-lived, Jacobinism remained a symbol of revolutionary theory and practice for the following century.

**Mechanical solidarity/society** (Durkheim): societies with a rudimentary occupational differentiation and a strong collective conscience in the form of a homogeneous and strictly enforced moral code reaffirmed by taboo and rituals.

**Military societies** (Spencer): pre-industrial societies with a rudimentary division of labour dominated by warrior caste and status relationships. Contrasts with **industrial societies.**

**Mode of production** (Marx): an analytical construct that contains **forces of production** and **relations of production**, which together define the socio-economic character of an epoch.

**Naturalism:** the belief that the methods of the natural sciences (however understood) are applicable to social life. See also **hermeneutics** and **positivism.**

**Objective culture** (Simmel): institutions, practices and social forms take on a life independent of their creators and threaten to stifle human creativity.

**Organic solidarity/society** (Durkheim): societies with complex divisions of labour and weak collective conscience, since moral codes are diverse and a high value is placed on individual freedom. The 'cult of individuality', which gave human rights sacred significance, would provide a moral basis for social integration.

**Positivism** (Comte): this rejected metaphysical thinking and proposed a unity and hierarchy of sciences based on methods of observation, experiment and comparison, which aimed to demonstrate general laws of social life. Later positivism took various forms and lost its association with Comte, but remained committed to **naturalism.**

**Postmodernism:** a diffuse intellectual movement in the social sciences, arts, architecture and literature that rejects universalist **Enlightenment** 'narratives', such as reason and progress, in favour of celebration of diversity, fragmentation and aesthetic irony.

**Rationalization** (Weber): tendency of worldviews to become increasingly systematic, exclude the unpredictable and eliminate magic. Contrasts with **charisma.**

**Rational-legal legitimation** (Weber): belief in the legality of enacted rules and the right of those elevated to authority to enact them – closely associated with the spread of bureaucracies.

**Relations of production** (Marx): the social (class) relations of ownership and non-ownership of the **forces of production.**

**Social action** (Weber): meaningful conduct orientated to the expectations of other people.

**Social contract:** the claim, associated with Hobbes, Locke and Rousseau, that just government is based on a voluntary and rational surrender of sovereignty by the people to a ruler, who in turn has an obligation to rule in the general interest.

**Social facts** (Durkheim): these exist prior and external to individuals, whom they constrain; language is a good example, though Durkheim's primary interest was in moral systems as social facts.

**Social formation** (Marx): the ensemble of social relations that contain both the dominant **mode of production** and earlier modes, e.g. rural smallholdings within capitalism.

**Socially necessary labour time** (Marx): the part of the working day during which workers create sufficient value to reproduce their subsistence needs. The level of development of the industry in question and the prices of basic necessities determines this. Marx suggests that wages will tend to equate with necessary labour time because the price of labour (like other commodities) will approximate its reproduction costs

**Society,** *sui generis***:** the view of society (e.g. in Marx and Durkheim) as an emergent level of reality analytically independent from individuals and thus subject to processes that can be understood only with reference to other social forces.

**Substantive rationality** (Weber): to secure the provision of a population (or group) with goods and services in accordance with the ethical requirements of a system of norms.

**Surplus value** (Marx) (= surplus labour, surplus labour time): the portion of the working day during which workers produce value that is appropriated by the capitalist.

**Traditional action** (Weber): action rooted in fixed bodies of customary habits and beliefs.

**Typification** (Simmel): process whereby **forms of association** are created and sustained by abstracting individuals into social types (e.g. stranger, friend, parent, lover, bureaucrat).

**Use value** (Marx): the universal quality of goods to be of some use to their owner. Though termed 'value' this is not measurable. Contrasts with **exchange value**.

**Value relevance** (Rickert, Weber): purposes that guide our choice of methods and topics for sociological enquiry. Methodological differences (e.g. between natural and social sciences) lie in their respective research objectives rather than in inherently different subject matters.

**Value-rational action** (Weber): striving for a substantive goal (e.g. salvation) through calculated means.

**Verstehen** (Weber): method of understanding action by situating it in the context of an actor's meanings.

# Sociology websites

There are now many social science sites on the web and the following are a selection relevant to social theory. Many of these are interlinked. These are accurate at the time of going to press but URLs can become outdated and change location. Updated links can generally be found through **Yahoo! Social Science/ Sociology**. Of particular relevance to this book are the following:

**Dead Sociologists Society**
http://www.pscw.uva.nl/sociosite/TOPICS/Sociologists.html [extracts and commentary on most classical sociologists]

**Rousseau's Homepage**
http://www.wabash.edu/Rousseau/

**The Durkheim Page**
http://eddie.cso.uiuc.edu/Durkheim/

**Auguste Comte** et le positivism/and positivism (in French and English)
http://www.hgx-hypersoft.com/clotilde/

**Marx/Engels Archive**
http://csf.Colorado.EDU/psn/marx/Archive/
[an excellent site with photo gallery, the full or part text of most of Marx and Engels' texts, letters and interviews, with links to other relevant sites]

**Georg Simmel Online**
http://www.socio.ch/sim/index_sim.htm

**Verstehen, Max Weber's Home Page**
http://msumusik.mursuky.edu/~felwell/http/weber/whome.htm

## OTHER SITES OF INTEREST

**SocioWeb**
http://www.socioweb.com/~markbl/socioweb/

**SocioSite**
http://www.pscw.uva.nl/sociosite/

**WWW Virtual Library: Sociology**
http://www.mcmaster.ca/socscidocs/w3virtsoclib/index.htm

**Yahoo! Social Science/Sociology site**
http://www.yahoo.com/Social_Science/Sociology/

# Bibliography

Abel, T. (1929) *Systematic Sociology in Germany*. New York: Octagon Books.

Adorno, T. (1991) *The Culture Industry*, ed. J. M. Bernstein. London: Routledge.

Adorno, T. and Horkheimer, M. (1973) *Dialectic of Enlightenment*. London: New Left Books.

Albrow, M. (1990) *Max Weber's Construction of Social Theory*. London: Macmillan.

Alexander, J. C. (1983) *Theoretical Logic in Sociology, Vol. 3, The Classical Attempt at Theoretical Synthesis: Max Weber*. London: Routledge and Kegan Paul.

Alexander, J. C. (1989) *Structure and Meaning: Relinking Classical Sociology*. New York: Columbia University Press.

Alexander, J. C. (ed.) (1990) *Durkheimian Sociology: Cultural Studies*. Cambridge: Cambridge University Press.

Alexander, S. (1990) Women, class and sexual differences, in T. Lovell (ed.) *British Feminist Thought*. Oxford: Blackwell.

Althusser, L. (1965) *For Marx*. London: New Left Books.

Anderson, R. J., Hughes, J. A. and Sharrock, W. W. (eds) (1986) *Classic Disputes in Sociology*. London: Allen and Unwin.

Arato, A. (1974) Neo-idealist defense of subjectivity, *Telos*, 21: 108–61.

Aron, R. (1970) *Main Currents of Sociological Thought*, 2 vols. New York: Doubleday.

Atkinson, M. (1968) On the sociology of suicide, *Sociological Review*, 16(1): 83–92.

Auerbach, N. (1982) *Woman and the Demon: The Life of a Victorian Myth*. London: Harvard University Press.

Avineri, S. (1968) *The Social and Political Thought of Karl Marx*. Cambridge: Cambridge University Press.

Bach, M. (1990) Individualism and legitimation: paradoxes and perspectives of the political sociology of Emile Durkheim, *Archives Européennes de Sociologie*, 31: 117–40.

Barkin, K. (1970) *The Controversy Over German Industrialization 1890–1902*. Chicago: University of Chicago Press.

Barnes, H. (ed.) (1969) *Introduction to the History of Sociology.* Chicago: University of Chicago Press.

Barran, P. and Sweezy, P. (1966) *Monopoly Capital.* New York: Monthly Review Press.

Barrett, M. (1988) *Women's Oppression Today: The Marxist-Feminist Encounter.* London: Verso.

Bauman, Z. (1978) *Hermeneutics and Social Science.* London: Macmillan.

Bauman, Z. (1988) Exit visas and entry tickets: paradoxes of Jewish assimilation, *Telos,* 77: 45–78.

Bauman, Z. (1992) *Intimations of Post-Modernity.* London: Routledge.

Bebel, A. ([1879] 1970) *Women Under Socialism.* New York: Free Press.

Beccaria, C. ([1764] 1963) *On Crime and Punishment.* New York: Bobbs and Merrill.

Beetham, D. (1985) *Max Weber and the Theory of Modern Politics.* London: Allen and Unwin.

Beetham, D. (1991) *The Legitimation of Power.* London: Macmillan.

Ben-David, J. (1962–3) Professions in the class system of present-day societies, *Current Sociology,* 12: 247–330.

Bendix, R. (1966) *Max Weber: An Intellectual Portrait.* Berkeley: University of California Press.

Benoit-Smullyan, E. (1969) The sociologism of Emile Durkheim and his school, in H. Barnes (ed.) *An Introduction to the History of Sociology.* Chicago: University of Chicago Press.

Berger, P. and Luckman, T. (1967) *Social Construction of Reality.* Harmondsworth: Penguin.

Berki, R. N. (1983) *Insight and Vision: The Problem of Communism in Marx's Thought.* London: Dent.

Berman, M., (1985) *All That is Solid Melts into Air.* London: Verso.

Bernstein, E. ([1899] 1961) *Evolutionary Socialism, a Criticism and Affirmation.* New York: Schocken Books.

Bleicher, J. (1982) *The Hermeneutic Imagination.* London: Routledge.

Blumenberg, H. (1983) *The Legitimacy of the Modern Age.* London: MIT Press.

Bonald, M. de (1864) *Oeuvres Complètes,* 3 vols. Paris: Migne.

Bottomore, T. B. and Frisby, D. (1990) Preface to the second edition, in G. Simmel *The Philosophy of Money.* London: Routledge.

Bottomore, T. B. and Nisbet, R. (eds) (1978) *History of Sociological Analysis.* Oxford: Blackwell.

Bottomore, T. B. and Rubel, M. (eds) (1970) Introduction to *Karl Marx, Selected Writings in Sociology and Social Philosophy.* Harmondsworth: Penguin.

Bowler, P. (1984) *Evolution: The History of an Idea.* London: University of California Press.

Bruns, G. (1992) *Hermeneutics Ancient and Modern.* London: Yale University Press.

Buck-Morss, S. (1977) *The Origins of Negative Dialectics.* Hassocks: Wheatsheaf.

Burrows, J. W. (1966) *Evolution and Society.* Cambridge: Cambridge University Press.

Cahnman, W. J. (ed.) (1973a) *Ferdinand Tönnies: A New Evaluation.* Leiden: Brill.

Cahnman, W. J. (1973b) 'Tönnies and Marx: evaluation and excerpts', in W. J. Cahnman (ed.) *Ferdinand Tönnies.* Leiden: Brill.

Cameron, R. (1966) *France and the Economic Development of Europe*. Chicago: MIT Press.

Camic, C. (ed.) (1997) *Reclaiming the Sociological Classics: The State of Scholarship*. Oxford: Blackwell.

Carlebach, J. (1978) *Marx and the Radical Critique of Judaism*. London: Routledge.

Caute, D. (1988) *The Fellow Travellers: Intellectual Friends of Communism*. London: Yale University Press.

Chalcraft, D. (1994) Bringing the text back in – on ways of reading the iron cage metaphor in the two editions of *The Protestant Ethic*, in L. Ray and M. Reed (eds) *Organizing Modernity*. London: Routledge.

Chalmers, A. (1978) *What is This Thing Called Science?* Milton Keynts: Open University Press.

Chambers, R. ([1844] 1994) *Vestiges of the Natural History of Creation*. Chicago: University of Chicago Press.

Child, J. (1970) Organizational structure, environment and performance: the role of strategic choice, *Sociology*, 6(1): 2–22.

Clarke, S. (1994) *Marx Theory of Crisis*. New York: St Martin's Press.

Cohen, J. L. (1987) *Class and Civil Society: The Limits of Marxian Critical Theory*. Amherst: University of Massachusetts Press.

Collins, R. (1980) Weber's last theory of capitalism – a systematization, *American Sociological Review*, 45. 925–42.

Collins, R. (1986) *Weberian Sociological Theory*. Cambridge: Cambridge University Press.

Collins, R. and Makowsky, M. (1984) *The Discovery of Society*. New York: Random House.

Comte, A. (1824) *System of Positive Polity*, 4 vols. New York: Franklin.

Comte, A. (1858) *Catechism of Positive Religion*. London: Chapman.

Comte, A. (1974) *The Crisis of Industrial Civilization*, ed. R. Fletcher. London: Heinemann Educational.

Comte, A. ([1830] 1975) *Cours de philosophie positive*, 2 vols. Paris: Herman.

Comte, A. (1976) *The Foundation of Sociology*, ed. K. Thompson. London: Nelson.

Condorcet, M. J. A. ([1794] 1976) Sketch for the Historical Picture of the Progress of the Human Mind, in K. M. Baker (ed.) *Selected Writings*. Indianapolis, Ind: Bobbes-Merrill.

Connerton, P. (ed.) (1976) *Critical Sociology*. Harmondsworth: Penguin.

Cooley, C. H. (1902) *Human Nature and the Social Order*. New York: Free Press.

Coser, L. A. (1977) *Masters of Sociological Thought*. New York: Harcourt Brace.

Coser, L. A. (1991a) Georg Simmel's style of work, in L. J. Ray (ed.) *Formal Sociology*. Aldershot: Edward Elgar.

Coser, L. A. (1991b) George Simmel's neglected contributions to the sociology of women, in L. J. Ray (ed.) *Formal Sociology*. Aldershot: Edward Elgar.

Craib, I. (1997) *Classical Social Theory*. Oxford: Oxford University Press.

Crook, S. (1991) *Modernist Radicalism and its Aftermath*. London: Routledge.

Crow, G. (forthcoming) *Social Solidarities: Causes, Contexts and Consequences*. London: Macmillan.

Darwin, C. ([1859] 1964) *Origin of Species*. Cambridge: Cambridge University Press.

Davis, M. (1973) Georg Simmel and the aesthetics of social reality, *Social Forces*, 51: 320–29.

Delanty, G. (1997) *Social Science: Beyond Constructivism and Realism*. Buck-ingham. Open University Press.

Dilthey, W. (1862) *Aus Schleiermachers Leben*. Berlin: Reimer.

Dilthey, W. (1976a) The rise of hermeneutics, in P. Connerton (ed.) *Critical Sociology*. Harmondsworth: Penguin.

Dilthey, W. (1976b) *Dilthey: Selected Writings*, ed. H. P. Rickman. Cambridge: Cambridge University Press.

Dilthey, W. (1985) Awareness, reality: time, in K. Mueller-Vollmer (ed.) *The Hermeneutics Reader*. Oxford: Basil Blackwell.

DiMaggio, P. and Powell, W. (1983) The iron cage revisited, *American Sociological Review*, 48: 147–60.

Douglas, J. (1966) *The Social Meanings of Suicide*. Princeton, NJ: Princeton University Press.

Draper, H. and Lipow, A. (1976) Marxist women vs bourgeois feminism, *Socialist Register*, 176–226.

Durkheim, E. (1933) *Division of Labour in Society*. London: Collier Macmillan (first published 1895).

Durkheim, E. ([1895] 1964) *Rules of Sociological Method*. New York: Free Press.

Durkheim, E. (1965) *Montesquieu and Rousseau*. Michigan, Ann Arbor Press.

Durkheim, E. (1969a) Individualism and the intellectuals, *Political Studies*, 17: 14–30.

Durkheim, E. (1969b) *Journal Sociologique*, ed. and int. J. Duvignaud. Paris: Presses Universitaires de France.

Durkheim, E. (1969c) Note sur la notion de civilisation, *Journal Sociologique*, 681–85.

Durkheim, E. (1969d) Deux lois d'évolution pénale, *Journal Sociologique*, 244–73.

Durkheim, E. (1969e) La prohibition de l'inceste et ses origines, *Journal Sociologique*, 37–101.

Durkheim, E. ([1897] 1970) *Suicide*. London: Routledge.

Durkheim, E. (1972) *Selected Writings*, ed. and int. A. Giddens. Cambridge: Cambridge University Press.

Durkheim, E. ([1912] 1976) *Elementary Forms of the Religious Life*. London: Allen and Unwin.

Durkheim, E. (1979) Durkheim's review of Georg Simmel's *Philosophie des Geldes*, *Social Research*, 46(2): 321–8.

Durkheim, E. ([1950] 1992) *Professional Ethics and Civic Morals*. London: Routledge.

Eisenstadt, S. N. (1968) *The Protestant Ethic and Modernization: A Comparative View*. New York: Basic Books.

Eldridge, J. (1994) Work and authority: some Weberian perspectives, in L. Ray and M. Reed (eds) *Organizing Modernity*. London: Routledge.

Engels, F. ([1884] 1968) Origin of Family, Private Property and the State, in K. Marx and F. Engels *Selected Works*, London: Lawrence and Wishart.

Etzioni, A. (1997) *The New Golden Rule: Community and Morality in a Democratic Society*. London: Profile Books.

Evans, R. (1976) *The Feminist Movement in Germany 1894–1933*. London: Sage.

Evans, R. (1979) *The Feminists*. London: Croom Helm.

Evans, M. (1987) Engels: materialism and morality, in J. Sayers, M. Evans and N. Redclift (eds) *Engels Revisited*. London: Tavistock.

Fehér, F. (ed.) (1990) *The French Revolution and the Birth of Modernity*. Oxford: University of California Press.

Ferguson, A. ([1767] 1966) *An Essay on the History of Civil Society*. Edinburgh: Edinburgh University Press.

Feuerbach, L. ([1841] 1957) *Essence of Christianity*. New York: Harper.

Fischoff, E. (1944) The Protestant ethic and the spirit of capitalism: the history of a controversy, *Social Research*, 11: 54–77.

Fletcher, R. (1971) *The Making of Sociology*, vols 1 and 2. London: Joseph.

Foucault, M. (1979) *Discipline and Punish: The Birth of the Prison*. Harmondsworth: Penguin.

Fraser, N. (1995) From redistribution to recognition? *New Left Review*, July/ August (212): 68–93.

Frisby, D. (1981) *Sociological Impressionism: Reassessment of Georg Simmel's Social Theory*. London: Heinemann.

Frisby, D. (1990) Introduction to the translation, in G. Simmel, *The Philosophy of Money*. London: Routledge.

Frisby, D. (1994) *Georg Simmel*. London: Fontana.

Frisby, D. and Featherstone, M. (eds) (1997) Introduction to the texts, in G. Simmel, *Simmel on Culture*, London: Sage.

Gadamer, H. G. (1976) *Philosophical Hermeneutics*. Berkeley: University of California Press.

Gadamer, H. G. (1993) *Truth and Method*. London: Sheed and Ward.

Gane, M. (1993) *Harmless Lovers? Gender, Theory and Personal Relationships*. London: Routledge.

Gane, M. (1996) Engendering the end of European history: Auguste Comte's cult of woman at the heart of the western republic, *Renaissance and Modern Studies*, 39: 15–26.

Gane, M. and Tribe, K. (eds) (1992) *the Radical Sociology of Durkheim and Mauss*. London: Routledge.

Gay, P. (1962) *The Dilemma of Democratic Socialism*. London: Collier.

Gay, P. (1996) *Enlightenment: The Science of Freedom*. London: Norton.

Gerth, H. H. and Mills, C. W. (eds) (1948) *From Max Weber*. London: Routledge.

Giddens, A. (1971) *Capitalism and Modern Sociological Theory*. Cambridge: Cambridge University Press.

Giddens, A. (1973) *Class Structure of the Advanced Societies*. London: Hutchinson.

Giddens, A. (1978) *Emile Durkheim*. London: Fontana.

Giddens, A. (1979) *Studies in Social and Political Theory*. London: Hutchinson.

Giddens, A. (1990) *The Consequences of Modernity*. Cambridge: Polity.

Giddens, A. (1994) *Beyond Left and Right*. Cambridge: Polity.

Goffman, E. (1959) *The Presentation of Self in Everyday Life*. New York: Doubleday.

Gouldner, A. (1963) Anti-Minotaur: the myth of a value-free sociology, in M. Stein and A. Vidich (eds) *Sociology on Trial*. Englewood Cliffs, NJ: Prentice Hall.

Gouldner, A. (1976) *The Dialectic of Ideology and Technology*. London: Macmillan.

Granovetter, M. and Swedberg, R. (1992) *The Sociology of Economic Life*. Boulder, CO. Westview.

Green, R. W. (ed.) (1959) *Protestantism and Capitalism: The Weber Thesis and its Critics*. London: Heath.

Greenfeld, L. (1992) *Nationalism: Five Roads to Modernity*. Cambridge, MA: Harvard University Press.

Habermas, J. (1972) *Knowledge and Human Interests*. London: Heinemann.

Habermas, J. (1976) *Legitimation Crisis*. London: Heinemann.

Habermas, J. (1984) *Theory of Communicative Action*, vol. 2. London: Heinemann.

Habermas, J. (1987) *The Philosophical Discourse of Modernity*. Cambridge: Polity.

Haines, V. A. (1997) Spencer and his critics, in C. Camic (ed.) *Reclaiming the Sociological Classics*. Oxford: Blackwell.

Hamilton, P. (ed.) (1990) *Emile Durkheim: Critical Assessments*, 4 vols. London: Routledge.

Hamilton, P. (ed.) (1991) *Max Weber: Critical Assessments*, 4 vols. London: Routledge.

Harvey, D. (1994) *The Condition of Postmodernity*. Oxford: Blackwell.

Hazard, P. (1965) *European Social Thought in the Eighteenth Century*. Harmondsworth: Penguin.

Heater, D. (1990) *Citizenship: The Civic Ideal in World History, Politics and Education*. London: Longman.

Heberle, R. (1973) The sociological system of Ferdinand Tönnies, in W. J. Cahnman (ed.) *Ferdinand Tönnies*. Leiden: Brill.

Hegel, G. ([1805] 1949) *Phenomenology of Mind*. London: Allen and Unwin.

Hegel, G. ([1821] 1967) *Philosophy of Right*. Oxford: Oxford University Press.

Hegel, G. (1969) *Science of Logic*. London: Allen and Unwin.

Heidegger, M. ([1927] 1996) *Being and Time*. New York: State University Press.

Heilbron, J. (1995) *The Rise of Social Theory*. Cambridge: Polity.

Hekman, S. (1983) *Max Weber and Contemporary Social Theory*. Oxford: Robertson.

Hekman, S. (1986) *Hermeneutics and the Sociology of Knowledge*. Cambridge: Polity.

Hennis, W. (1987) Personality and life orders: Max Weber's theme, in S. Lash and S. Whimster (eds) *Max Weber, Rationality and Modernity*. London: Allen and Unwin.

Hill, C. (1965) *Intellectual Origins of the English Revolution*. Oxford: Clarendon.

Hobbes, T. ([1651] 1994) *Leviathan*. London: Everyman.

Holmes, L. (1992) *The End of Communist Power*. Cambridge: Polity.

Honneth, A. and Joas, H. (eds) (1991) *Communicative Action: Essays on Jurgen Habermas's The Theory of Communicative Action*, trans. J. Gaines and D. L. Jones. Oxford: Polity.

Horkheimer, M. (1982–3) Egoism and the freedom movement, *Telos*, 54: 10–60.

Houlton, R. (1996) Classical social theory, in B. S. Turner (ed.) *Blackwell Companion to Social Theory*. Oxford: Blackwell.

Hughes, H. S. (1974) *Consciousness and Society*. St Albans: Paladin.

Hughes, J. A. (1990) *The Philosophy of Social Research*. London: Longman.

Hughes, J. A., Martin, P. J. and Sharrock, W. W. (1995) *Understanding Classical Sociology*. London: Sage.

Hume, D. ([1748] 1975) *Enquiries Concerning Human Understanding*. Oxford: Clarendon.

Humphries, J. (1987) The origin of the family: born out of scarcity not wealth, in J. Sayers, M. Evans and N. Redclift (eds) *Engels Revisited*. London: Tavistock.

Israel, J. (1971) *Alienation: From Marx to Modern Sociology*. Boston, MA: Allyn and Bacon.

Joll, J. (1973) *The Second International 1889–1914*. London: Routledge.

Kaiser, T. (1980) Politics and political economy in the thought of the Ideologues, *History of Political Economy*, 12(2): 141–60.

Kalberg, S. (1997) Max Weber's sociology: research strategies and modes of analysis, in C. Camic (ed.) *Reclaiming the Sociological Classics*. Oxford: Blackwell.

Kant, I. ([1784] 1970) An answer to the question: what is enlightenment?, in H. S. Reiss (ed.) *Kant: Political Writings*. Cambridge: Cambridge University Press.

Keat, R. (1971) Scientific knowledge and the problem of naturalism, *Journal for the Theory of Social Behaviour*, 1: 3–17.

Kitch, M. J. (ed.) (1967) *Capitalism and the Reformation*. London: Longman.

Kolakowski, L. (1972) *Positivist Philosophy*. Harmondsworth: Penguin.

Kolakowski, L. (1989) *Main Currents of Marxism: Its Rise, Growth and Dissolution*, 3 vols. Oxford: Oxford University Press.

Körner, S. (1977) *Kant*. Harmondsworth: Penguin.

Kuhn, T. (1970) *Structure of Scientific Revolutions*. Chicago: University of Chicago Press.

Kumar, K. (1995) *From Post-Industrial to Post-Modern Society*. Oxford: Blackwell.

LaCapra, D. (1972) *Emile Durkheim: Sociologist and Philosopher*. Ithaca, NY: Cornell University Press.

Landes, J. (1981) Feminism and the internationals, *Telos*, 49: 117–26.

Larrain, J. (1979) *The Concept of Ideology*. London: Hutchinson.

Lash, S. (1987) Modernity or modernism? Weber and contemporary social theory, in S. Lash and S. Whimster (eds) *Max Weber, Rationality and Modernity*. London: Allen and Unwin.

Lash, S. and Urry, J. (1994) *Economies of Signs and Spaces*. London: Sage.

Lash, S. and Whimster, S. (eds) (1987) *Max Weber, Rationality and Modernity*. London: Allen and Unwin.

Lehmann, H. and Roth, G. (eds) (1993) *Weber's 'Protestant Ethic': Origins, Evidence, Context*. Cambridge: Cambridge University Press.

Lehmann, J. (1993) *Deconstructing Durkheim: A Post-Post-Structuralist Critique*. London: Routledge.

Lehmann, J. (1994) *Durkheim and Women*. London: University of Nebraska Press.

Levine, D. (1997) Simmel reappraised: old images, new scholarship, in C. Camic (ed.) *Reclaiming the Sociological Classics*. Oxford: Blackwell.

Lichtheim, G. (1969) *Marxism*. London: Routledge.

Locke, J. ([1699] 1884) *Some Thoughts Concerning Education*. Cambridge: Cambridge University Press.

Locke, J. ([1680] 1960) *Two Treatises on Government*, ed. P. Laslett. Cambridge: Cambridge University Press.

Locke, J. ([1681–3] 1980) *Second Treatise on Civil Government*, ed. C. B. Macpherson. Indianapolis, Ind: Hackett.

Löwith, K. (1982) *Max Weber and Karl Marx*. London: Allen and Unwin.

Löwy, M. (1979) *Marxisme et romantisme revolutionaire*. Paris: Le Sycomore.

Lukács, G. ([1923] 1968) *History and Class Consciousness*. Cambridge, MA: MIT Press.

Lukács, G. (1980) *The Destruction of Reason*. London: Merlin.

Lukes, S. (1973) *Emile Durkheim: His Life and Work*. Harmondsworth: Penguin.

Lyotard, J-F. (1990) *The Postmodern Condition*. Manchester: Manchester University Press.

McClelland, J. S. (1996) *A History of Western Political Thought*. London: Routledge.

MacIntyre, A. (1987) *After Virtue*. London: Duckworth.

Mackinnon, M. H. (1994) The longevity of the thesis: a critique of the critics, in H. Lehmann and G. Roth (eds) *Weber's Protestant Ethic: Origins, Evidence, Contexts*. Cambridge: Cambridge University Press.

Maistre, J. de ([1796] 1974) *Considerations on France*. Montreal: McGill.

Makkreel, R. (1975) *Dilthey: Philosopher of the Human Studies*. Princeton, NJ: Princeton University Press.

Malthus, T. ([1798] 1888) *Essay on the Principle of Population*. London: Reeves and Turner.

Mandeville, B. ([1729] 1924) *Fable of the Bees, Or Private Vices, Publik Benefits*. Oxford: Clarendon Press.

Mann, T. ([1928] 1960) *The Magic Mountain*. Harmondsworth: Penguin.

Markham, F. (1964) Introduction to H. Saint-Simon, *Social Organization, the Science of Man and other Essays*. New York: Harper and Row.

Marshall, G. (1982) *In Search of the Spirit of Capitalism*. London: Hutchinson.

Marx, K. ([1844] 1964) *Economic and Philosophical Manuscripts of 1844*. New York: International Publishers.

Marx, K. ([1847] 1966) *The Poverty of Philosophy*. Moscow: Progress Press.

Marx, K. ([1875] 1968) *Critique of the Gotha Programme*, in K. Marx and F. Engels *Selected Works*. London: Lawrence and Wishart.

Marx, K. ([1862] 1969) *Theories of Surplus Value*, vol. 2. Moscow: Progress.

Marx, K. (1970) *Critique of Hegel's Philosophy of Right*. Cambridge: Cambridge University Press.

Marx, K. ([1857–8] 1973) *The Grundrisse*. Harmondsworth: Penguin.

Marx, K. ([1867] 1976) *Capital: A Critique of Political Economy*, vol. 1. Moscow: Progress.

Marx, K. (1978) *Selected Writings*, ed. D. McLellan. Oxford: Oxford University Press.

Marx, K. and Engels, F. ([1848] 1967) *Manifesto of the Communist Party*. Moscow: Progress.

Marx, K. and Engels, F. ([1884] 1968) *Selected Works*. London: Lawrence and Wishart.

Marx, K. and Engels, F. ([1846] 1974) *The German Ideology*. London: Lawrence and Wishhart.

May, T., (1996) *Situating Social Theory*. Buckingham: Open University Press.

Mead, G. H. (1933) *Mind, Self and Society*. Chicago: Chicago University Press.

Menczer, B. (1952) *Catholic Political Thought 1789–1848*. London: Burns Oates.

Merton, R. (1990) *Puritanism and the Rise of Modern Science: The Merton thesis*, ed. I. B. Cohen, K. E. Duffin and S. Strickland. New Brunswick, NJ: Rutgers University Press.

Mészáros, I. (1975) *Marx's Theory of Alienation*. London: Merlin.

Milbank, J. (1993) *Theology and Social Theory*. Oxford: Blackwell.

Misztal, B. (1996) *Trust in Modern Societies: The Search for the Bases of Social Order*. Cambridge: Polity.

Mommsen, W. (1987) Personal conduct and societal change, in S. Lash and S. Whimster (eds) *Max Weber, Rationality and Modernity*. London: Allen and Unwin.

Mommsen, W. (1991) Max Weber as a critic of Marxism, in P. Hamilton (ed.) *Max Weber: Critical Assessments*, vol. 1. London: Routledge.

Montesquieu, C. ([1748] 1949) *Spirit of the Laws*. Lodnon: Collier–Macmillan.

Morgan, L. H. (1877) *Ancient Society*. Chicago: Kerr.

Morrison, K. (1995) *Marx, Durkheim, Weber*. London: Sage.

Müller-Vollmer, K. (ed.) (1986a) *The Hermeneutics Reader: Texts of the German Tradition from the Enlightenment to the Present*. Oxford: Basil Blackwell.

Müller-Vollmer, K. (1986b) Language, mind and artifact: an outline of hermeneutic theory since the Enlightenment, in Müller-Vollmer (ed.) *The Hermeneutics Reader*. Oxford: Basil Blackwell.

Nedelmann, B. (1991) Individualization, exaggeration and paralysation: Simmel's three problems of culture, *Theory, Culture and Society*, 8(3): 169–94.

Nisbet, R. (1967) *The Sociological Tradition*. London: Heinemann.

Nisbet, R. (1986) *Conservatism*. Buckingham: Open University Press.

Novak, M. W. (1976) An introduction to reading George Simmel's sociology, *Sociological Inquiry*, 46(1): 31–9.

Offe, C. (1984) *Contradictions of the Welfare State*. London: Hutchinson.

Ortega y Gasset, J. ([1930] 1961) *The Revolt of the Masses*. London: Unwin.

Outhwaite, W. (1975) *Understanding Everyday Life*. London: Allen and Unwin.

Outhwaite, W. (1987) Laws and explanations in sociology, in R. J. Anderson, J. A. Hughes and W. W. Sharrock (eds) *Classic Disputes in Sociology*. London: Allen and Unwin.

Outhwaite, W. (1996) Introduction to H. Andersen and L. B. Kaspersen (eds) *Klassisk og moderne samfundsteori – en Introduktion*. Copenhagen: Hans Reitzels Forlag. English version (1999) *Classical and Modern Social Theory*. Oxford: Blackwell.

Palmer, R. (1969) *Hermeneutic Interpretation Theory in Schleiermacher, Dilthey, Heidegger and Gadamer*. Evanston, IL: Northwestern University Press.

Pappenheim, F. (1959) *The Alienation of Modern Man: An Interpretation Based on Marx and Tönnies*. New York: Monthly Review Press.

Parsons, T. (1949) *The Structure of Social Action*. New York: Free Press.

Parsons, T. (1973) A note on *Gemeinschaft* and *Gesellschaft*, in W. J. Cahnman (ed.) *Ferdinand Tönnies*. Leiden: Brill.

Pearce, F. (1989) *The Radical Durkheim*. London: Unwin Hyman. Heinemann Educational.

Peel, J. D. Y. (1971) *Herbert Spencer: The Evolution of a Sociologist*. London: Heinemann Educational.

Pellicani, L. (1988) Weber and the myth of Calvinism, *Telos*, 75: 57–85.

Pickering, M. (1993) *Auguste Comte: An Intellectual Biography*, vol. 1. Cambridge: Cambridge University Press.

Pinel, P. ([1806] 1962) *A Treatise on Insanity*. New York: Hafner.

Popper, K. (1970) *The Poverty of Historicism*. London: Routledge and Kegan Paul.

Porter, R. and Teich, M. (eds) (1981) *The Enlightenment in National Context*. Cambridge: Cambridge University Press.

Rachfahl, F. (1968) Kalvinismus und Kapitalismus, in J. Winchelmann (ed.) *Max Weber, Die protestantische Ethik II*. Munich: Siebenstern Taschenbuch.

Ray, L. J. (1978) Habermas, legitimation and the state, *Journal for the Theory of Social Behaviour*, 8(2): 149–64.

Ray, L. J. (1986) The Protestant ethic debate, in R. J. Anderson, J. A. Hughes and W. W. Sharrock (eds) *Classic Disputes in Sociology*. London: Allen and Unwin.

Ray L. J. (ed.) (1991) *Formal Sociology: The Sociology of George Simmel*. Aldershot: Edward Elgar.

Ray, L. J. (1993) *Rethinking Critical Theory*. London: Sage.

Ray, L. J. (1996) *Social Theory and the Crisis of State Socialism*. Cheltenham: Edward Elgar.

Ray, L. J. and Reed, M. (eds) (1994) *Organizing Modernity: New Weberian Perspectives on Work, Organization and Society*. London: Routledge.

Ray, L. J. and Sayer, A. (eds) (1999) *Culture and Economy after the Cultural Turn*. London: Sage.

Razzell, P. (1977) The Protestant ethic and the spirit of capitalism: a natural scientific critique, *British Journal of Sociology*, 28: 17–37.

Reed, M. (1992) *The Sociology of Organizations*. London: Harvester Wheatsheaf.

Reedy, W. J. (1994) The historical imaginary of social-science in postrevolutionary France: Bonald, Saint-Simon, Comte, *History of the Human Sciences*, 7(1): 1–26.

Rengger, N. J. (1995) *Political Theory, Modernity and Postmodernity*. Oxford: Blackwell.

Rickman, H. P. (ed.) (1976) Introduction to *Dilthey: Selected Writings*. Cambridge: Cambridge University Press.

Rigby, T. H. and Fehér, F. (eds) (1982) *Political Legitimation in Communist States*. New York: St Martin's Press.

Ritzer, G. (1983) *Contemporary Sociological Theory*. New York: Knopf.

Ritzer, G. (1994) *Sociological Beginnings*. New York: McGraw-Hill.

Robertson, R. (1933) *Aspects of the Rise of Economic Individualism*. Cambridge: Cambridge University Press.

Rossi, A. S. (ed.) (1973) *The Feminist Papers*. London: Columbia University Press.

Roth, G. (1987) Rationalization in Max Weber's developmental history, in S. Lash and S. Whimster, *Max Weber, Rationality and Modernity*. London: Allen and Unwin.

Rousseau, E. ([1762] 1968) *The Social Contract*. Harmondsworth: Penguin.

Rousseau, J.-J. ([1762] 1974) *Emile*. London: Dent.

Rousseau, J.-J. ([1754] 1992) *Discourse on the Origin of Inequality*. Indianapolis, Ind: Hackett.

Runciman, W. G. (1998) The selectionist paradigm and its implications for sociology, *Sociology* 32(1): 163–88.

Saint-Simon, H. (1964) *Social Organization, the Science of Man and other Essays*. New York: Harper and Row.

Saint-Simon, H. (1966) *Oeuvres*, vol. 1. Paris: Anthropos.

Saint-Simon, H. (1975) *Selected Writings on Science, Industry and Social Organization*, ed. and trans. K. Taylor. London: Croom Helm.

Samuelsson, K. (1961) *Religion and Economic Action: A Critique of Max Weber*. London: Heinemann.

Say, J. B. ([1803] 1821) *A Treatise on Political Economy* (2 vols). London.

Sayers, J., Evans, M. and Redclift, N. (eds) (1987) *Engels Revisited: New Feminist Essays*. London: Tavistock.

Scaff, L. A. (1988) Weber, Simmel and the sociology of culture, *Sociological Review*, 36(1): 1–30.

Scaff, L. A. (1989) *Fleeing the Iron Cage: Culture, Politics, and Modernity in the Thought of Max Weber*. Berkeley: University of California Press.

Schleiermacher, F. D. (1977) *Hermeneutics: The Handwritten Manuscripts*, ed. H. Kimmerle; trans. J. Duke and J. Forstma. Missoula, MT: Scholars Press.

Schleiermacher, F. D. (1985) General hermeneutics, in K. Müller-Vollmer (ed.) *The Hermeneutics Reader*. Oxford: Basil Blackwell.

Schluchter, W. (1987) Weber's sociology of rationalism and the typology of religions rejections of the world, in S. Lash and S. Whimster (eds) *Max Weber, Rationality and Modernity*. London: Allen and Unwin.

Schutz, A. (1972) *Phenomenology of the Social World*. London: Heinemann.

Seé, H. (1959) Contribution of the Puritans to the evolution of modern capitalism, in R. W. Green (ed.) *Protestantism and Capitalism*. London: Heath.

Seidman, S. (1983) Modernity, meaning and cultural pessimism in Max Weber, *Sociological Analysis*, 44(4): 267–78.

Seidman, S. (1994) *Contested Knowledge*. Oxford: Blackwell.

Shilling, C. (1993) *The Body and Social Theory*. London: Sage.

Shklar, J. N. (1987) *Montesquieu: Pioneer of the Sociology of Knowledge*. Oxford: Oxford University Press.

Shope, J. H. (1994) Separate but equal – Durkheim's response to the woman question, *Sociological Inquiry*, 64(1): 23–36.

Simmel, G. (1971) *On Individuality and Social Forms*. Chicago, Ill: University of Chicago Press.

Simmel, G. ([1900] 1990) *The Philosophy of Money*, ed. T. Bottomore and D. Frisby. London: Routledge.

Simmel, G. ([1916] 1997) The crisis of culture, in D. Frisby and M. Featherstone (eds) *Simmel on Culture*. London: Sage.

Smith, A. ([1759] 1976a) *Theory of Moral Sentiments*, ed. D. D. Raphael and A. L. Macfie. Oxford: Clarendon.

Smith, A. ([1784] 1976b) *An Inquiry into the Nature and Causes of the Wealth of Nations*. Oxford: Clarendon Press.

Smith, R. (1997) *Fontana History of the Human Sciences*. London: Fontana.

Solomon, R. C. (1983) *In the Spirit of Hegel: A Study of G. W. F.'s Phenomenology of Spirit*. Oxford: Oxford University Press.

Spencer, H. (1873) *The Study of Sociology*. New York: Appleton.

Spencer, H. (1881) *The Principles of Psychology*, 2 vols, 3rd edn. London: Williams and Norgate.

Spencer, H. (1883–5) *The Principles of Sociology*, 3 vols. London: Williams and Norgate.

Spencer, H. (1884) *The Principles of Biology*, 2 vols. London: Williams and Norgate.

Spencer, H. (1887) *First principles*. London: Williams and Norgate.

Spencer, H. ([1879] 1978) *The Principles of Ethics*. Indianopolis: Liberty Classics.

Spencer, H. (1904) *An Autobiography*, 2 vols. New York: Appleton.

Sprinzak, E. (1972) Weber's thesis as an historical explanation, *History and Theory* 11: 294–320.

Stark, D. (1991) Comment, in P. Bourdieu and J. Coleman (eds) *Social Theory for a Changing Society*. Boulder, CO: Westview.

Stern, F. (1974) *The Politics of Cultural Despair*. London: University of California Press.

Swingewood, A. (1985) *A Short History of Sociological Theory*. London: Macmillan.

Szacki, J. (1979) *History of Sociological Thought*. London: Aldwych Press.

Szamuely, T. (1988) *The Russian Tradition*. London: Fontana.

Tawney, R. H. (1975) *Religion and the Rise of Capitalism*. Harmondsworth: Penguin.

Taylor, C. (1979) *Hegel and Modern Society*. Cambridge: Cambridge University Press.

Tenbruck, F. H. (1959) Formal sociology, in K. H. Wolff (ed.) *Georg Simmel*. Columbus: Ohio State University Press.

Thompson, E. P. (1978) *The Poverty of Theory and Other Essays*. London: Merlin.

Thönnessen, W. (1969) *The Emancipation of Women*. London: Pluto.

Tokei, F. (1972) Lukács and Hungarian culture, *New Hungarian Quarterly*, 13(47).

Tönnies, F. (1971) On *Gemeinschaft* and *Gesellschaft*, in M. Truzzi (ed.) *Sociology: The Classic Statements*. New York: Oxford University Press.

Tönnies, F. (1973) *Community and Association (Gemeinschaft und Gesellschaft)*. London: Harper.

Toumlin, S. (1990) *Cosmopolis: The Hidden Agenda of Modernity*. Chicago: University of Chicago Press.

Trevor-Roper, H. (1963) Religion, the Reformation and social change, *Historical Studies*, 4: 18–44.

Turgot, A. ([1750] 1913) Discourses on the successive progress of the human mind, in *Oeuvres*, vols 315–16. Paris: Alcan.

Turner, B. S. (1987) The rationalization of the body: reflections on modernity and discipline, in S. Lash and S. Whimster (eds) *Max Weber, Rationality and Modernity*. London: Allen and Unwin.

Turner, B. S. (1992) *Max Weber: From History to Modernity*. London: Routledge.

Turner, B. S. (ed.) (1996) *Blackwell Companion to Social Theory*. Oxford: Blackwell.

Turner, S. P. (ed.) (1996) *Social Theory and Sociology: The Classics and Beyond*. Oxford: Blackwell.

Voltaire, F. M. (1994) *Political Writings*, ed. and trans. D. Williams. Cambridge: Cambridge University Press.

Vromen, S. (1987) George Simmel and the cultural dilemma of women, *History of European Ideas*, 8(4–5): 563–78.

Vucht Tijssen, L. van (1991) Women and objective culture: Georg Simmel and Marianne Weber, *Theory Culture and Society*, 8(3): 203–18.

Wagner, P. (1994) *A Sociology of Modernity: Liberty and Discipline*. London: Routledge.

Walker, A. (1978) *Marx: His Theory and its Context*. London: Longman.

Wallerstein, I. (1990) The French Revolution as a world-historical event, in F. Fehér (ed.) *The French Revolution and the Birth of Modernity*. Oxford: University of California Press.

Walton, J. and Gamble, A. (1972) *From Alienation to Surplus Value*. London: Sheed and Ward.

Weber, Marianne (1998) Women's special cultural tasks, in P. M. Lengermann and J. Niebrugge-Brantley (eds) *The Women Founders: Sociology and Social Theory, 1830–1930*. New York: McGraw-Hill.

Weber, Max (1927) *General Economic History*. London: Allen and Unwin.

Weber, Max (1964) *Theory of Social and Economic Organization*, trans. A. M. Henderson and T. Parsons. Glencoe, NY: The Free Press.

Weber, Max ([1920] 1965) *The Sociology of Religion*. London: Methuen.

Weber, Max (1974) *Protestant Ethic and the Spirit of Capitalism*. London: Allen and Unwin.

Weber, Max (1978a) Anti-critical last word on 'the Spirit of Capitalism', *American Journal of Sociology*, 283: 1,105–31.

Weber, Max ([1913] 1978b) *Economy and Society*, 2 vols, ed. G. Roth and C. Wittich. London: University of California Press.

Weber, Max (1978c) *Weber: Selections in Translation*, ed. W. G. Runciman. Cambridge: Cambridge University Press.

Weingartner, R. H. (1959) Form and content in Simmel's philosophy of life, in K. H. Wolff (ed.) *Georg Simmel*. Columbus: Ohio State University Press.

Weinstein, D. and Weinstein, M. (1993) *Postmodern(ized) Simmel*. London: Routledge.

Wellmer, A. (1971) *Critical Theory of Society*. New York: Seabury Press.

White, L. W. (1969) Henry Morgan: pioneer in the theory of social evolution, in H. Barnes *Introduction to the History of Sociology*. Chicago: University of Chicago Press.

Wilson, S. (1973) The antisemitic riots of 1898 in France, *Historical Journal*, 16(4): 789–806.

Winch, P. (1958) *The Idea of a Social Science*. London: Routledge.

Wistrich, R. S. (1992) *Antisemitism: The Longest Hatred*. London: Thames Mandarin.

Wittfogel, K. (1963) *Oriental Despotism*. New Haven, CT: Yale University Press.

Wolff, K. H. (ed.) (1959) *Georg Simmel, 1858–1918: A Collection of Essays*. Columbus: Ohio State University Press.

Wollstonecraft, M. ([1792] 1975) *Vindication of the Rights of Women*, ed. M. Kramnick. Harmondsworth: Penguin.

Wood, A. (1996) Marx against morality, in P. Singer (ed.) *Companion to Ethics*. Oxford: Blackwell.

Zeitlin, I. M. (1968) *Ideology and the Development of Sociological Theory*. Englewood Cliffs, NJ: Prentice Hall.

# Index

SITUATING SOCIAL THEORY

Tim May

> ... very substantial and reliable introduction to social theory, imagin-
> atively written and extremely readable.
>    William Outhwaite, Professor of Sociology, University of Sussex

This original and approachable text examines contemporary social theory
in the context of its traditions and historical development.

The book begins by charting the history of social theory, examining its
development in terms of the Enlightenment project and the cultural and
intellectual contexts in which theorists worked and constructed their ideas.
It then goes on to examine hermeneutics, phenomenology, pragmatism,
critical theory, structuralism, systems theory and feminisms. In outlining
the main ideas behind these traditions, the form and content of modern
social theory is situated within its historical antecedents, enabling the
reader actively to explore the arguments and reflect upon their strengths
and weaknesses.

The book then examines schools of thought and social theorists that represent the current terrain of social theory, including Goffman, ethnometh-
odology, symbolic interactionism, Giddens, Habermas, Foucault, Bourdieu,
feminisms and postmodernism. The chapters follow a common format,
locating the main ideas in terms of relevant traditions and historical context, discussing how theories have subsequently developed, and examining
the modifications, applications and critiques of these ideas. Throughout,
a focus on the relationship between agency, ideas on the social self and
social structure provides a thematic coherence.

*Situating Social Theory* is designed as an invaluable text for intermediate
undergraduate courses within sociology and the wider social sciences, and
it will provide an essential source of reference for advanced undergradu-
ates and postgraduate researchers.

## Contents

272pp    0 335 19286 6 (Paperback)    0 335 19287 4 (Hardback)

KNOWING THE SOCIAL WORLD

Tim May and Malcolm Williams

- What is the relationship between philosophy, social theory and empirical research?
- In what ways can we claim to 'know' the social world?
- What are the properties of the social world and their implications?

This ground-breaking and multi-disciplinary book brings together a distinguished team of leading thinkers to discuss issues surrounding and informing questions such as: what is the 'social', in what ways can we 'know' it, and how can our findings be validated? These issues are discussed in an accessible way, including the relationship of philosophical and research issues to each other, the nature of social reality, properties that may be ascribed to the social, research accounts and rhetorical 'persuasion', and the relations between 'gender and knowing'. The overall concern of the book is to clarify how and in what ways we can claim to know the social world and what implications and consequences this may have for social scientific practice.

For too long philosophers, social theorists and methodologists have talked past each other, often unaware of the mutually beneficial insights that each offers the other. This book is intended to contribute to a more constructive encounter and dialogue in order to advance understanding of the problems and possibilities surrounding the quest to know the social world. With this overall aim in mind, it will be essential reading for students and researchers in the social sciences.

### Contents
*Introduction: knowing the social world – The social world as knowable – Naturalisms and anti-naturalisms – When the knower is also the known – Social properties and their basis – Social theory and the analysis of society – The reality of social domains: implications for theory and method – Relationism, cubism, and reality: beyond relativism – Feminists' knowledge and the knowledge of feminisms: epistemology, theory, methodology and method – Quantitative and qualitative research strategies in knowing the social world – Reflections and reflexivity – References – Name index – Subject index.*

208pp    0 335 19767 1 (Paperback)    0 335 19768 X (Hardback)

## CONTEMPORARY SOCIAL AND POLITICAL THEORY
## AN INTRODUCTION

**Fidelma Ashe, Alan Finlayson, Moya Lloyd, Iain MacKenzie, James Martin, Shane O'Neill**

'. . . the book is excellent and should do really well. It is well written and comprehensive, and it meets the needs of sociologists.'

John Scott, University of Essex

- What have been the major innovations in contemporary social and political thought in the twentieth century?
- How have these ideas challenged the canon?
- What are the implications of these new ideas for our understanding of key theoretical concepts?

This new and accessible introduction to contemporary social and political theory examines the impact of new ideas such as feminist theory, post-structuralism, hermeneutics and critical theory. The innovations brought by these currents to the intellectual traditions of Europe and America are outlined and assessed. Designed for the newcomer to theory, no previous knowledge is assumed and a student-friendly approach is adopted throughout.

Rather than focus on individual thinkers, the authors take a 'conceptual' approach by examining contemporary theories through themes such as 'rationality', 'power', 'the subject', 'the body' and 'culture'. Each chapter considers the evolution of a concept and examines the major debates and transformations that have taken place in that area. The needs of the undergraduate are kept in mind at all times and, in addition to an extensive bibliography, the book contains a useful glossary of key terms and concepts.

*Contents*
*Preface – Rationality – Social criticism – Language – Power – The subject – The body – Culture – The social and the political – Glossary –Bibliography – Index.*

224pp    0 335 19624 1 (Paperback)    0 335 19625 X (Hardback)